EMPRESS *of* ROME

EMPRESS *of* ROME

The Life of Livia

MATTHEW DENNISON

Quercus

First published in Great Britain in 2010 by
Quercus
21 Bloomsbury Square
London
WC1A 2NS

A CIP catalogue record for this book is available
from the British Library

ISBN 978 1 84916 110 7

Text and plates designed and typeset by Ellipsis Books Limited, Glasgow
Printed and bound in Great Britain by Clays Ltd. St Ives plc

For Gráinne
– like Livia, *'probitate, forma [mulierum] eminentissima'*

. . . 'These literary gatherings get a little on my nerves,' Judy said, 'I sometimes wish I'd married a plumber.'

'Even a plumber, my dear,' Arnold said with a constrained twist of his lips, 'would, one imagines, take a certain interest in his work.'

'Yes, but a plumber finishes his work when he finishes it,' said Judy. 'He isn't always talking and thinking about plumbing. He doesn't go to plumbing lunches and plumbing teas and plumbing conversaziones. He doesn't give lectures on plumbing.'

Richmal Crompton, *Family Roundabout*, 1948

Contents

Author's Note

For British television viewers of the 1970s, Livia loomed large in the history of ancient Rome. Jack Pulman's thirteen-part small-screen adaptation of Robert Graves's novel *I, Claudius* promulgated a version of events in which Livia played a leading and decisive role. Even for the armchair student of Roman history, this is cause for surprise. Neither the Republic nor the principate recognized the vesting of formal power of this sort in women's hands. What then was Livia up to? Who was deceiving whom?

The Pulman–Graves account of the founding of the Roman Empire owed much to the work of Publius or Gaius Cornelius Tacitus. Tacitus's *Annals of Imperial Rome*, written early in the second century, is an intensely vivid record of the Rome of the first emperors. Its purpose was more than reportage. 'It seems to me a historian's foremost duty,' Tacitus wrote with tub-thumping moral afflatus, 'is to ensure that merit is recorded, and to confront evil words and deeds with the fear of posterity's denunciations.' A number of evil deeds he placed squarely at Livia's feet.

Tacitus considered himself without partisanship. Other surviving ancient texts – painting different portraits of Livia and her actions – suggest that Livia would not have agreed. Without seeking out undiscovered fragments, lost inscriptions or unknown papyri, I have revisited these other sources and a wealth of scholarship arising from them, alongside Tacitus's account. My intention has been to create a portrait of Livia that, no less remarkable than the scheming villainess of the Tacitus–Graves–Pulman triad, is more finely balanced, more equivocal – and less indebted to burlesque.

This book was written with the assistance of a generous award from The Society of Authors. To The Society, and particularly the members of the distinguished judging panel under the chairmanship of Antonia Fraser, I express my grateful thanks.

As ever, I am grateful to those many people who, in different ways, provided help with the writing of this book. In Italy, Sir Timothy and Lady Clifford offered hospitality, kindness and inspiration at a critical moment; without their intervention, this book would not have been written. Other friends were generous in their hospitality throughout the research period: Jim and Fern Dickson, Claudia Joseph, Cathy Davey, and Ivo and Pandora Curwen.

I am grateful to those people who read, answered questions and offered advice on the manuscript, including Dr Adrian Goldsworthy, Kathryn Jones of The Royal Collection and, especially, John Everatt, an inspirational classics master and a patient reader. The staff of The Library of the Societies for the Promotion of Hellenic and Roman Studies and The London Library were helpful, as was Ann Price of Denbigh Library in North Wales, who mastered for me the inter-library loan scheme. I am grateful to my agent, Georgina Capel, and my editor Richard Milbank.

Immense thanks, of course, are due to the unsung behind-the-scenes efforts of my wonderful parents, my father-in-law and above all my beloved wife, Gráinne, for so much patience, encouragement and love.

'Few women of real nobility have received such venomous treatment as Livia.'

J. P. V. D. Balsdon, *Roman Women:*
Their History and Habits, 1962

'Of all the Roman empresses, Livia may be said to have done the greatest honour to her dignity, and to have best supported the character of it. Augustus owed a considerable part of his glory to her, and not only consulted her in the most important and difficult affairs, but generally took her advice.'

'... it cannot be denied that there was a great deal of art and cunning in her manner of proceeding, which the emperor did not find out till it was too late.'

'... not even Augustus, with all his art and skill, could avoid being deceived by her. She knew well how to take full advantage of his weakness, and acquired such an ascendancy over him that nothing could resist it; and Caesar, master of the world, might very properly be said to be slave to Livia.'

J. R. de Serviez,
The Roman Empresses, 1718

'In the domestic sphere she cultivated virtue in the time-honoured fashion, she was affable beyond what was approved in women of old, a headstrong mother, a compliant wife, a good match for the intrigues of her husband and the hypocrisy of her son.'

Publius Cornelius Tacitus,
The Annals of Imperial Rome

'No Roman woman ever wielded such power and influence as Livia.'

Donald R. Dudley,
The World of Tacitus, 1968

Livia, Augustus and the Julio-Claudian Dynasty

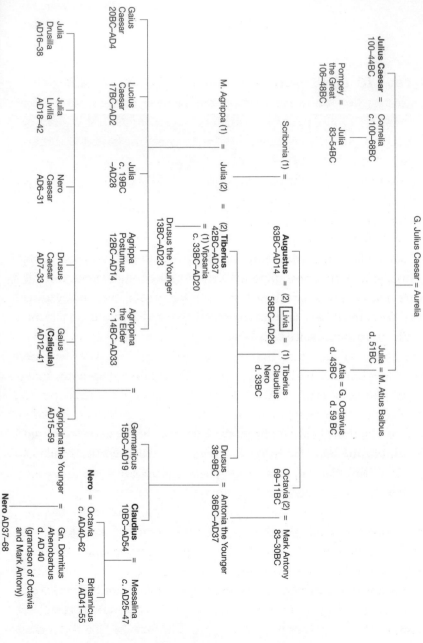

Bold type denotes emperor

Livia was the wife of **Augustus** (r. 31BC–AD14). She was the mother of **Tiberius** (r. AD14–37) through her first husband, Tiberius Claudius Nero. She was the great-grandmother of **Caligula** (r. AD37–41) through her younger son Drusus. She was the grandmother of **Claudius** (r. AD41–54), also through her younger son Drusus. She was the great-great-grandmother of **Nero** (r. AD54–68) through her younger son Drusus via her great-granddaughter Agrippina the Younger.

PREFACE

'He chopped down the family tree'

'It seems to me,' offers the narrator of Tennyson's poem 'Lady Clara Vere de Vere', published in 1842, '"Tis only noble to be good. Kind hearts are more than coronets, and simple faith than Norman blood.'

A century after Tennyson, in a spirit of benign flippancy, those lines inspired a black and white film which remains, on both sides of the Atlantic, among the most popular comedies ever made in Britain. *Kind Hearts and Coronets*, advertised in 1949 with the slogan 'He chopped down the family tree', tells the story of Louis Mazzini, the child of a late-Victorian mésalliance between an English noblewoman and an Italian opera singer. On her death, the family of Louis's mother, the D'Ascoynes, refuses to admit her body to the family crypt. Louis avenges this indignity by removing every D'Ascoyne who stands between him and the family's title. Eight deaths later, he finds himself, as he had intended, Duke of Chalfont. Although the contributions of Evelyn Waugh and Nancy Mitford – both at intervals canvassed for assistance – failed to make it to the final cut, it is a slick piece of screenwriting. It is proof, too, that the oldest jokes can be the best.

Almost two thousand years before the cameras began rolling at Ealing Studios, a man born Tiberius Claudius Nero became second emperor of Rome – despite sharing no blood ties with his predecessor, Augustus. Tiberius was the son of Augustus's wife Livia and her first husband Nero. Livia's second marriage, like that of Mazzini and his D'Ascoyne bride, was the union of a woman of lofty breeding and ancient lineage and a man, in relative terms, of unknown background. With ill grace, Augustus adopted

1

his stepson as his heir five months short of Tiberius's forty-sixth birthday. In poor health and nearing the considerable age of seventy, Augustus justified his action 'for reasons of state'. It was not a choice born of affection and he came to it only after exhausting a number of alternatives.

Between Tiberius and the throne had stood at various moments five or possibly six candidates preferable to Augustus, as well as Augustus himself. All died unexpectedly, in each case in circumstances which remain in part unresolved. Of those six deaths five were attributed by at least one ancient author to the malign intervention of Tiberius's mother. Livia's scheming, her malevolence and, above all, her unbridled maternal ambition and lust for power, so the story goes, jibbed at nothing in pursuit of the throne for her son and a perpetuation through him of her own influence in Rome. She is Louis Mazzini without the smiling insouciance, let loose on a stage set that is larger and darker than the comic opera buffoonery of the latter's mise en scène – like Tennyson's Lady Clara Vere de Vere, a woman of position but cold heart, rejoicing in inflicting cruelty.

In *Kind Hearts and Coronets*, Mazzini writes his memoirs and cheerfully confesses to his dastardly exploits. Livia left no corresponding confession. Nor would she have, since in fact no evidence connects her with the deaths of Marcellus, Marcus Agrippa, Gaius and Lucius Caesar, Agrippa Postumus, Germanicus – or even Augustus. Frequently Livia was hundreds of miles away when her 'victim' died of fever or a battle-wound. On the principle of 'Where there's a will, there's a way', distance apparently proved no obstacle to this mistress of the dark side. In almost every instance her weapon was poison. Against both reason and probability, we are asked to believe that, Mazzini-like, she 'chopped down the family tree'.

Livia's true 'crime' was not murder but the exercise of power. In a society so assertively masculine that its historians avoided mentioning women save as exemplars of outstanding virtue or vice – or, in the unique but vexed case of Cleopatra, as a ruler in her own right – Livia created for herself a public profile and a sphere of influence. The wife of one *princeps* ('leading citizen') of Rome, she became the mother of his successor after a series of unforeseeable deaths. In the early years of Tiberius's reign she was acknowledged by several sources as almost his equal in power. Unofficially she was hailed as 'Mother of Her Country'. But any power she exercised was always circumscribed. Assiduously she confined her visible sphere of influence to acceptable, traditionally female areas. That she won public plaudits for her contribution to Roman life was in itself enough to condemn her – in the eyes not only of contemporaries but also of influential later writers.

Her posthumous deification in AD 41 did not guarantee Livia respect. Tacitus condemned her to eternal Grand Guignol in his revisionist *Annals*, published less than a century after her death. His portrait of a 'feminine bully', a malevolent stepmother and an 'oppressive mother' both to her family and the Roman state eventually inspired the Livia of Robert Graves's ripping yarn, *I, Claudius*. Once Graves's novel became an acclaimed television series in 1976, Livia acquired two lives, that emerging from the scant evidence of the surviving contemporary sources, advanced by scholars, and the stronger meat from which actress Siân Phillips conjured the Livia of the popular imagination. In seeking to create a portrait of Livia, it is necessary to steer between the two.

It would be preposterous to suggest that *Kind Hearts and Coronets*, a piece of postwar levity dressed up in pastiche Edwardian frou-frou, was inspired by Tiberius's accession to supreme power in ancient Rome, or to mine it or the poetry of Tennyson for clues to elucidate our reading of that earlier event; this is not my intention. Robert Hamer's comedy does not draw on historical sources. Possibly the mésalliance of Mazzini's mother recalls the operetta-style marital career of the Habsburg princess Louise of Tuscany, who, divorced from the Crown Prince of Saxony in 1903, four years later married an Italian musician, Enrico Toselli, to the consternation of the courts of Europe. But the connection is tenuous. The point of interest is that, for sixty years, a sophisticated but featherlight comedy of multiple murder has delighted audiences throughout the English-speaking world without any of them imagining there is any truth behind the story. In the case of Livia and Tiberius, readers – and latterly television viewers – have treated a story of comparable plot and similar ghoulishness with greater credulity. What in *Kind Hearts and Coronets* is obviously fiction, in the lost world of ancient Rome becomes believable, despite the origin of Livia's rumoured misdeeds lying with authors who neither pretended nor attempted impartiality and made no effort to substantiate their claims. The truth, as so often, appears richer and stranger than fiction.

'The first forty-two years of the Queen's life,' Lytton Strachey wrote in *Queen Victoria*, 'are illuminated by a great and varied quantity of authentic information. With Albert's death a veil descends.' Just such a veil has descended over much of Livia's life. Periodically, she is absent from or discounted by the sources, or otherwise obscured by the corrupting effect of ancient historians' animosity towards women in general and those closest to the workings of empire and the Julio-Claudian ascendancy in particular. Given such depredations – silence concerning Livia's childhood, virtual silence about her later years – it is not possible to write a conventional biography of this woman who died almost two thousand years ago or, with authority, as Robin Lane Fox once wrote of Alexander the Great, to pretend to certainty in her name. This book is part quest, part cautious conclusion.

CHAPTER 1

'Superbissima'

The walls of the atrium were lined with wooden cupboards, a honey-comb of boxes, each with its own door. Open or closed, there was no secret about the contents of the cupboards. Nor could there be, in this the most public room of the house, accessible to every visitor, invited or unknown. In time, the atrium or main hall would all but disappear from Roman houses, re-imagined as little more than a passageway from the elaborate doors on to the street, closed only in times of mourning, to the private realm within. In the dying days of the Republic, the atrium continued to extend its welcome.

That welcome was more a matter of form than of comfort. This busy room was sparsely furnished. Many objects distracted the eye; few offered respite to tired limbs or indeed the anxious petitioner.

On festival days, when the household altar shone red with the blood of animal sacrifice, the doors of the wooden cupboards stood open. A label, the *titulus*, marked each one, explaining the precise nature of its contents. Or perhaps, not so much its nature as its achievements. For the atrium's wooden cupboards, called *armaria*, contained the past – moments frozen in time, like the blown birds' eggs and preserved but-terflies of Victorian naturalists.

Roman *armaria* displayed the wax ancestor masks of the city's patri-cian nobility, each a cross between a portrait bust and a death mask, framed inside its box. These were the *imagines maiorum* of ancient Rome, recorded in the second century BC by the Greek historian Polybius and described two hundred years later by Pliny the Elder as the archetypal example of traditional Roman domestic art.[1] Today no trace of them remains, except in the written sources. Each mask personated a significant member of the family in whose atrium it stood. Its wooden cupboard was by way of a shrine.

Inclusion within the gallery of *imagines* was a question of hurdles successfully jumped. The subject must be dead; must in its lifetime have held public office above the rank of junior magistrate or 'aedile' – and must, of course, have been a man. We cannot know the quality of craftsmanship, whether the wax was tinted, how the hair was treated or the masks made. All that survive are the complementary accounts of Polybius and Pliny and the less fragile record preserved in stone portrait busts, which presumably shared predominant characteristics with their wax counterparts. Worn or carried by the actors employed in Roman funeral processions, *imagines maiorum* were at the same time realistic in appearance and functional, with holes for the eyes and breathing.[2] They were a public face of Rome's oldest love affair, its romanticizing of its own noble and strenuously masculine history. In Rome, history and legend merged. Even politicians, once dead, became masks for actors, the makers of history mere ciphers in a pageant, reputation a matter for a strolling player. In the Roman Republic, immortality was a reward for public service. The records of the *tituli* were businesslike, impersonal. It was not a sentimental society. Daily, domestic animals – chickens and lambs – found their throats slit in appeasement of gods who offered no lifeline of eternal redemption. A dish of blood spilt on the altar was enough to hold heavenly ire at bay.

What did he see, the visitor to the atrium of this Roman townhouse on a January day in 58 BC? He glimpsed the populous rollcall of honour of one of Rome's greatest families. A fire had been lit – for today a child was born. Slaves would tend the fire for eight days, until the child received its names in a ceremony of purification known as the *dies lustricus*. For eight days the flames of the symbolic fire would lick reflections across the waxy contours of the ancestor masks so proudly displayed in their wooden cases. In vain the *armaria* sought to shield their splendid contents from the heat of the day and the fire's dark smoke. The ancestor masks in question represented the family immortalized by Livy as '*superbissima*', 'excessively haughty', a family almost as old as Rome itself and, like Rome, by turns savage and cruel, distinguished and beneficent: the family of the Claudii.

Its newest member would never be commemorated by a waxen image. She was a girl. Instead, within a century, her cult would be worshipped across the breadth of the Mediterranean world and beyond; her features chiselled from marble and basalt in temples remote from Rome; her name invoked in marriage ceremonies and written histories and inscribed on provincial coinage alongside the legend 'Mother of the World'; her likeness affiliated to personifications of an empire's chosen virtues. At the *dies lustricus* she received from her family two names: Livia Drusilla. For much of her life – and by history – she would be known by the former.

The name of Livia has survived through two millennia, even into generations unfamiliar with ancient history and Rome's written sources. It resonates beyond the confines of any *armarium* or noble atrium, bolder but less easily read than the soft translucency of a portrait carved from wax. It is spiced with accretions of legend and malice . . . sharp-tasting . . . contentious . . . perhaps even dangerous. Its associations embrace good and bad: synonymous with lust for power or the exemplary virtue Romans prized in their women. Livia is a villain; Livia is a victim.

Ancient historians set no store by childhood. Even the contemporary biographies of great men divulge few details of their subjects' earliest years. Since the ancients believed that character was static – it emerged fully formed and neither developed nor altered over time – they had recourse only to their subjects' active years. Childhood simply reflected in a distant, smaller mirror adult truths, as when Suetonius tells us of the Emperor Tiberius, 'His cruel and cold-blooded character was not completely hidden even in his boyhood.'[3]

The whole picture as it appeared to ancient historians is to modern eyes frustratingly incomplete, little more than the terse statements of public office contained in the *tituli* of the aristocratic atrium. How much less, then, do we know of the lives of Roman women. They were excluded by Rome's constitution from holding public office and by extension – as well as by custom – from the ranks of the ancestor masks. Restrictions on their public role inevitably limited what writers could know about them.[4] As the commentator Asconius indicated as early as the first century, it was often impossible simply to identify, let alone elaborate, the wives of even the most prominent men. Across the gulf of two millennia, Roman women's early lives have mostly disappeared from view. Livia's is no exception.

Neither the time nor the place of Livia's birth is known to us. Since no other city of the Roman empire afterwards claimed her as its daughter, it seems safe, in the absence of contradictory information, to assume that she was born in Rome. Modern opinion fixes that event in the year 58 BC, though the ancient sources also offer the previous year, 59, as a possibility. Although the Roman calendar differed significantly from our own, the date 30 January can be stated with reasonable certainty.

The atrium was a place of business, a room of passage and of display, the 'great grand hall' that Vitruvius insisted upon for 'gentlemen who must perform their duties to the citizenry by holding offices and magistracies'.[5] Here the citizenry and a senator's clients – those to whom, as patron, he owed a moral and legal obligation – came to call, to petition or entreat in a morning ritual called the *salutatio*. Aristocratic Roman townhouses of the Republic, unassuming in appearance, lined the city's streets and thoroughfares, and opened directly upon the public way. Only one door admitted entrance from the outside, open throughout the hours of daylight. Inside, at the end of a passage, lay the atrium, flooded with light on account of its open roof and lined with ancestor masks, labelled in their boxes like latter-day portraits or the stuffed natural-history specimens of country-house corridors. Painted family trees, also displayed on the walls of the atrium, made clear the relationships of those eyeless forebears. Somewhere near at hand stood a mighty chest, bound with metal and apparently immoveable. The *arca* contained family papers, some no doubt relating to the faces in the cupboards. It may also have symbolized, and indeed contained, the family's riches. An altar served to honour the *lares*, the spirits of dead ancestors which, like the *imagines*, benignly looked down on the household.

The nature of the visitor's business mattered little. He could not doubt where he stood, nor the source of authority of those he visited. At a glance he absorbed twin concerns of Rome's governing elite: family pride and a microscopic view of Roman history seen through the prism of family greatness. Under the Roman Republic – an oligarchy of office-holding aristocratic families – these galleries of pallid likenesses perpetuated the human scale of politics. They provided too the backdrop of aristocratic childhood.

Beyond the atrium unfolded more private regions of the house, accessible to intimates: friends and family, favoured clients and colleagues. The master of the house conducted public business in the atrium or the adjoining *tablinum*, a shop window of a room displaying records of official transactions.[6] Here clients requested favours or payment in return for votes – or, like one disaffected poet, presented themselves in their smartest clothes to bolster the master's prestige: 'You promise me three *denarii* and tell me to be on duty in your atria, dressed up in my toga. Then I'm supposed to stick by your side ...'[7] Private dealings were reserved for the *cubiculum*, which combined the functions of bedroom and study. It lay beyond the *tablinum*, on the other side of the peristyle. Privacy meant remoteness from the street – from the clamorous, odoriferous tumult of Rome that lapped about the ever-open doors of the grandest houses.

There could be no work on a day like this. Outside, Rome the colossus pursued an unceasing roundelay. The streets rang with innumerable noises: the continuous clatter of building work and that seething, vociferous mass that later drove Martial the epigrammatist to the country – in times of plenty, schoolmasters, bakers, coppersmiths and gold beaters, exchange clerks, soldiers and sailors with bandaged bodies, begging Jews and bleary-eyed matchsellers, all at loose in the crowded city.[8] In times of famine, intermittent through the years of Livia's childhood, the baying of crowds bent on slaughter, arson and mischief jack-knifed through busy streets.[9] Inside, a semblance of calm prevailed. We do not know the whereabouts of Livia's father at the time of her birth. A supporter of Rome's new governing trio of Julius Caesar, Pompey and Crassus – the First 'Triumvirate' – he may have been sent in 59 BC on a fund-raising journey to Alexandria on Egypt's Mediterranean coast. Had he returned by the end of January of the following year, he would have found himself at home, in a room near to that in which his wife was confined, awaiting the birth of their child.

His was not a lonely vigil. At the onset of labour, slaves carried messages to relatives and political associates. Their presence alongside Livia's father fulfilled a traditional requirement that senatorial births be witnessed[10] – though from their non-vantage point in a neighbouring room, none of the watchers witnessed anything but the prospective father's nerves. Five years before the birth of Livia, Suetonius records that Gaius Octavius, the father of Octavian, the future Emperor Augustus and Livia's second husband, arrived late for the Senate's debate on the Catiline Conspiracy. The confinement of his wife Atia had detained him.[11] Since Octavius felt able to miss so critical a debate, at a moment when not only Rome but a number of Italian towns were threatened with armed insurrection, it is safe to assume that childbed attendance by fathers was common practice, at least among Rome's senatorial class.

A father's place, however, was not in the labour room itself. There, the expectant mother toiled in a women's world, attended by slaves, her midwife and often her mother and female relatives. If she was a woman of means, as Livia's mother was, the slaves who ministered to her would have belonged to her personally, not part of the joint marital property, just as her husband owned outright his valet and secretaries. Their faces at least would have been familiar to their mistress. In anticipation of a happy outcome, it is likely that a wet nurse was also to hand.

The newborn baby was placed on the ground, ideally in a beam of sunlight. Romans embraced ritual and superstition: they welcomed natural signs which could be interpreted as good omens. Suetonius records a birth in AD 37 that occurred at dawn. 'The sun was rising and his earliest rays touched the newly born boy almost before he could be laid on the ground, as the custom was.'[12] This crowning by nature proved an accurate foreshadowing. The boychild was Nero, who afterwards, by a roundabout route, inherited Rome's imperial throne.

Admitted at last to the birthing chamber, the father lifted up his newest infant. Symbolically he raised the child – an acknowledgement of paternity and a statement of intent: the child would be allowed to live. For Roman fathers who were the senior living male of their family possessed by ancient acquiescence a power of life and death. That ability, sanctioned by society, was to decide whether a baby should be tended and cared for or exposed at birth, abandoned to certain starvation. Livia's father chose life. Among those who made a different decision for the offspring of their family were the Emperors Augustus and Claudius.

It was cause for moderate rejoicing. In Roman society a daughter could not bestow on her family the prestige a son might bring – even if she became a Vestal Virgin and enjoyed, in addition to a blameless reputation, the highest legal protection of the Roman state, that of sacro-sanctity. But daughters had their uses politically, through the agency of marriage. Roman history abounds with fathers and brothers who exploited the marital careers of their daughters and sisters to advance, or even revive, family influence.[13] Daughters as well as sons inherited the right to own and display ancestor masks. Into the atria of other pow-erful, noble houses Roman daughters carried the symbols of their fore fathers' greatness. It was part of belonging to the special club that was Rome's governing elite. In the century before the birth of Christ, the last of the Roman Republic, blood and ink would be spilled to ensure that club's survival. The sacrificial victims in this instance were fellow Romans.

More precarious in January 58 was the survival of the infant Livia Drusilla. Mortality rates in ancient Rome were alarmingly high. One in three babies died before the end of their first year,[14] while half of all Roman children failed to reach their fifth birthday.[15] Overcrowding and the waves of visitors who flocked to Rome as the centre of a far-flung trading network led to frequent epidemics in the capital. August was the cru ellest month, followed by September, weeks of searing heat and flour-ishing ailments. Aqueducts carried fresh water to parts of the city but standards of sanitation were low. The living conditions of the rich ought to have mitigated these endemic scourges: cooking and bathing were separate in the houses of Rome's first citizens, which also included pri-vate lavatories. Despite this, ignorance of the role of human waste in the spread of disease remained widespread. Food poisoning, too, regu-larly exacted its tariff.[16] The case of Cornelia, celebrated mother of the Gracchi brothers in the second century BC, illustrates the fragility of infant life in Rome: of Cornelia's twelve children, only three survived to adulthood. Infant mortality was simply a fact of life. It is this which provides the context for an otherwise brutal-sounding letter by Seneca. The philosopher counsels a father to grieve moderately at the death of his young son. The boy, Seneca indicates, was too small to be of any social importance; his loss is less significant than would be that of a friend.[17] Possibly Seneca's view of small boys was shaped by his experience as boyhood tutor to the Emperor Nero.

For the moment, all was happiness, signalled by the lighting of the symbolic fire in the atrium. Later, Livia's 'witnesses' would light similar fires on the altars of their own household gods. As soon as news of the birth was widely known, other guests arrived, their purpose curiosity and congratulation. In his miscellany of excerpts, *Athenian Nights*, the Latin author Aulus Gellius recorded one such visit. Friends embraced the new father, asking him for details of his wife's labour and its outcome. 'It had been protracted, and the newly delivered young mother was asleep, so they could not see her. Her mother was also present and clearly in charge of the practicalities, for she had already decided to engage wet nurses to spare her weakened daughter the strain of breast-feeding.'[18]

Livia's mother, too, had recourse to wet nurses. By the last years of the Republic the practice was virtually universal among upper-class Roman mothers. The written sources are vocal in their disapproval. Aulus's hero Favorinus replies to the new grandmother's assertion of her daughter's exhaustion and unfitness for the task, 'Dear lady, I beg you, let her be more than half a mother to her son.' At length he outlines the philosophical arguments in favour of mothers feeding their children,[19] including the striking suggestion that a nurse's milk contains the equivalent of moral ectoplasm, transmitting her moral character to the child she suckles.[20] Other writers dwell on those exemplary women, like Licinia, the wife of Cato the Elder, who bucked the trend and suckled their children themselves. But the sources were written by men. Like the ancestor masks in their wooden cupboards, they embodied an outlook shaped by the certainty of Rome as a man's world.

We do not know at what stage Livia Drusilla of the Claudii absorbed this truism. Her future career would show that she had done so and done so well. But the writers were seldom satisfied. It is a feature of much of Livia's historiography, though not to the same extent of her life, that she consistently inspired in male commentators ambivalence or worse, betrayed in sinister insinuations and dark rumours reproduced with relish. Over time, the grounds of that ambivalence would be made clear. On 30 January, 58 BC she was simply a baby.

CHAPTER 2

In the beginning . . . were the Claudii

In ancient Rome there were powerful reasons for marriage aside from love. Chief among them were politics and money. Was it politics, money or the quest for a wife which in 60 or 59 BC took Marcus Livius Drusus Claudianus, future father of Livia, to the Campanian town of Fundi?

Inland from the Tyrrhenian Sea, on the Via Appia, the principal route from Rome to Italy's heel, the ancient Volscian town of Fundi was commended by Livy for the 'Roman sentiments' it had demonstrated as early as 330 BC, and would later be colonized by veteran soldiers of the Emperor Augustus.[1] The town lay alongside marshy vineyards, the Ager Caecubus, which Pliny remembered for the rich, full flavour of their wine.[2] Since Fundi's only recorded economic role was shipment of this Caecuban wine, it is unlikely that Marcus was drawn there by financial affairs. Nor did Fundi possess, or aspire to, political significance or influence. How, then, did Marcus find himself in Fundi, agreeable home town of Alfidia, his future wife and afterwards Livia's mother?

It is possible that Marcus did not visit Fundi at all. Instead, Marcus Alfidius, Alfidia's father, a man with an eye to a prize, may have chosen to broadcast his daughter's charms in Rome. Indolent patrician youths could not be expected to travel in pursuit of a partner so far from the capital as Fundi, a journey of more than fifty miles. Yet for the socially or politically ambitious parent, a Roman bridegroom offered richer pickings than any home-grown suitor. Naturally the rich made demands of their own, namely further riches in the form of a substantial dowry, but this Marcus Alfidius was both willing and able to satisfy. There is also the possibility that Livia's father discovered Fundi while staying close by. Today remains of ancient villas litter the vicinity. They are Roman country escapes rather than principal dwelling places, close to the seaside with tranquil lakes and mountains nearby, a retreat for the urban rich.

For Marcus Livius Drusus Claudianus was surely rich. He found himself the happy possessor of a double inheritance. In addition to the wealth of his biological parents, of whom we know nothing save that they were Claudians, Marcus benefited from a second stroke of notable good fortune. He was the adopted son of a man whom the Greek historian Diodorus Siculus would afterwards describe as the richest man in Rome:[3] Marcus Livius Drusus, senator and tribune. The son of a tribune of the same name, Drusus had exploited his considerable wealth - and the freedom from factional allegiance it granted him - to propose swingeing legislative reform, notably the extension of Roman citizenship into the regions of Italy. Inevitably his plans aroused unease among Rome's conservative governing body, the Senate. In 91 BC, in the atrium of his house on the Palatine, Drusus was fatally stabbed. The murder weapon was a suitably lethal-sounding leather worker's knife.[4]

Drusus's assassination has one happy outcome for the modern reader. It offers us a definite pointer to Livia's father's age. Adoption was widespread in Roman life. Unlike modern adoption, it did not arise from the unwillingness or inability of a child's biological parents to take care of it; nor did it imply that the child's parents had died or divorced. Romans were frequently adopted as adults, even, as would be the case with Livia, in extreme old age. The process was a means of strengthening ties between families and clans - and calls of affection reverberated less insistently than the claims of politics and economics. Marcus may have been adopted in Drusus's will. The alternative and more likely course - one which would explain his use of the name Marcus, which was not typical of patrician Claudians - was that Drusus adopted his 'son' during the boy's lifetime. This suggests that Marcus was born not later than around 93 BC, placing him in his mid-thirties or upwards at the time of Livia's birth. Such a relatively advanced age for a Roman noble to become a father might in some instances indicate that the bridegroom had been married before: in Marcus's case, corroborative evidence is lacking. We can conclude with greater certainty that there was a marked difference in age between Marcus and his wife.

In the event, Marcus Alfidius raised no objections to his daughter's marriage on grounds of age. He is unlikely to have raised objections at all, but rather opted to play the role of chief advocate and presiding Cupid. Twice over, by birth and by adoption, Alfidia's husband stood in the first rank of Rome's great families. It was not a boast Alfidius or his daughter could match.

Ancient Rome was quite clear about what constituted conferring a favour in marriage. If the alliance were one between wealth and birth, the concessions were made by the party of ancient lineage, that partner who furnished the atrium of the marital home with his or her entitlement of mask-filled *armaria*. The spouse who was simply wealthy occupied the junior position.

Half a century before Livia's birth, Julius Caesar's aunt married a man who seven times held the consulship. Consuls were the Roman Republic's highest-ranking executive officers, empowered for twelve-month terms to mastermind Rome's principal civil and military programmes. Gaius Marius's unprecedented achievement was to hold repeatedly a position which Roman law had previously forbidden to be held by the same individual twice in a decade. His achievement was doubly impressive. For Marius was the first member of his family to enter politics. This made him, in Roman terms, a *novus homo* or 'new man', and stacked the odds against him: the Roman constitution disdained outsiders. His ascent was copiously rewarded with power, influence and wealth. To this he added status in the form of his marriage to Julia.

Julia, as her name suggests, was a member of the Julian clan, one of Rome's oldest aristocratic families. It mattered little whether the Julians at that point retained their wealth or prominence. In marrying a man of obscure origin, it was Julia who bestowed the favour. Marius, endowing Julia with his sumptuous worldly goods – which included a house on the Sacra Via close to the Forum at the very heart of Rome – received the honour. At his aunt's funeral, Julius Caesar expressed forcefully the way of the Roman world: 'My Aunt Julia's family is descended on her mother's side from kings and on her father's side from the immortal gods.'5 There was no room to argue. Nor would many in Rome have thought to do so.

The Alfidii were not patrician. They were also, as we have seen, not Roman in origin. In 60 BC, when Marcus extended the benison of his gentle breeding and multiple *armaria*, no Alfidius had held the great offices of the Roman state. In Fundi the family were aristocrats, Alfidia's father a town councillor. Such claims cut no mustard in Rome. There the Alfidii were so little known that subsequent generations confused them with the similarly named Aufidii, giving rise to speculation that Livia's forebears had been senators, gastronomes and even peacock farmers. In Rome, Alfidia's only consequence lay in her dowry.

The Romans were pragmatic about money. Just as they considered a rich woman fortunate to marry a distinguished man, independent of his financial condition, so they applauded the nobleman's good sense in choosing a rich wife. Her fortune, they saw, would enable him to pursue his birthright, the *cursus honorum* or 'course of honours', that sequence of public offices from which, under the Roman oligarchy, men of non-patrician background (Gaius Marius was an exception) were carefully excluded.[6] The Romans did have a concept of mésalliance – a senator marrying a prostitute or freedwoman, for example – but Marcus's marriage to Alfidia fell outside its bounds. By the end of the Republic, half a century of civil wars had left the ranks of the patricians too depleted to permit marriage exclusively between families of similar standing. Only three patrician families – the Metelli, the Ahenobarbi and the Caepiones – cocked a snook at changing mores and resisted marrying non-nobles.[7] Added to this, under the Republic, Romans' first concern was with paternal descent, making Alfidia largely insignificant in Livia's make-up. When Mark Antony poured scorn on the humble origins of Octavian, Livia's future husband, it was his father's family who concerned him: 'one great-grandfather who was a freedman and a rope-maker from the country round Thurii and another of African extraction who first sold scent and later bread at Aricia.'[8] Antony ignored Octavian's mother, Atia. Comfortably patrician, she was also, through her relationship to Julius Caesar, niece to a god.

Although Livia and Mark Antony would occupy opposing sides in the battle for supremacy in Rome – a battle won as much with words as through armed combat – it is significant that, Alfidia's municipal origins notwithstanding, Mark Antony did not disparage Livia's ancestry.

In Roman terms the background of Marcus Livius Drusus Claudianus and his daughter was unimpeachable.

In the beginning, more or less, were the Claudii. Seven years after the expulsion of Rome's seventh and last king, with the advent of the Roman Republic arrived in the city a Sabine leader described by Livy as 'harsh by nature'. He was Attus or Attius Clausus, founding father of the Claudii. Clausus evidently combined harshness with determination: within a decade the immigrant from Regillum had been appointed consul. During the next four and three-quarter centuries – the lifespan of the Republic – Clausus's family would attain twenty-seven further consulships, five dictatorships, seven censorships, six triumphs and two ovations in Suetonius's reckoning of their exceptional tally. It was an achievement none could match. The Claudii became one of only five families said to occupy a special, elevated subgroup of their own, the '*maiores*' – along with the Aemilii, Cornelii, Fabii and Valerii. A Claudius was among the ten patricians or 'Decemvirs' who, in 451 BC, took the place of that year's consuls, entrusted with the task of codifying Rome's ancient laws. Livia's family found themselves authors of Rome's first written legal charter, the Twelve Tables.

In the following century, the Claudii branded their physical imprint on Rome – and on the Italian mainland at the same time. Appius Claudius Caecus, censor, consul and dictator, provided Rome with her first aqueduct, the Aqua Appia. He also spearheaded construction of the road which bore his name, the Via Appia. That southerly thoroughfare connected Rome to Capua via Aricia and Fundi, slicing through the foul-smelling malarial swamps of the Pomptine Marshes whose night-croaking frogs were audible to Cicero and Horace.[9] Among Appius's children were a brace of sons: Publius Claudius Pulcher, Claudius 'the Fair', and Tiberius Claudius Nero, the surname, Nero Suetonius tells us, Sabine for 'strong and energetic'.[10] From them descended the family's twin branches, the Claudii Pulchri and Claudii Nerones. Most historians accept Suetonius's assertion that Livia's paternal grandfather, Marcus's biological father, was a Claudius Pulcher, either Gaius or Appius. Both held the consulship. In time Livia would marry a Neronian cousin and reunite in the blood of their children the twin threads of the earlier Appius's legacy.

It would be fanciful to expect that legacy to be one of virtue uncorrupted. As if the tag of excessive haughtiness were not enough, Livy went a step further and labelled the Claudii in addition '*crudelissima*', 'exceedingly cruel'. Suetonius, who prided himself on the rigour of his investigations into family history, consigned Livia's family to posterity as 'violent and arrogant';[11] we do not know the extent to which he had Livia in mind. Stories of unedifying Claudian hauteur shadow the ancient sources. Through works by Livy, Suetonius, Cicero, Cassius Dio and even the sycophantic Valerius Maximus marches the parade of offenders: the Decemvir Appius Claudius, whose unrelenting lustful harassment of the youthful Verginia resulted in her father stabbing her to preserve her honour; Publius Claudius Pulcher, to whose contempt for the gods was attributed devastating naval defeat in the First Punic War, with loss of life and ships; Appius Claudius Pulcher, denied a military triumph only to stage it himself independently, taking with him as protection in his chariot his daughter Claudia, a sacrosanct Vestal Virgin; and Publius Clodius Pulcher, arch-enemy of Cicero, accused of incestuous relations on a grand scale.

How far can we trust such accounts? With the exception of Cicero's letters and speeches, most were written comfortably after the event. If we are deceived in them, what is their authors' intent? Is their purpose to present an accurate portrait of a prominent family? Do they deliberately denigrate the Claudian inheritance at a time when the Claudians best known to their readers were Livia, her son Tiberius or the three Julio-Claudian emperors who succeeded him? Such a purpose illuminates the reputation of later Claudians and cannot be discounted from our ultimate evaluation of their characters. Suetonius's tag of violence and arrogance is one which would raise its head more than once in the lives of both Livia and her elder son.

On 30 January 58 BC expectations for the infant Livia Drusilla were straightforward. If the gods spared her, she would grow up to become the wife and mother of upstanding Roman men devoted to the good of the state. No one present in Marcus's house the day Alfidia gave birth anticipated Livia wielding the power of a decemvir or holding a naval or military command – and indeed she did none of these things. In her education there would be precepts from the past. She must learn from the *women* of her family. Through their ranks, too, flowed ebb tides of good and bad.

At a point between high and low tide on an April day in 204 BC, the people of Rome gathered at the harbour of Ostia, west of the city. The Second Punic War against Carthage, referred to by Romans as the war against Hannibal, had already lasted fifteen years. On that April day, a metaphorical sun was shining. The Sibylline Books had advised the transfer to Rome of a black stone emblem of the goddess the Romans called Cybele, the 'Great Mother', a deified personification from ancient Phrygia of the Earth Mother. An oracle of the Books had promised that, close on the heels of the goddess, peace would come to Rome. Later, Roman authorities would regard Cybele's cult with antipathy, wary of the frenzy of her worship: clashing cymbals, beating drums and howling eunuch priests, the Galli. In 204 BC the Senate requested the man considered Rome's *vir optimus* ('best man'), Publius Cornelius Scipio Nasica, to greet the statue at the harbourside. He was accompanied by a deputation of the city's most virtuous matrons. Among them was a woman of the Claudii, Claudia Quinta. We do not know the grounds for her inclusion. Her beauty, Ovid recalled, was a match for her high birth.[12] Her reputation, as Livy recorded, was doubtful.

What happened next is uncertain, lost amid the romantic impulses of later chroniclers. The harbour at Ostia was prone to silting – today the town stands at a remove of several kilometres from the sea, cut off by centuries of sandbanks. The ship bearing the Great Mother ran aground on silt or sand. Every effort made to move her failed. Until Claudia Quinta stepped forward. 'They say I am not chaste . . . If I am free of crime, give by thine act a proof of my innocence and, chaste as thou art, do thou yield to my chaste hands.'[13] The ship proceeded on its course. The statue was borne triumphant back to Rome, passed along the line of matrons to the Temple of Victory on the Palatine. Claudia's virtue, once questioned, was set in stone. Her own statue would shortly be erected in the temple porch, close to that of the Great Mother. As if to silence history's doubters, the statue twice survived destruction by fire. Three years later, the Second Punic War ended in victory for Rome.

The legend of Claudia Quinta proved long-lasting. A medieval wood-cut depicts a wimpled Claudia accomplishing her feat of strength singlehanded, pulling the ship to shore with no more than a silken girdle. At the end of the fifteenth century the Sienese painter Neroccio de' Landi chose Claudia Quinta as one of seven literary and biblical paragons for a domestic commission illustrating the nature of virtue.

But if Claudia's virtue was not forgotten, it suffered a temporary eclipse in the year of Marcus and Alfidia's marriage.

In 61 BC a woman of the Claudii became the mistress of an unmarried man six years her junior. Their affair lasted three years. It terminated acrimoniously in 59, when the woman took a new lover. He was younger still, twelve years younger than she was. He was also, unfortunately, a friend of the woman's former lover. His name was Marcus Caelius Rufus, an ambitious aristocrat from Picenum. His sights were set not so much on his high-born mistress as a future senatorial career which he afterwards pursued with vigour. His friend's ambitions were not political, although he too was of equestrian rank and, lovelorn, would serve on the staff of the governor of Bithynia. His name was Gaius Valerius Catullus. In a sequence of poems which continues to be read more than two thousand years later, Catullus charted the progress and collapse of his affair with his Claudian mistress. He called her Lesbia. She was almost certainly Clodia Metelli, a descendant of Appius Claudius and wife of Quintus Metellus Celer, praetor and Governor of Cisalpine Gaul. Thanks to Catullus she is, after Cleopatra, the most infamous love object of the ancient world.

Clodia was one of six siblings. Each enjoyed a reputation for erratic behaviour and sexual unorthodoxy. In addition to her affair with Catullus, which began while her husband was alive and ended in the year of his death (this, some said, caused by poisoning at Clodia's hands), Clodia was suspected of incest. Her sibling paramour was her youngest brother, that Publius Clodius Pulcher who, like Clodia herself, earned Cicero's opprobrium. According to her brother-in-law

Marcus Lucullus, Clodia shared her brother's favours with both her sisters.

Were their friends sympathetic to Marcus and Alfidia, as they waited to witness Livia's birth in January 58? Seldom had the Claudian name been of greater prominence. Clodius, despite his aberrances, rode the crest of a wave. As tribune of the plebs, he was responsible for four bills passed in the month of Livia's birth. One in particular earned him widespread popular support. It involved reorganization of the State-subsidized supply of grain throughout Italy: chief among its provisions was the award of a regular free dole of grain to citizens in Rome.[14] By birth, of course, Clodius was disqualified from occupying the powerful position of tribune of the plebs. But in April 59 he had forsworn patrician status to be adopted by a plebeian and become himself of non-senatorial, plebeian rank.

Vengeful and unforgiving, Cicero was poised to demolish for ever vestiges of Clodia's reputation. Pungent rumours of her dire doings circulated throughout Livia's infancy. Cicero's chance came in April 56. His speech in defence of Caelius Rufus broadcast Clodia's disgrace across Rome – and across the divide of the centuries to modern readers. There are powerful reasons for doubting that either sibling had enhanced the Claudian name.

Happily, Marcus belonged by adoption to a different family. The Livii Drusi had achieved distinctions as great as the Claudii if fewer of them, in their case a total of eight consulships, two censorships, three triumphs and a dictatorship.[15] Marcus's adoptive father, Marcus Livius Drusus, had won popular acclaim for his proposal to extend Roman citizenship without forfeiting or denying his patrician rank. For his troubles he had been murdered. Kinship with a martyr to the cause of the common man would hinder neither Marcus nor his infant daughter.

As he lay dying, Velleius Paterculus records, Marcus Livius Drusus gave voice to a characteristically Roman last utterance: 'When will the State have another citizen like me?'[16] Not, certainly, in the person of his granddaughter Livia. Throughout her long life Livia resisted martyrdom to any cause. Cautious of controversy, careful to circumvent censure, she bent her instincts on survival. Not for her Drusus's contentious public utterances. Perhaps she drew inspiration from her namesake, her great-aunt Livia, wife of the consul Publius Rutilius Rufus. That Livia, Pliny tells us, survived to the remarkable age of ninety-seven.[17]

CHAPTER 3

'Innocent of guilt'

Livia was just months old when traces of her inheritance were erased from the streets of Rome. This came about through a combination of gang violence, animosity between leading citizens and a voluntary exile.

The house of Livia's adoptive grandfather stood on the Clivus Victoriae on the northwest side of the Palatine Hill, Republican Rome's favourite residential quarter. It had been built earlier the same century by an architect whose remit was clear. 'If you have any kind of skill,' Marcus Livius Drusus had instructed him, 'you will build my house so that no matter what I'm doing, everyone can see it.'[1] Grandiloquent as such a sentiment may have sounded, Drusus's insistence on transparency would cost him dear. Within years of its completion, as we have seen, the house became the site of his murder.

It probably did not, however, immediately devolve upon his adopted son, Marcus Livius Drusus Claudianus. Rome had no principle of primogeniture. Even if Marcus were his 'father's' foremost heir, he would have been legally prevented from receiving the latter's fortune outright. Instead Drusus's house was sold. Its site retained for the moment associations with its builder and, indirectly, with Marcus and his fledgling family.

But it was not to last. In 62 BC, the house was sold again, on this occasion for the considerable sum of three and a half million sesterces.[2] The vendor was Marcus Licinius Crassus, the purchaser Cicero. Whether either rebuilt Drusus's house – a frequent undertaking among the contemporary Roman elite – we do not know.

It was in the same year that Cicero had embarked on a collision course with Livia's troublesome kinsman Publius Clodius Pulcher. He destroyed the latter's alibi in a scandalous trial involving all-female religious rites and Clodius's secret affair with Julius Caesar's wife Pompeia. The ill feeling of that trial harrowed fertile ground which, as we know, six years later erupted into ugly bloom. Clodius and Cicero stood as prosecution and defence at the trial of Clodia's former lover and Cicero's erstwhile protégé Marcus Caelius Rufus. Cicero, on that occasion, emerged the victor. In the intervening years, however, Clodius had exploited his position as tribune of the plebs to make the waters of Rome as hot as possible for his opponent, and in the spring of 58 Cicero had departed the city for voluntary exile. His absence was of short duration – but long enough to enable a pro-Clodian rabble to raze his house, formerly the home of Livia's grandfather, scatter his furniture and statues, and annexe areas of the site for projects of Clodius's own, including, in Cassius Dio's account, the dedication of a temple of Liberty.[3]

Where, then, was Marcus and Alfidia's house, in which Livia was born and where she would spend the greater part of her childhood? The answer, of course, is probably lost. The Clivus Victoriae ascended the Palatine from the Velabrum, the low valley between the Palatine and Capitoline hills bookended by the Forum and the cattle market. Popular and prestigious, it was home to much of senatorial Rome, not only Cicero but also Clodius and, at least until the year before Livia's birth, the faithless Clodia – a motley agglomeration of neighbours for a young girl. If, as seems probable, Marcus's house was close by, Livia would spend almost the whole of her long life in this select enclave on Rome's most sacred hill. Within walking distance lay the Temple of Victory – and that statue of Claudia Quinta which stood as a perpetual memorial to the heights attainable by Claudian womanhood.

It was an environment calculated to foster family pride. Souvenirs of five hundred years of Claudian distinction lined the walls of Marcus's atrium. They spilled over into the adjoining *alae* or wings – a wax mask for each of the holders of those twenty-eight Claudian consulships, the generations of censors and dictators, winners of triumphs and ovations. Supplementary were the accretions of Livii Drusi office-holders. 'There could not be a more beautiful or ennobling sight for a young man eager for fame and respect,' Polybius had written of such a display. 'For who would not be inspired to see the images of those men renowned for their excellence . . . The greatest result is that young men are thus inspired to undertake anything for the public good in the hope of winning the glory that attends on brave men.'[4]

Polybius's focus, characteristic of the ancient world, was masculine endeavour. In the century after the historian's death, is it not possible that such a display, glimpsed daily, exerted a similar enchantment over a daughter of the Claudii and Livii Drusi? Hostile ancient sources notwithstanding, there is little to suggest that at any point in her life Livia's ambitions significantly transgressed accepted boundaries of the female sphere – and much to the contrary. Her self-perception confined itself within the perimeters Rome prescribed for its women: she was daughter, wife and mother. But at a relatively early age, in marrying Octavian, Livia embraced eminence apparently without fear. When that association brought her fame, she took pains to ensure that fame was accompanied by respect. We cannot know what in her own mind constituted the grounds of that respect: her position as wife of Rome's first citizen . . . or an awareness of her unique inheritance of two families' greatness, renown for excellence spanning half a millennium . . .

'I read over your letters again and again, and am continually taking them up, as if I had just received them; but, alas! this only stirs in me a keener longing for you,' Pliny the Younger wrote to his wife Calpurnia.[5] 'You cannot believe how much I miss you. I love you so much and we are not used to separations. So I stay awake most of the night thinking of you . . .'[6] Thanks to publication of his letters within his own lifetime, Pliny's marriage to Calpurnia is among history's most famously happy. If that happiness was exceptional, such an outcome was not, insofar as Pliny allows us to discern, a source of surprise to him. 'What less could be expected?' he once asked Calpurnia's aunt Hispulla.[7] His reaction is evidence that, by the beginning of the second century AD, at least some upper-class Romans regarded marriage not simply as a response to social, political and economic pressures, but a personal union promising ideally emotional fulfilment to both partners.

It is impossible to offer more than the most conjectural picture of the emotional climate in which Livia spent her childhood. Were Marcus and Alfidia happy? We do not know. Did they expect to find happiness in marriage a century and a half before Pliny married Calpurnia? Perhaps. Marcus, by one account, had his peccadilloes. Again Marcus Caelius Rufus and Cicero intrude into Livia's sphere. In 50 BC, Caelius Rufus wrote to his mentor. Livia's father, probably at that point a praetor, was presiding over a court. The cases under review all violated the Scantinian law. That vintage piece of Republican legislation penalized homosexual acts,[8] if a reference in Quintilian is correct, 'criminal fornication' between men and 'free-born boys' – young men who were not slaves.[9] Quintilian records a fine in one instance of ten thousand sesterces. Caelius Rufus makes no comment beyond asserting the irony of Marcus, in implementing the Lex Scantinia, being in a position to censure others.[10]

We are not compelled to conclude from this that Livia's father was unfaithful to her mother with a succession of Roman youths, but the possibility exists. Taunts of homosexuality were common among Rome's magistrate classes. Roman society did not regard such transgressions in the same light as may modern readers, although it drew the line at passive homosexuality and incest. No recorded response of Alfidia's survives. She may sensibly have concluded that 'free-born boys' represented a lesser challenge than Marcus taking a mistress. Such a reaction would be in keeping with the policy advocated for husbands by the eminent contemporary writer Varro: 'A husband must either put a stop to his wife's faults or else he must put up with them. In the first case he makes his wife a more attractive woman, in the second he makes himself a better man.'[11] The first course, it goes without saying, was not open to Alfidia. It is unlikely that Livia was aware of this aspect of her parents' lives, if indeed it existed. There is no evidence of a divorce between Marcus and Alfidia nor, save in Caelius Rufus's correspondence, of scandal attaching to either of them.

Latin does not contain a word specifically for baby. While this should not be interpreted as proof that individual Romans were uninterested in their infant offspring, it is indicative of a broader detachment. The Romans recognized the extent to which babies required and merited adult attention. Lucretius, in his history of the natural world, acknowledges that human children are more helpless in their early stages than the young of any other species.¹² What Romans did not perpetuate in relation to babies and small children was a culture of doting.

Tacitus was one of several ancient writers to decry the ubiquity of wet-nursing. He applauded those mothers who fostered a closer bond with their babies, but he did not idealize the menial aspects of child-care. In the *Dialogues*, he attributes to the orator Vipstanus Messalla sentiments expressive of traditional Roman philosophy. 'In the early days, every child born of a good mother was reared not in the dismal room of a mercenary nurse, but in the lap of its own mother, enfolded in her care. Such a woman took particular pride in being described as looking after her home and devoting herself to her children.'¹³ A mother's pride, however, stuck at physical drudgery. That side of childrearing was entrusted to slaves. Slaves, like later nurserymaids, exercised the day-to-day care of children. Their responsibility lasted throughout the period of *infantia*, which Quintilian indicates continued until around the child's seventh birthday, the point at which, typically, formal learning began.¹⁴ In wealthy households like that of Livia's parents, this task would have been shared by several slaves, even if the family numbered only one child. The child enjoyed both its mother's care and affection and that of its attendant slaves.

All the pointers indicate that Livia was an only child. The sources do not record any siblings and none is known to have come forward during the long period of Livia's public prominence, when close relationship to the wife of Rome's emperor would have been obviously advantageous. Added to this is the fact that Marcus, adopted as a child by Drusus, in turn himself adopted a son.

His choice fell on a scion of the Scribonius Libo family. The boy in question was the eldest son of Lucius Scribonius Libo, consul in 34 BC. In keeping with standard practice, he took the name Marcus Livius Drusus Libo and as such would himself attain the consulship under the empire of Livia's second husband.

Through his biological father, Marcus's adopted son was a nephew of Scribonia, who later preceded Livia as the wife of Octavian. Indirectly, therefore, by adopting Libo and uniting the two families more closely,

Marcus may have been instrumental in bringing together Livia and the husband who catapulted her name into the history books. None of this, of course, can have been in Marcus's mind at the time and it seems probable, since we hear of no relationship existing between Livia and her adopted brother, that Libo's adoption was accomplished at the very end of Marcus's life, perhaps even in his will. Since Livia was already married by this time and no longer living with Marcus and Alfidia, she and Libo, though near contemporaries in age,[15] may have been virtual strangers to one another.

Despite the example of Cornelia of the Gracchi with her twelve children, Livia's only-child status was not particularly unusual. Upper-class families of the late Republic invariably extended to no more than two or three children. In part this was attributable to high rates of infant mortality and the hazards of childbirth to mothers, but only in part. In the absence of primogeniture, Romans avoided excessive division of patrimony and estates.[16] Society women, we are told by commentators from Seneca to Juvenal, were adept at avoiding pregnancy, as much for the preservation of their good looks as their health.[17] It was part of an argument which had raged almost from the Republic's origins. Although the Romans possessed no formal definition of marriage before Modestinus in the early third century AD,[18] there had long been an acceptance that the purpose of marriage was children – in the case of the upper classes, those children the Republic required for its continued smooth running. Eunomia, in Plautus's comedy of the early second century BC, *The Pot of Gold*, counsels her brother to action which will do him everlasting good: marriage 'to produce children'.[19] Augustus later castigated unmarried and childless men for failing to carry out 'any of the duties of men' and expressed the wish that they 'did not exist at all'.[20] Actress and emperor issued advice which senatorial Romans before and after Marcus found all too easy to disregard.

There were advantages for Livia, of course. The Romans' espousal of a recognizable small nuclear family created bonds of intimacy between parents and their offspring, even in the absence of any widespread fondness for small children. The management by slaves of the more arduous aspects of childcare, together with the limited number of children in most households, in some cases enabled significant parental involvement in the nursery.

The Emperor Augustus, in sentiments attributed to him by the Greek historian Cassius Dio, commended parenthood as a means of self-perpetuation. 'Is it not a joy to acknowledge a child who possesses the qualities of both parents, to tend and educate a being who is both the physical image of yourself, so that, as it grows up, another self is created? Is it not blessed, on quitting this life, to leave behind as successor ... one that is your own, born of your own essence, so that only the mortal element of you passes away, while you live on in the child that succeeds you?'[21] But there are notable suggestions that this essentially egocentric view did not predominate. Plutarch records that even Cato the Censor, a strict traditionalist in matters relating to the family, made a habit unless prevented by public duty of being present at his son's bathtime, while Aulus Gellius devoted to his literary life only time left over from the more pressing duties of administering his estate and attending to his children's education.[22] According to Lucretius, young men's funeral services of the late Republic, the period of Livia's childhood, included a stock lament that a deceased father would never again have his children run to him to be kissed and lifted to his breast.[23] Cato himself may have been a forbidding figure, but such instances indicate that, at least within the confines of the home, Roman fathers were able to enjoy openly affectionate relations with their children.

It is a picture that is sometimes difficult to reconcile with that of the archetypal Roman mother. Tradition – beloved of upper-class Romans – made clear demands on the Republic's mothers. Their purpose was not primarily, as it is understood today, the creation of a secure and loving environment. Senatorial mothers carried within them the blueprint of an ideal Roman. Their task was to realize that blueprint.

Emphasis rested on discipline, moral vigilance and ethical rigour.[24] It was a stern code which made greater provision for the good of the State than that of mother or child. 'Had I a dozen sons, each in my love alike,' says Shakespeare's Volumnia, mother of Coriolanus, 'I had rather had eleven die nobly for their country than one voluptuously surfeit out of action.'[25] The ancient sources reveal how near the mark was Shakespeare's estimate. The poet Horace refers to time dragging for the children of widows, bound by maternal authority, while Cicero mentions the severe punishments meted out by mothers or teachers for breaches of mourning.[26] Although it was the senior male of a Roman household, the *paterfamilias*, who exercised power by right of law – the so-called *patria potestas*, by which the *paterfamilias* possessed the right of life and death, as well as ongoing control of his children's financial affairs – in practice the male and female roles of father and mother were not sharply differentiated. Both held authority. Neither served as sole provider of a child's quantum of love and kindness. Both felt in equal measure the responsibility imposed by past exempla.

Even the most deeply cherished theories cannot consistently reap results. The history of Republic and Empire alike abounds with men and women who failed to meet – or chose to bypass – the exacting standards Rome sought to impose by ancient precept. Parents and especially children resisted the pale inspiration of wax ancestor masks, the stirring didacticism of those documents of family greatness hidden in the *arca*. They were the targets of Velleius Paterculus, writing Rome's history at the beginning of the first century AD: 'The older discipline was discarded to give place to the new. The state passed from vigilance to slumber, from the pursuit of arms to the pursuit of pleasure, from activity to idleness.'[27] They ignored Horace's poetic warning:

> Roman, you may be innocent of guilt,
> Yet you shall pay for each ancestral crime,
> Until our mouldering temples are rebuilt
> And the gods' statues cleansed of smoke and grime.[28]

Livia was not among their number, as her future career will show, although, as time passed, few around her matched her determined self-control. As an adult married to Rome's first emperor, she embraced and embodied age-old concepts of ideal Roman womanhood, her public persona a deliberate sop to nostalgia for a mythical, more virtuous past. Her outlook was shaped by the demands made on her by her husband, at a moment of constitutional innovation, to exemplify cultural norms, and by her consciousness of her own place in the long continuum of Roman history. She accepted that that place was hers in the first instance by dint of birth. Her education began early – in the atrium of her father's house, where the smoke of daily sacrifice scorched the cheeks of veteran *imagines*, and at her mother's knee.

CHAPTER 4

'Virility to her reasoning power'

In 50 BC Cicero was buying and Marcus was selling. The commodity being traded was a garden. The business of its purchase occupied a succession of letters between Cicero and a Roman knight called Atticus.

Undoubtedly, Marcus jeopardized the deal's smooth progress by digging in his heels over price. Cicero drove a hard bargain. In his case, reluctance to compromise on price arose from dissatisfaction with the goods in dispute. Marcus's garden had not been the orator's first choice. Of the names on Atticus's shortlist, only Marcus was prepared to sell.

Cicero's instructions to Atticus entrusted the equestrian with a degree of responsibility. 'If you ask, what is it I wish for? First, Scapula's gardens, then Clodia's; afterwards, if Silius refuses and Marcus is unreasonable, those of Cusinius and Trebonius ... But if you prefer Tusculanum, as you have signified in some of your letters, I shall not object to it.'[1] Of these seven options two – the gardens of Clodia and Marcus – would recur throughout the letters. Atticus, clearly, cared little for the latter. 'Though you say you quite revolt from Marcus's gardens,' Cicero replied to him, 'yet I must be content with those, unless you can find something else. The building I do not regard.'[2] It was a half-hearted endorsement. Later Cicero wavered. In a subsequent letter, he told Atticus, 'Those of Silius and of Marcus do not appear to me sufficiently respectable for a family residence. How would it become one to remain for any length of time in such a villa as that? I should therefore prefer, first, Otho's; and next to that, Clodia's. If nothing can be done, either some stratagem must be practised upon Marcus, or I must be content with Tusculanum.'[3]

In the event, evidently, nothing could be done, and Atticus's stratagem prevailed with Marcus. Cicero himself provides us with a clue to the motives of Livia's father in selling his gardens. In discussing Clodia's resistance to Atticus's approaches, he writes, 'I do not suppose . . . that she will sell; for she takes pleasure in it and is in no want of money.' [4] It is unlikely, in a city as crowded as Rome, that Marcus, like Clodia, did not also take pleasure in his property. Perhaps, then, Marcus was indeed in want of money.

How had this come about? We can be reasonably certain that Marcus had received a significant inheritance from Drusus. In addition, Alfidius probably provided his daughter with a handsome dowry, her entrée to such glittering marriage stakes. Under Roman law of this period, Marcus was entitled to mortgage any property included in Alfidia's dowry for his own use without Alfidia's consent. That there is no evidence to suggest he did this may in itself tell us something positive about the nature of Livia's parents' marriage.

By the time of Cicero's purchase, nine years after Marcus and Alfidia's marriage, Marcus had attained the rank of praetor, one of the Republic's senior magistracies with a powerful judicial role, as we have seen. The praetorship was an elected position. In ancient Rome, victory in the hustings seldom came cheap.

The satirist Juvenal famously denounced the political disengagement of Romans who craved, he claimed, only two things in return for their loyalty: bread and circuses. His was not a solitary lament. Five years before Livia's birth, Cicero defended Lucius Licinius Murena against a charge of bribery in the consular elections. His speech contained valuable lessons for every politically ambitious Roman. His point was simple: 'The Roman people . . . love public magnificence.'[5] Cicero illustrated his argument with reference to a case from the end of the second century BC.

The senatorial career of Quintus Tubero had stalled at the position of praetor. Tubero was mean; his parsimony cost him votes and esteem. Asked to oversee banquet preparations at the funeral of the Punic War hero Scipio Africanus, Tubero 'used goatskins to cover his wretched Punic stools, and set up Samian crockery, as if indeed it were Diogenes the Cynic who were dead and not as if they were doing honour at his death to that great man Africanus.'[6] Punic or Carthaginian stools were low, narrow benches, Samian crockery the inexpensive red earthenware used by Romans as everyday table- and kitchenware; goatskins, too, clearly fell short of expectations. It was not the route to Romans' hearts, and Quintus Tubero, despite first-rate patrician connections, paid with his career. Julius Caesar, by contrast, achieved electoral victory in 65 BC partly as a result of his lavish spending on renovation of the Appian Way.

There had been too many politicians among the Claudii and Livii Drusi for Marcus not to have learned so fundamental a lesson. The demands of public life on the private purse were urgent and pressing. Votes existed for the buying, popular support for the wooing with bribes. Clients too exacted their fistful of silver. It is quite possible that it was the cost of politics which necessitated Marcus's sale to Cicero – a case of losing one part of Rome in order to win over another.

We cannot assess the nature of Marcus's financial needs. Nor can we form an estimate of whether their extent was such as to impact on Livia's childhood. Marcus had family connections in Pisaurum. A Roman colony of the second century BC, northeast of Rome on the Via Flaminia, Pisaurum was described by Catullus as 'sickly.'[7] Marcus's connections with the 'sickly' colony evidently continued to play a part in his life, since Cicero referred to him mockingly as Pisauran – scarcely a compliment in the light of Catullus's estimate. Cicero's reference may further suggest that Marcus retained property in the colony. In 42 BC Livia would give birth to her first child, Tiberius. In the following century, according to Suetonius, a belief was widespread 'that Tiberius was born at Fundi'.[8] Mistakenly, it was assumed that Livia had returned for her confinement to her grandparents' house outside Rome. If an association between Livia and Fundi remained current, perhaps she or her mother had inherited property in the town, which they visited intermittently.

The likelihood that Livia's parents continued to own and administer property in both Pisaurum and Fundi allows us to discount Marcus's decision in 50 BC to sell land in Rome to Cicero as proof of large-scale financial difficulties. Instead we can conclude that anxieties of this sort were sufficiently manageable as not to disturb Livia's childhood – which may, in part, have been spent agreeably at family properties in Umbria and Campania: a peripatetic aristocratic life of the sort outlined in Cicero's letters. In later life, despite unimaginable resources, Livia espoused a lifestyle of understated luxury at odds with that of Romans unaccustomed to wealth.

Two years previously, when Livia was six, a man who would later loom large in the early years of her marriage had found himself the victim of popular fury. That man was Marcus Aemilius Lepidus. The future Triumvir was named as *interrex* in the tense days following the murder of that vexatious Claudian, Livia's kinsman Clodius. The nomination was not without its dangers – in this case the storming of Lepidus's house by incensed pro-Clodian plebs. Asconius recalled the scene. 'Then [the mob] broke through the gateway with all manner of violence and pulled down his ancestral portraits [the *imagines maiorum*], broke up the symbolic marital couch of his wife Cornelia, a woman whose chastity was considered an example to all, and also vandalized the weaving operations which, in accord with ancient custom, were in progress in the entrance hall.'[9]

As in Lepidus's atrium, so in that of Marcus and numberless Roman patricians. The masculine element dominated but did not overwhelm the space. Records of male achievement lined the walls – those ancestor masks commemorating holders of the great magistracies of the State. In the centre of the room stood potent symbols of Roman womanhood. The *lectus genialis*, a low couch, represented the matrimonial bed. Nearby a loom or looms, tall and broad and workable only by a standing weaver, indicated traditional feminine activity – woolworking, '*lanificium*', weaving specifically. Since weaving required both light and space, the atrium, with its expansive layout and roof open to the sky, was the obvious place.

The mob that threatened Lepidus, while sparing the senator himself, destroyed every cherished building block of patrician domesticity. Trampled underfoot was the sanctity of past, present and future. Each was represented in the atrium: in the ancestor masks of a distinguished family; the looms on which a devoted wife wove cloth for her husband; and the marriage bed in which successive generations were faithfully conceived. Daily, entering or leaving the atrium, Livia would have been aware of the room's contents. Over time she would have learned their symbolic import. The vigorously masculine world of Rome sought in these concrete signifiers to encompass a woman's whole existence.

As with so many aspects of Roman women's lives, our picture of daughters' education in the late Republic is a moth-picked patchwork. Mothers exercised a supervisory role in their children's education. Overwhelmingly, this role was one of moral guidance. Intellectual instruction was entrusted to a slave or *pedagogus* who was bought or hired to teach children at home.

In order for a mother's supervision to be effective, women required at least basic literacy. In many upper-class families, among whom education was held in high esteem, women's accomplishments extended far beyond the rudimentary. Caecilia Attica, daughter of Cicero's secretary Atticus, was taught by a slave as a young child, before receiving instruction from the famous freedman *grammaticus* Quintus Caecilius Epirota, whom her father hired to advance her education a stage further. Although traditionally Roman education for girls had emphasized moral virtues and skills that were predominantly domestic over academic accomplishments, by the end of the Republic, bilingualism was increasingly prevalent in senatorial nurseries, apparently in the form of reading and writing in addition to the spoken word. Girls as well as boys learned both Greek and Latin. Pompey's daughter Pompeia began reading Homer sometime after her eighth birthday.[10]

It is impossible to know if there was a sense of going through the motions in all this. The purpose of boys' education was to produce adept public speakers, skilled in oratory and rhetoric. Seriousness, loyalty and courage were the qualities valued by the Republic. Such aims never motivated a girl's upbringing, even in cases like Livia's where a daughter was an only child. Most girls of the senatorial class would be married before the age at which young men completed their studies and made their first public speech: any education on which they embarked was invariably left unfinished.

In this Livia was typical of girls of her class, marrying for the first time when she was either fifteen or sixteen. The highest expectation of a Roman daughter was that she display the sterling qualities of her father, an outcome which, though commended, was not considered likely. Cicero records one exceptional case, that of Laelia. 'It was my good fortune more than once to hear Laelia, the daughter of Gaius [Laelius], speak, and it was apparent that her careful usage was coloured by her father's elegance of speaking, and the same was true of her two daughters.'[11] As in so many other aspects of their lives, Roman women were a conduit for the transmission of masculine virtues or the preservation of male distinction. Behaviour which earned praise was that in which the 'female' was submerged in the 'male'. It is characteristic of Roman thought in this matter that women received ready compliments for their resemblance, in mind or character, to their fathers rather than their mothers.[12] Women themselves, as if to prove the strength and efficacy of the tradition, did not jib at this extremity of self-denial. In the elegy Propertius wrote for Cornelia, the stepdaughter of Livia's future husband Octavian, Cornelia roots her claim to exceptional merit in two sources: her adherence to that code of behaviour prescribed for respectable Roman noblewomen and her illustrious kinsfolk.[13]

Always hovering near the surface was the Roman conviction that women were intellectually and temperamentally different from their menfolk. The Jewish philosopher Philo, a near contemporary of Livia's, who may have encountered her towards the end of her life, characterized a woman's world as of the senses, a man's as of the mind.

The truth was that Romans mistrusted erudite women. Discussing Pompey's wife Cornelia, who had been taught literature, music and geometry and had 'listened with profit' to lectures on philosophy, Plutarch took pains to reassure his readers that Cornelia remained nevertheless 'free from the distasteful pedantry which such studies confer upon women'.[14] Juvenal's disparagement of a later generation of Roman bluestockings is a desperate plea for a return to traditional values of female ignorance and silent submission. It betrays more than a hint of fear.

The woman who begs as soon as she sits down to dinner to discourse on poets and poetry . . . rattles on at such a rate that you'd think all the pots and pans in the kitchen were crashing to the floor and that every bell in town was clanging. All by herself she makes as much noise as some primitive tribe chasing away an eclipse ... Wives shouldn't try to be public speakers; they shouldn't use rhetorical devices; they shouldn't read all the classics – there ought to be some things women don't understand.[15]

By contrast, Agricola's mother Julia Procilla earned Tacitus's praise for her careful supervision of her son's education. She checked his enthusiasm when he showed more interest in studying philosophy than was suitable for a Roman senator.[16] The evidence of the sources suggests that Livia successfully avoided both overtly intellectual interests and Juvenalian garrulousness. The only ancient author able to quote her speech at length is Cassius Dio: in his own words, he attributes to Livia sentiments she may or may not have expressed.

In early imperial Rome, a Stoic philosopher earned fame and renown. His name was Gaius Musonius Rufus and his diatribe 'Should daughters be educated in roughly the same way as sons?' has led some commentators mistakenly to claim him as an early feminist. Musonius Rufus's argument was that since women are capable of the same virtues as men, their progress towards those virtues ought to take the form of similar teaching. For virtues, do not read intellectual prowess. 'I do not mean to say,' surviving fragments tell us, 'that women should possess technical skill and acuteness in argument, which would be rather superfluous, since they will philosophize as women.'[17] Instead, the Stoic's reasoning was fundamentally conservative. His treatise 'That women too should study philosophy' expressed a point of view that such study was the vehicle of transforming women into good wives, mothers and housekeepers. It enabled them to control their emotions, suppress the selfish instinct and love and care for their husband and children.[18] In short, it was a catalyst to ideal womanly behaviour as understood by Roman men.

Livia's education aimed at instilling adult qualities from as early an age as possible. This was in keeping with the broader belief that children were simply smaller versions of their adult selves, alike in character. The death of Fundanius's daughter Minicia while still a young child inspired an encomium from Pliny that sums up the general approach: 'She already possessed the wisdom of old age and the dignity of a *matrona* without losing her girlish sweetness and the modesty of a virgin.'[19] If such steadfast maturity could be harnessed to properly 'masculine' strength of mind, the result would be a prodigy indeed.

Were these efforts successful in Livia's case? Did the reading of ancient texts, the transcribing of particularly elevating lines of poetry or drama, the reiteration of age-old precepts and Alfidia's moral steerage create a woman worthy of Marcus's senatorial career and the dazzling achievements of her Claudian and Livii Drusan predecessors? Livia's future conduct will prove that they did. It was more than sycophancy that inspired Philo's assessment that Livia rose high above her sex because the excellence of her education 'gave virility to her reasoning power'.[20] Suetonius records a telling detail. In the years to come, Augustus took pains not to embark on serious discussions with Livia without first having committed his thoughts to a small notebook. Did the most powerful man in the world fear, respect or simply recognize the sharpness of his wife's intellect? Suetonius offers an apparently simple explanation. He acted as he did 'lest he should say too much or too little when speaking off the cuff'.[21] We must form our own conclusions.

The challenge of Livia's public life – for the moment far in the future – was to contain praiseworthy 'virile' reasoning within the sanctioned bounds of her feminine calling. Insofar as her detractors were concerned, she failed. At a remove of two millennia, we can discern in Livia's example an early, accomplished mastery of a near-impossible conjuring trick. Her life offers proof that historically a woman, working outside the channels of officialdom, could achieve significant goals – by sublimating the appearance of self-motivation within the schemes of powerful men.

Chief among Livia's weapons was homespun. As emperor it suited Augustus to be married to a woman who practised the old Roman customs of home-weaving, just as it suited Livia to exult in the role of domestic Penelope learned from Alfidia in Marcus's atrium. In the minds of both was a tradition of household weaving begun in the Republic's infancy and still practised in the sixth century AD.[22]

Once, Romans spun and wove wool at home through necessity. As the empire grew, Egypt, Greece and the Near East supplied Rome with linen, tapestry and dyed woollen fabrics. Even silk was available to those prepared to pay. By the time of Livia's birth, Columella recorded, readymade fabrics were a fact of Roman life. [23] But the loom remained, a nimble monolith, visible to all in the aristocratic atrium. That it served a more than decorative purpose is evident from the numbers of slaves employed in its service. In Rome, the vault of the Statilius Taurus family included the ashes of eight spinners, one supervisor of the wool, four patchers, four weavers, two dyers and four fullers. In time, Livia's own *columbarium* would accommodate the remains of two supervisors of the wool, two fullers and five patchers [24]

By then, old associations had transformed the Roman loom into more than a frame for weaving. It was a symbol of matronly virtue, as if its taut strings permitted no slackening of the moral fibres. It represented the submission of the self that was the ultimate aim, according to Roman men, of every Roman woman – days spent in peaceable industry for the benefit of husband and children. As the ideal woman suckled her babies, so too she clothed them, protecting them from the harshness of the world outside in layers of woollen homespun. Not without reason did the Roman bride carry a spindle and a distaff. It was a fallacy, of course, a fantasy, but it bolstered the status quo and promised to preserve the eternal verities of a Roman state built on masculine achievement and the attendant succour of women and household gods.

As a married woman and empress of Rome, Livia, assisted by her propagandist husband, took pains to present herself as the archetypal Roman matron. This meant denying that her own very new role was anything but the acme of very old Roman aspirations. Central to her personal myth-making were the homely traditions of the great days of the Republic, a simplified vision of a time before luxury and vice softened Roman sinews. Livia's renown emphasized the extent to which she embodied cherished Roman virtues. She herself became the symbolic thread spun by ancient forebears and woven into the emperor's new clothes which her husband claimed she made for him on the household loom. Livia's, so the story went, was the quintessential Roman upbringing and education. It may not have been so far from the truth.

CHAPTER 5

A young man of noble family,
of native talent and moderation?

The goal, of course, was marriage. The great men whose likenesses survived in sculpted wax, the legendary women who bore and tended them
– all, by and large, were married. Roman men had joked since time
immemorial that it was impossible to enjoy a really harmonious life
with a wife at your side. Most, like the senator Quintus Caecilius Metellus
Macedonicus in the century before Livia's birth, would have conceded
that, without a wife, there was no sort of life at all.[1] There were excep-
tions, but these were the few not the many. Once every five years, daughters of the upper classes were chosen as children to serve the goddess
Vesta. Thereafter, eternally virgin, they guarded Rome's sacred flame.
Vestal Virgins were seldom plucked from families with only one child.
Sacrosanct chastity would not be Livia's portion.

Livia's marriage is the first event since her birth which we can infer
with certainty. Here again, however, we must assume a date. From the
birth of her first child in November 42, it is reasonable to conclude that
Livia was married either in the previous year – 43 BC – or early in 42.
She would have been fifteen, at most sixteen.

This was not unusual. Teenage pregnancies were widespread in contemporary senatorial Rome. Girls were often married by the age of
fourteen and frequently earlier, although officially the law frowned
on marriage before a girl's twelfth birthday. Plutarch is one of several
writers whose reservations about 'childish' brides survive on record. Still,
the custom persisted. Pliny's friend Fundanius was a philosopher with

43

progressive views on women's education. But when his daughter Minicia died at the age of thirteen, invitations to her wedding had already been despatched.[2]

The rationale was twofold. Romans had taken on board a correspondence earlier propounded by Aristotle of the virtue of women (a euphemism for sexual continence) and the vigour of the state. It thus became imperative that means be found of safeguarding female virtue, ideally by channelling the sex urge. Marriage was the safest sanctioned outlet. As the onset of sexual desire in women was fixed by ancient doctors at the beginning of puberty, specifically menstruation, this was the obvious time to harness those feelings within the respectable confines of a suitable alliance. The need was felt to be especially pressing in the case of girls who ate a lot but did little work[3] – a curious intimation that female libido in ancient Rome peaked among greedy teenage girls of the leisured classes. Surviving funerary inscriptions emphasize that women of the senatorial class did indeed marry younger than their lowlier counterparts.

It was partly a case of *carpe diem*. The Augustan poet Horace caught the mood:

> Life's short. Even while
> We talk Time, hateful, runs a mile.
> Don't trust tomorrow's bough
> For fruit. Pluck this, here, now.[4]

Even among adults life expectancy was short. One modern study set the median age of death for women of the Roman Empire at twenty-seven.[5] The task that upper-class girls were required to accomplish was therefore restricted to a narrow window. In their hands rested the future of the state. They must produce the next generation of Rome's rulers.

Given their importance, aristocratic marriages were mostly arranged. The contracting parties were the husband or husband's father and the wife's father or brother. Like so much in Rome, the choice of a spouse was men's business, managed in order to create alliances that were firstly political and afterwards economic or social. By the time of Livia's marriage, Roman women's position was such that fathers might consult their daughters' inclinations. But the truth remained that so long as a daughter was under her father's legal guardianship – within his *potestas* – her only grounds for refusing his choice were if the husband-to-be could be shown to be morally unfit.[6] Since sons too were bound by paternal authority, they faced similar restrictions. In their case, only a bride of notoriously bad character could be rejected.[7] Where first marriages were concerned, it would be a remarkable girl indeed who succeeded in acquiring a notoriously bad character by the age of fourteen. In the light of her subsequent behaviour such a reputation is unlikely in Livia's case.

For the father of the bride, a daughter's marriage was an event of some significance. Cicero described his daughter Tullia's marriage as his 'top domestic priority'[8] – despite the fact that, on this occasion, the marriage in question was Tullia's third and that Cicero, absent from Rome as governor of the eastern province of Cilicia, would ultimately acquiesce in Tullia and her mother Terentia making the choice of husband themselves. It is likely that Marcus regarded Livia's marriage in similar fashion, as Livia herself would certainly have understood.

We do not know whether Roman girls thought of their marriage in any romantic light. That they should would appear to indicate a society in which hope perpetually triumphed over experience. Like much in Livia's upbringing, her attitude towards her eventual marriage – which she accepted as fore-ordained and unavoidable – was shaped by precept and example. She was familiar with Marcus and Alfidia's marriage and those, presumably, of their friends. Family history furnished further instances. Many offered distinctly troubling pause for thought, like the recent extreme case of Clodia and Quintus Metellus Celer, a union coloured by infidelity, accusations of incest and rumours of murder by poisoning. Livia's grounds for hope lay in her relationship with her father. In these matters, even the most devoted father could rate highly the exigencies of self-interest. The one factor of which the teenage Livia can have been sure was that her husband would not be her immediate contemporary. Upper-class Roman men invariably married on the cusp of their first magistracy, the quaestorship.[9] At the end of the Republic, the minimum-age qualification for quaestors was thirty, ensuring that Livia's husband would be at least double her age. That rule, and many like it, was about to be broken. But neither Livia nor Marcus could have known that.

Rome, unlike ancient Greece, did not segregate men and women. In the city itself, the Forum, the Senate House and almost all public monuments formed a men-only world from which women were excluded.[10] But the business of state was not confined to these precincts of the city centre. The houses of Rome's ruling elite encompassed public as well as private life; their internal planning did not enforce male and female zones. Spaces like the atrium and the *tablinum* existed to accommodate at home the same public role the Roman father espoused in the Forum or Senate House. At recognized periods of each day – notably the morning *salutatio*, when clients and colleagues petitioned the resident magistrate – the private realm of the Roman house functioned as workplace. The *salutatio* was no place for children. But for the inquisitive, perspicacious child, this window on to Roman politics in the raw must have operated like a barometer, offering at least scratch readings of the shifting pulse rate of the great city outside. Was it possible that, approaching marriageable age, Livia Drusilla of the Claudii was unaware of the tenor of Roman politics to which Marcus devoted his days? Did she sense the seismic upheaval that, throughout her childhood, threatened Rome in the person of a single ambitious patrician? Did Marcus betray to her his fears for the future of the system with which their family was inextricably caught up? Probably not. Marcus may not have defined those fears, even to himself. But Rome's governing elite formed a hermetic coterie. Their gossip, which must intermittently have reached Livia's ears, inevitably touched on politics. She surely knew the name of Julius Caesar.

Marcus Livius Drusus Claudianus belonged, as we have seen, to two of Rome's most distinguished senatorial families. Their joint record of service matched the lifespan of the Republic. For almost five centuries, Claudii and Livii Drusi had striven for the good of the state, that *res publica* the Romans regarded so highly. In doing so they had inevitably also served themselves well. Marcus can be forgiven for making an equation between the good of the state and his own welfare. Their fortunes were bound closely together.

Politically, Rome was a conservative body. Witness the reluctance of the populace to vote for *novi homines*, those men like Gaius Marius whose family names were unknown in the senatorial records. Ditto the belief, genuinely held, that the son of a dutiful, upright father would himself be dutiful and upright. 'Brave noble men father brave noble children,' wrote Horace. 'In bulls and horses likewise the male's stamp shows clearly; we never find fear bred from fierceness, eagles hatching doves.'[11] Marcus's political philosophy was rooted in the preservation of the Republic. In the building blocks of the Republic's government lay the foundations of his life of privilege, wealth and power. When forces moved to challenge that structure and the future of the Republic appeared imperilled, it was not to be expected that Marcus would act otherwise than in the Republic's defence. And so, through a mixture of self-interest and good intentions, at a moment of unprecedented upheaval, Marcus, seeking a son-in-law who was also a political ally, backed the losing side. He dragged with him into the maelstrom his daughter Livia.

In 44 BC, the year of Livia's fourteenth birthday, a victorious general exchanged his laurel wreath for a leafy circlet made of gold. He wore with it the red-purple tunic and toga associated by Romans with military conquest, and red calf-length leather boots which, he claimed, had once formed part of the ceremonial dress of the kings of Alba Longa. He was Julius Caesar. At the beginning of the year, his position as dictator of Rome, traditionally granted for six months at times of national emergency, was declared permanent; he held the censorship lifelong. In all but name he had achieved the unthinkable and become king of the world's proudest republic. Rome was turned on its head. The ramifications of Julius Caesar's eminence were complex and radical, and would alter the course of many Roman lives, Livia's among them.

'I love and I hate,' Catullus had confessed of his Claudian mistress 'Lesbia' in the preceding decade. Henceforth Rome would love and hate Caesar. For while ordinary Romans loved the man whose statue they inscribed even in his own lifetime 'To the Unconquered God',[12] too late the city's nobles succumbed to justifiable anxiety. Caesar's formal powers, bestowed on him in principle by those same nobles acting as the Senate, exceeded all previous awards. Such a monopoly operating long-term was irreconcilable with Rome's traditional government by elected magistrates culled from the city's first families.

Something had to give and famously did so on the Ides of March. A conspiracy of senators, sixty in total, murdered Julius Caesar on the March morning a soothsayer had warned him would prove fearful. We do not know if Marcus was among their number. Caesar's life was extinguished by twenty-three stab wounds. The deed was witnessed by the assembled Senate, conspirators and non-conspirators alike. In its aftermath, once civil war had become inevitable, all faced the same choice. On which side did they stand? For or against the dead man's cause? Were they tyrannicides or Caesarians? Despite his dalliance with Caesar's Triumvirate in 59, Marcus chose to oppose those loyal to Rome's erstwhile master. So, too, did the man he had chosen as Livia's husband. In both cases it proved the wrong decision.

Since politics among the Roman elite was a family affair, it should not surprise us that the marriages contracted by noble families served as litmus tests of political allegiance. Marcus's choice of a husband for his only daughter was motivated by political gain. His candidate, lauded by Cicero as 'a young man of noble family, of native talent, and moderation',[13] ought to have proved a useful ally. He was even a kinsman, though we cannot be sure of the proximity of the two families' connection.

His name was Tiberius Claudius Nero and, in marrying Livia, he achieved a form of immortality. Thanks to the circumambulatory nature of fate, it was Nero's names – and, in some instances, his genes – which were ultimately bequeathed, via Livia, to Rome's first imperial dynasty. Like Marcus and his daughter, Nero was a Claudian – as his name suggests one of the Nerones. The lesser of the family's two branches, the Nerones had not held the consulship for more than a century and a half. Whatever Marcus's hopes for his son-in-law – and Cicero's encomium notwithstanding – Tiberius Claudius Nero was not the man to revive their laggardly fortunes. His marriage to Livia would prove a questionable alliance for Marcus's family and an ambiguous testament to Marcus's good judgement. It would also test Livia on a personal level.

Four years before Marcus served as praetor, Nero proposed himself as prosecutor in a highly publicized extortion trial. It was his first recorded appearance in the Roman public arena. His attempt, though unsuccessful, was not disgraceful and again earned Cicero's plaudits. Indeed, Cicero remained impressed by Nero, later choosing him as Tullia's third husband – an unsuccessful conclusion to that 'top domestic priority', since Tullia, in her father's absence, had availed herself of an alternative suitor, leaving Nero still up for grabs. Possibly Cicero's interest was instrumental in raising Nero's profile. Although a further seven years would pass before his marriage to Livia, their engagement may have been of long standing, brokered by Marcus in the wake of Tullia's rejection. Clearly Nero inclined towards an alliance of some prominence, as it was he who had proposed himself to Cicero rather than vice versa. The proposal occurred in the year of Marcus's praetorship. Marcus's high office, publicized on account of his application of the Scantinian Law, combined with Livia's exemplary pedigree, which Tullia could not rival, may well have rendered marriage to his 'cousin' just as attractive to Nero as marriage to Cicero's daughter. Happily, by the time that marriage took place, following Caesar's assassination, both men inhabited similar political territory. It had not always been so.

At moments in the previous two decades Marcus and Nero had each adopted a course in relation to Julius Caesar that was frankly opportunistic. Marcus, as we have seen, curried favour with the First Triumvirate of Caesar, Pompey and Crassus. We do not know if he succeeded in his attempt to secure for himself a commission fundraising in Alexandria the year before Livia's birth. Following the collapse of the Triumvirate in 53, he played his hand with greater circumspection. Crassus's death pitted Pompey against Caesar. There is no record of Marcus declaring himself for either, although it is reasonable to surmise that, confronted by Caesar's decidedly un-Republican vaunting ambition, his sympathies lay with Pompey. Pompey, however, was killed in 48. Thereafter Marcus's course mostly fades from view.

At the very point when we assume Marcus had turned away from Caesar, Nero embraced him. In 48 Nero became one of Caesar's quaestors. The appointment took him from Rome to Alexandria, once Marcus's proposed destination. There he commanded Caesar's fleet. In Alexandria, for the one and only time in a notably chequered career, he acquitted himself with distinction: Suetonius asserts that it was Nero who was 'largely responsible' for the Caesarian victory in the Alexandrian War.[14] Whatever the truth of this assessment, Caesar himself was apparently pleased with his acolyte. He rewarded Nero with a priesthood and, two years later, a commission of some prestige: the foundation of two veterans' colonies in southern Gaul on the sites of modern Arles and Narbonne.

Did absence in Gaul make the heart grow fickle or was Nero simply a man always ready to back the frontrunner? On his return to Rome following Caesar's death, he discarded his Caesarian colours. He made a singular proposal in a debate in the Senate – special rewards for the tyrannicides Brutus and Cassius for their role in the misdeed which had robbed Nero of an indulgent master. Cicero, more circumspect, suggested an amnesty for past evils.[15]

The result was that by the summer of 44 BC Nero and Marcus found themselves politically united. Both opposed the forces loyal to Caesar's memory, led for the moment by Mark Antony but shortly to be ranged behind the dictator's great-nephew Octavian. Both, as would eventually become apparent, had miscalculated – though modern sympathies may incline more towards Marcus, the less overtly self-motivated of the two. Sure of the path he had chosen, Marcus, went one step further. He consigned all his eggs to a single basket. He engaged his only daughter Livia Drusilla to the turncoat Nero. It is not an action any Roman father would have undertaken lightly. We do not know how long the union had been in Marcus's contemplation. The engagement of Tiberius Claudius Nero and Livia Drusilla would not, as events unfolded, form the precursor to a marriage of great duration.

CHAPTER 6

'Night would last for ever'

Across the city a dark pall descended. It hid the sun and an acrid fog cloaked the streets. On distant Sicily, Etna had erupted – not puffs of smoke but balls of flame, according to reports. Such was the heat of the blast, Livy tells us, that it was felt across the Strait of Messina.[1] Fallout has been traced as far as Greenland. 'The sun, when Caesar fell, had sympathy for Rome –' Virgil wrote later. 'That day he hid the brightness of his head in a rusty fog/ And an evil age was afraid his night would last for ever.'[2] Volcanic gloom clouded much of the year 44 BC. Crops failed, Plutarch records, from lack of sunlight and warmth. It was surely symbolic.

Was any aspect of Livia's engagement conventional, bar the safely patrician status of her Claudian husband? These were remarkable times in Rome's history, unsettled and unsettling, the political sands quicksands, the centre of power in flux. Two years before Caesar's death, Cicero – never at a loss for words – had taken it upon himself to advise the dictator, 'It is for you alone, Caesar, to bring back to life all that you see in ruins ... you must restore honesty and trust ...'[3] Caesar's murder and its aftermath left Rome more deeply fragmented than before. A broken world, it offered opportunities to the resourceful, as Livia's second husband, Octavian, would prove in spectacular fashion, and pitfalls for the unwary, as her first husband amply demonstrated.

But revolution in Rome was not an act of volcanoes or the weather any more than it was the result of mass uprising. In Rome revolution was an upper-class affair. Regimes toppled, as Caesar fell, to the pressure of disaffected insiders. While the Senate debated its course, ordinary Romans pursued their daily business, muttering about the portent of the iron-red fog. So long as the streets remained free from fighting and fear, Roman life continued its familiar round. Throughout 44 and for much of 43, Caesar-less Rome struggled to recover a semblance of normality. A race had begun to decide the city's new master. All too soon that race would erupt into blood and iron. For the moment, in Rome itself at least, swords were mostly sheathed. If Marcus had already reached an agreement with Nero, it would still have been possible at this point to celebrate the engagement publicly.

Livia and Nero's engagement party shared its name in Latin with the word for betrothal itself: *'sponsalia'*. Such parties were attended by a wide circle of guests, including politicians as well as relatives. The husband-to-be presented his betrothed with a ring, the *anulus pronubus*. According to Pliny the Elder, the ancient custom of an iron ring persisted; Tertullian suggests more plausibly *anuli* of gold.[4] Presents were exchanged which, by legal dispensation, could exceed the value otherwise imposed on gifts.[5] Whether Livia and Nero yet knew each other we will never discover. The likelihood of their acquaintance increases or dwindles depending on the point at which Marcus and Nero reached their agreement. Nor do we know the length of Livia's engagement or the date of her wedding, though many dates can probably be discounted as inauspicious, including the period of the Feast of the Dead, the Parentalia, in mid-February, and May, the month in which Romans sacrificed to their dead. We reach firmer ground when we consider the form their wedding took: several contemporary sources outline typical marriage procedure. Given the value placed by Romans on tradition, it is unlikely that Livia's wedding to Nero diverged significantly from accepted practice.

Livia was beautiful. On that even hostile sources agree. Ovid, not wholly reliably, commends her Venus-like form and Junoesque features from the misery of his Black Sea exile, when Livia was in her late sixties. She must have presented a striking appearance on her wedding day five decades earlier, in the first flush of youthful radiance.

On her head she wore a scarf-like veil of vibrant orange. The *flam-meum* did not, like modern bridal veils, cover her face: it was wrapped around her hair. Part of the ceremonial dress of the wife of the priest of Jupiter,[6] it was an antiquated detail, typical of Rome's romanticizing of its own past. A marjoram wreath held the *flammeum* in place.[7] Beneath the folds of flame-coloured tissue, Livia's hair – for the only time in a girl's life – was tortured into a cone-shaped arrangement at odds with current Roman fashion. With a ceremonial spear, her hair had been parted into six broad locks. Reasons for the spear are not clear – one author suggests the use specifically of a bent iron spearhead in order to dispel evil spirits resident in the hair.[8] The hair was plaited and the six plaits fastened into the required cone with woollen fillets. How much of this eccentric construction was visible beneath the orange veil remains uncertain. The Roman wedding dress was a *tunica recta*, a white woollen tunic woven on an upright loom like those of the aristocratic atrium. It was fastened around the waist by a woollen girdle, tied in an elaborate ceremonial knot. Unravelling the knot of Hercules was a bridegroom's first challenge. It may have been intended as a symbolic deterrent to yet more evil spirits. On her feet Livia wore slippers, known as *lutei socci*, of the same flame orange as her veil.

Even before the wedding began, there were ceremonies and acts of piety. A bride dedicated her childhood toys, including her dolls, and the toga worn by all Roman children, with its single scarlet stripe, to her father's household gods. Given the age at which aristocratic Roman girls married, this represents more than a token surrender of the past and is not without poignancy. If the family's shrine was in the atrium, the ceremony of dedication would have taken place within sight of the symbolic marriage couch which, today of all days, achieved a special significance. Beyond the atrium, the vestibule leading to the house's main entrance, and the entrance itself, were decorated with branches and flowers, the 'green gifts of Thessalian buds from fields and alps, from river banks where the light west wind has unsealed them' described by Catullus.[9]

The formal act of marriage scarcely existed as such – a characteristic instance of a very Roman discrepancy that religion, which coloured so many aspects of the city's life, notably politics, was virtually absent from areas which seem to modern readers quintessentially 'religious', such as the marriage service.[10] By way of formality it was traditional to divine omens. Cicero records that this was not priest's work, but that of a friend of the family.[11] In the unlikely event that he was able to discern any omens at all, the *auspex* present at Livia and Nero's wedding faced a difficult conundrum. What should he reveal to that happy assembly of Claudians? Livia's first marriage would be blighted by Nero's inability to keep pace with the switching tides of contemporary politics and his unerring instinct for backing a loser. Despite its short duration, it must frequently have felt to Livia like a test of stamina and endurance. Livia and Nero were probably married for a maximum of five years. It was a hair-raising, peripatetic interlude. Banishment, flight and terror were the gifts of Nero's household gods. Added to this, all too soon, came bereavement. The *auspex*, it is safe to assume, mentioned none of this.

As the light faded, Livia left Marcus's house for the final time. She set off on foot for the short journey to her new marital home, also on the Palatine. Possibly she was accompanied by flutes, as the dramatist Plautus suggests in his farce *Casina*.[12] Boys bearing torches almost certainly formed part of her procession. If she did not herself carry a spindle and distaff, tools of 'virtuous' weaving, an attendant did so on her behalf. The torches had been lit in Marcus's house – according to Varro, at the ceremonial hearth of the bride's atrium.[13] Possibly, obscene songs and jokes accompanied Livia's progress, an incursion of indecorousness wholly at odds with the austere, even forbidding rectitude she would later present to Romans' gaze. At her destination, she anointed the doorposts with oil and fat and decorated them with woollen fillets. She was carried over the threshold by her attendants. Inside the house, Nero offered his bride water and fire, symbols of the domestic concerns of the Roman matron. In her wake, Livia brought with her her entitlement of ancestor masks, a substantial portfolio – for the politician of acuity an inheritance equal in value to the largest dowry. Nero was not that politician.

On the following day, in a potentially nerve-racking ceremony, Livia made an offering to Nero's household gods for the first time. The blood, smoke and ash of sacrifice sealed her compact with her new husband. Henceforth her role was that later expounded by Plutarch in his *Advice* to *Bride and Groom*, standard lessons Alfidia had surely taught her daughter. 'The wife ought to have no feeling of her own, but she should join with her husband in seriousness and sportiveness and in soberness and laughter.'[14] Far from jibbing at such constraints, Livia made them – or at least the semblance of them – her life's study. It was not by accident that she would later be associated with *concordia*, the Roman concept of marital harmony, and serve as a model for wives across the Empire. In the short term, *concordia* made demands on a sixteen-year-old girl. Surviving records fail to provide grounds for hope that her marriage to Nero abounded in 'sportiveness' or 'laughter'. As she wrestled with adjustment to her new state, Livia was also – with good reason – becoming increasingly afraid for her father.

In November 43 three men met on an island. Appian, in his history of Rome's Civil War, places the island in the river Lavinius. It was situated between Bononia and Mutina in northern Italy, an undistinguished site for talks which would decide the mastery of the Roman world.

The men were not friends in any real sense. Nor were their long-term aims compatible. Two had fought as enemies within the last six months. One was, effectively, a makeweight. His name was Lepidus. We met him a decade earlier when, as *interrex*, he witnessed the storming of the atrium of his house by supporters of the murdered Clodius. Senior-most in years, he would become the junior partner of the three men gathered in uneasy truce on that nameless island.

His colleagues were Caesarians. Mark Antony had shared Caesar's last consulship and afterwards seized control of the dictator's financial affairs. Octavian, Caesar's great-nephew, had been adopted posthumously by Caesar at the age of eighteen. He sought from Mark Antony not only control of Caesar's finances, of which he was the principal heir, but leadership of the Caesarian cause, his real inheritance. At the battle of Mutina earlier the same year, Octavian had defeated Mark Antony. That victory went some way to redressing the balance of power between the two men, which was otherwise weighted heavily in Mark Antony's favour. Separately, Lepidus, Antony and Octavian had decided on amity. Collectively, they would attain the power they craved. Individually, they were later to re-evaluate their union.

They met for two days and reached decisions on the three major challenges that faced them. If they were to hold sway in Rome, in place of Brutus and Cassius and the tyrannicides bent on restoring the Republic to its former status quo, they must legitimize their power. To make that power a reality, they needed funds. To preserve their power from onslaughts, they required both money and the removal of their enemies.

The first point was easily settled. They overrode the abolition of the post of dictator which Mark Antony had enacted after Caesar's death, and decreed themselves joint dictators for a five-year period – a Commission of Three for the Ordering of the State, known to historians as the Second Triumvirate.[15] This agreed, the Triumvirs formulated a plan which reflected credit on none of them. They decided, for the second and last time in Roman history, to institute a Proscription, drawing up long lists of their intended victims. The 'proscribed' forfeited all their worldly goods, which were liquidated in order to fill the coffers of the ruling party. They also forfeited their lives. 'Proscripti' were marked men. Once their names had been displayed on notices posted in Rome, anyone might kill them with impunity. There were even incentives for those who delivered the head of a victim to the Triumvirs: a reward of 100,000 sesterces to a free man, 40,000 sesterces and a promise of freedom to a slave.[16] Inevitably most of the killings were undertaken by soldiers. The Proscriptions' first victim was the tribune Salvius. Soldiers decapitated him in front of his guests at a banquet which, with exemplary sangfroid, he had arranged knowing that it would be his last.[17] His bloody end soon became a statistic.

In total the Proscriptions of 43 accounted for the murder of three hundred senators and two thousand equestrians. The lists embraced such prominent figures as Cicero and Caesar's scholar-librarian Marcus Terentius Varro. Mark Antony sacrificed his uncle, Lucius Caesar, Lepidus his brother Paullus. Octavian, Suetonius records, 'proscribed even Gaius Toranius, his own guardian, who had been his father Octavius's colleague as aedile.'[18] It was a merciless interlude. Slaves sold their masters and even wives abandoned husbands, the senators Septimius and Salassus perishing with the connivance of their spouses.[19] Terror gripped the streets of Rome. Appian's account does not exaggerate. 'Many people were murdered in all kinds of ways, and decapitated to furnish evidence for the reward. They fled in undignified fashion, and abandoned their former conspicuous dress for strange disguises. Some went down wells, some descended into the filth of the sewers, and others climbed up into smoky rafters or sat in total silence under close-packed roofs. To some, just as terrifying as the executioners were wives or children with whom they were not on good terms, or ex-slaves and slaves, or creditors, or neighbouring landowners who coveted their estates.'[20] It was not to be expected that Marcus would escape.

We cannot be certain why the name of Marcus Livius Drusus Claudianus was added to the lists of the Proscripti. The sources do not reveal any particular relationship, good or bad, between Livia's father and the Triumvirs. The explanation surely lies, as one recent biographer has suggested, in Marcus's support in the Senate for a decree to place one of Caesar's most prominent assassins, Decimus Brutus, at the head of two legions.[21] The motion passed, Decimus Brutus exploited his military command against Mark Antony at the battle of Mutina. The Triumvirs demanded a high penalty for what Marcus may have justified to himself as an act of loyalty to the Republic.

Although Marcus did not in fact die as a result of the Proscriptions, time was running out for Livia's father. He did not survive to witness the birth of his first grandchild, a boy called Tiberius, on 16 November 42 – or the outcome of Nero's refusal in the same year to relinquish his praetorship at the appointed time.

CHAPTER 7

Fugitive

The man asking the questions was an historian, Livia's near-contemporary Velleius Paterculus.

'Who can adequately express his astonishment at the changes of fortune and the mysterious vicissitudes in human affairs? Who can refrain from hoping for a lot different from that which he now has, or from dreading one that is the opposite of what he expects?'[1]

The subject who had inspired these reflections was not 'he' at all, but Livia. It was the year 40 BC and Livia, 'most eminent of Roman women in birth, in sincerity and in beauty . . . was then a fugitive . . .'

It was not, of course, the outcome Marcus had intended in betrothing Livia to Nero. But Marcus was dead, killed in autumn 42 by his own hand in his tent in a military camp in Thrace. The battle of Philippi, 'sepulchre of citizens' as Propertius described it, represented Republican Rome's last stand. Caesar's assassins Brutus and Cassius were vanquished by Mark Antony and Octavian and a force of 100,000 men. With the battle lost, Velleius Paterculus tells us, Marcus and his fellow *proscriptus* Quintilius Varus, 'without making any appeal for mercy, ended their lives'.[2] Livia's father behaved as Rome's cult of *virtus* demanded, resolute in the determination never to give in, even in the face of defeat.[3] Among those who drove him to suicide was the future husband of his only daughter.

Married life should have been so different for Livia. Surviving epitaphs suggest a widespread model of marriage that is small-scale in its focus, mundane, safe in its predictability. Republican Rome denied even the richest, grandest women control over their lives. Instead, it outlined a template of hazardous childbirth and uneventful domesticity. 'Stranger, I have little to say,' announces one tomb inscription of the period. 'This is the unbeautiful tomb of a beautiful woman . . . She loved her husband with her heart. She bore two children . . . Her speech was delightful, her gait graceful. She kept house, she made wool. I have finished. Go.'[4] Livia, too, was a beautiful woman. She also bore Nero two children. As events will show, she may or may not have loved her husband with her heart. Later, in the course of her second marriage, she is recorded as making wool and weaving woollen cloth. But her first marriage afforded her all too little time for keeping house. In vain would she seek to emulate the subject of one glowing epitaph, who 'desired nothing more than that her house should rejoice'.[5] Among the short-term outcomes of Philippi was an all-pervasive uncertainty among the households of senatorial Rome. Domestic tranquillity was not the Triumvirs' first priority. The consul Pedius, who worked to mitigate the violence of the Proscriptions and shorten the victim lists, died, we are told, of exhaustion and despair.[6] It was that sort of time.

Marcus had died, as he had mostly lived, a man of principle. His final stand was in defence of the Republic. It was not a sacrifice Nero was prepared to match. Speedily the younger Claudian transferred his allegiance from the assassins to the Triumvirs. He placed his trust not in Caesar's adopted son Octavian – a political tyro and unknown quantity, his family newcomers to the senatorial ranks – but in Mark Antony, the Republicans' dictator. We cannot know the extent to which Nero shared with Livia the rationale behind his political oscillation, only that no record of open dispute between them survives.

'The ideal for a man,' Nicostratus would later write in his treatise *On Marriage*, 'is a kind wife who knows how to look after him. He can relax with her and confide all his secrets, even public business, to her since it is like confiding in himself.'[7] Nicostratus's 'ideal' depended on a husband for whom sharing secrets and public business represented a positive benefit. There is no evidence that Nero fell into this category. Nor would the discrepancy in age between Nero and Livia, and the latter's presumed political naivety, have encouraged him to confide in her. Nicostratus wrote at a time when the imperial system – notably the example set by Livia in her marriage to Augustus – had accustomed Roman men to women's closer knowledge of power. In 42 BC, so fundamental a shift in outlook remained remote. Nero's attitude probably corresponded more nearly to that of Sallust, whose *Conspiracy of Catiline*, published only two years earlier, contained a pithy demonization of Sempronia. Sempronia paid for her involvement in Catiline's plot by posthumous denunciation as a woman 'who had often committed many crimes of masculine daring', a weightier criticism in Rome than modern readers may suspect.[8] Sallust's Sempronia was dangerous. Interference in politics branded her a transgressive, even sexually predatory, figure. Neither Nero nor Livia herself would have wished Livia to follow her example.

In the short term at least, Nero deserves our leniency. With hindsight, we can see that by the end of 42 Rome's Republic was defeated both ideologically and as a means of government. Julius Caesar had recognized the signs of its decline, but his foresight, coloured by self-interest, was not widespread. Other men of senatorial rank shared Nero's uncertainty and his apparent belief that Mark Antony remained the Republic's torchbearer. Pledging his support for him in 42, Nero may have acted in good conscience, in defence of the system Claudians had upheld since the sixth century. Only Nero's subsequent vacillations undermine his claims to integrity.

For the moment, Livia's anxieties were smaller in compass, distinct from the hurly-burly of Rome's power-broking. By the end of 42 she found herself both bereft and elated, confronting the death of her father and the birth of her first child. Tipping the scales in the right direction, her husband's star also showed signs of ascendancy. Like Marcus before him, Nero – newly married and a father to boot – had been elevated to the praetorship.

'I did not take my father's line; His trade was silver coin, but mine Corinthian bronzes . . .' ran the doggerel scrawled during the Proscriptions on to the base of a statue of Octavian.[9] The double allusion is to the rumour that the fortunes of the Octavii derived from money-lending and to Octavian's reputed fondness for costly objets d'art looted from the houses of the *proscripti*. Corinthian bronze was an alloy of copper, silver and gold not necessarily manufactured in Corinth. It was used for a range of bibelots and trinkets, including portrait busts. Pliny, in his *Natural History*, valued it 'before silver and almost before gold'.[10] Its value to us is as an indicator of the splendour of the aristocratic Roman townhouse.

This was the environment Livia had inhabited as a child, one in which the mistress of one household, 'and not a particularly rich one', spent 150,000 sesterces on a wine ladle, while Cicero bought a table for the staggering sum of half a million sesterces, a seventh of his purchase price of Drusus's house on the Palatine.[11] At first, following her marriage to Nero, this remained Livia's environment. Although it is probably impossible to trace Nero's Palatine house, it is important to recognize this aspect of Livia's life and the extent to which her experience prior to the Civil War was circumscribed by luxury and the blithe assumptions of hereditary wealth. Those assumptions were swiftly challenged, hostage to Nero's declining fortunes.

Nero's praetorship was conducted against a backdrop of growing divisions between the Triumvirs. At the close of his term of office, when the judicious magistrate might have kept his head below the parapet, Nero refused to relinquish the fasces. Instead he allied himself with Lucius Antonius, Mark Antony's brother and consul for the year, and Antony's formidable wife Fulvia, daughter of Sallust's Sempronia. Lucius and Fulvia opposed Octavian's awards to the Caesarian veterans of Philippi of land which had been confiscated from Italian farmers. 'By making charges against Caesar before the veterans at the one moment, and at the next inciting to arms those who had lost their farms when the division of lands was ordered and colonists assigned, [Lucius] had collected a large army,' Velleius Paterculus reported.[12] Large it may have been, but effective it evidently was not – at least, not effective enough. Lucius and Fulvia established an insurrectionists' stronghold in Perusia, the modern-day Umbrian hill town of Perugia built high above the Tiber valley. There Nero, Livia and Tiberius followed Lucius. Octavian and his armies followed too. When Perusia fell, starved into submission, Nero alone of the city's Roman office-holders refused to capitulate.[13] In fear for his life he fled – and the family of Tiberius Claudius Nero found themselves on the run. Out of sight was the gilded world of the Roman townhouse, with its Corinthian bronzes and generous complement of slaves; untended the hearth of Nero's household gods where Nero spilt animal blood and Livia made obeisance; remote the relative freedom of the aristocratic wife's life in Rome, with its public baths and shops, galleries, gardens and colonnades. Nero and Livia travelled with a reduced party of attendants, possibly only Tiberius's wet nurse and a single general servant. This novel experience of the fugitive's life must have frightened both of them and was particularly arduous for Livia as the mother of a young baby. The years of danger had begun. His own poor judgement, added to Octavian's dexterity at manipulating a constantly shifting pattern of alliances, served to brand Nero a rebel with a losing cause.

For three years Nero, Livia and Tiberius travelled. They fled from Perusia to Praeneste, Praeneste to Naples, Naples to Sicily, Sicily to Athens. At last they reached Sparta, the Greek city which had once enjoyed Claudian protection and now, under altered circumstances, returned the favour. At first Nero continued his policy of active opposition to Octavian. In Naples, he had attempted to incite an uprising among the city's slave population. Again Octavian emerged victorious. Historians like Velleius Paterculus recount such incidents specifically from Livia's viewpoint, while both Velleius and Cassius Dio make much of Livia's flight from the man she would shortly marry. The former describes Livia as 'a fugitive before the arms and forces of the very Caesar who was soon to be her husband',[14] exploiting for dramatic effect an irony of hindsight. In his handling, there is something heroic about Livia's terrifying chase across Italy. His narrative seems to echo the pursuit of men and women by gods familiar from epic poetry. 'Pursuing bypaths that she might avoid the swords of the soldiers, and accompanied by but one attendant, so as the more readily to escape detection in her flight, she finally reached the sea and with her husband Nero made her escape by ship to Sicily.'[15] The truth cannot have been either romantic or picturesque. If Livia's spirits gave way, we are not aware of it. At a certain point, Nero, while remaining inimical to Octavian – Pliny described the men as enemies – eventually tired of direct engagement with his adversary; his subsequent course suggests instead a search for safe refuge. Perhaps he was moved to pragmatism by the plight of his wife and baby.

What was never in question was Livia's loyalty to her husband. Whether through affection, consciousness of her duty as a wife, or necessity – at some point, unsurprisingly, Nero's name was added to the list of the *proscripti* and Livia may have doubted whether she any longer had a house in Rome to return to – she remained at Nero's side. Although such behaviour was not unique at this time, it was considered exemplary, contrasting as it did with the bloodier paths chosen by the wives of Septimius and Salassus. It suggests forcibly that later efforts to present Livia as the archetypal virtuous Roman wife rested on solid foundations. The period of Nero's Proscription frightened, frustrated and humiliated Livia but did not find her wanting in steadfastness or courage. Like a man grasping at straws, Nero exhausted one by one those leaders who shared his opposition to Octavian. All in vain.

Sixty years later, the senator Aulus Caecina Severus argued the case for Roman governors travelling abroad without their wives: 'A female entourage stimulates extravagance in peacetime and timidity in war ... Women are not only frail and easily tired. Relax control, and they become ferocious ambitious schemers ... Wives attract every rascal in a province.'[16] In the midst of civil war, Livia gave the lie to Severus's words. Nero's flight across the ancient world presented her with every sort of challenge. Hurrying from Sparta for reasons now lost, 'she ran into a sudden forest fire which scorched her hair and part of her robe.'[17] It was night and both Livia and Tiberius might have been killed in the unexpected conflagration, but the sources record neither complaint nor recrimination from Livia. Not until her return to Rome did her support for the hapless Nero falter.

Nero's destinations had included Sicily. There Sextus Pompey, son of Pompey the Great, continued with some success to champion the cause of the Republic. Although Sextus's sister Pompeia indulged baby Tiberius with presents of a cloak, a brooch (presumably to fasten the cloak) and some gold buttons, for Nero the detour proved less rewarding. There was no warm welcome from the man whose father Marcus had served almost twenty years earlier. Haughty in defeat, Nero claimed that Sextus had failed to treat him with proper respect. The small family of Claudii were soon on their travels again.

But Sextus did not forget his unwelcome visitors. In the summer of 39 BC he made a fragile pact with the Triumvirs. The Treaty of Misenum, though of short duration, included what amounted to a pardon for Sextus's allies. Among those exiles whose names would be removed from the lists of the proscribed was Tiberius Claudius Nero. Inevitably, absolution did not come cheap. Nero could expect the restoration of no more than a quarter of his property: the remainder was annexed by the State. At last he and his family could return to Rome in safety.

It was to be a summer of surprises. As autumn approached, Livia could no longer disguise the fact that, for the second time, she was pregnant. How she greeted this news we do not know. She was nineteen years old. Her father was dead, perhaps her mother too (Alfidia's death is not mentioned in the sources). Her husband, though undoubtedly courageous, had shown himself inadequate to the challenges posed by Rome's political turmoil. Nero had lost his fortune as well as his credibility as a statesman; by serendipity he had escaped with his life. As future events would reveal, he may also by this point have forfeited Livia's affections. As summer turned to autumn, questions of loyalty and affection increasingly occupied Livia's thoughts. The biggest surprise of 39 was still to come.

CHAPTER 8

'The whimsicality of fate'

In 56 BC 'a highly respected man of noble character', Quintus Hortensius Hortalus, asked his friend Cato the Younger for the hand of his
daughter Porcia in marriage. Cato demurred. Porcia was already mar
ried. Cato was married, too – to his second wife Marcia, by whom he
had three further children. Undeterred, Hortensius evolved another plan.
Plutarch tells us that '[he] wanted not only to be Cato's intimate friend
but also to unite their families and their future descendants'. So he
switched his attentions from Porcia, 'and boldly asked Cato to give him
his own wife [Marcia], who was still young and fertile'. At the time Hortensius was nearing sixty, Cato almost forty and Marcia little more than
twenty-five. Cato and Marcia showed every sign of affection. More than
this, Marcia was pregnant. 'Cato, however, seeing how eager and determined Hortensius was, did not oppose him, but told him that they had
to ask Marcia's father, Philippus, for consent. After Philippus had been
consulted and had given his approval, he engaged Marcia to Hortensius
in the presence of Cato, who had also given his consent.' What Marcia
thought we do not know. In the previous generation, Sulla's stepdaughter
Aemilia had entered a similar compact with extreme reluctance. Heavily
pregnant, she found herself divorced at speed from her husband Marcus
Acilius Glabrio. In his place Sulla married her to Pompey the Great. His
motives were political. Shortly after, Aemilia died in childbirth.

As peace returned to Rome with the cessation of civil war, it was
Cato's acquiescence, not Marcia's or Aemilia's sacrifice, which Romans
would have reason to remember.

*

It was not friendship which had drawn the Triumvirs to Sextus Pompey in the summer of 39 BC but fear. The people of Rome were hungry. Famine gripped the city. From his island base, Pompey wielded significant naval power. His control of the seas was more than tactical: it enabled him to disrupt shipments of grain from Sicily to Rome. Although Roman politics, unlike those of Revolutionary France, did not pivot on the price of a loaf of bread, restricted food supplies in the capital provided a recipe for disaffection. Riots and demonstrations rent the streets. Romans had grown unused to iron rations. 'We want the parrotfish, transplanted from distant shores; we want fish from the Syrtes that cost a shipwreck to bring to Rome: we're tired of grey mullet. We fancy a mistress not a wife. Roses are out: we want cinnamon,' Petronius would write, only partly in jest. Sallust traced the Roman taste for luxury and soft living as far back as the middle of the second century BC; perhaps the habit had become ingrained.[2] Octavian dared not risk any meddlesome rabble-rouser who attributed shortage of food to his own continuing hostile relations with Pompey. He learnt his lesson the hard way, after being stoned in the Forum by an angry mob, and made with reluctance a makeshift peace.

For Nero and Livia, exiles no longer, this sense of Rome's diminished munificence came very close to home. Nero's proscription may have cost them their house on the Palatine; undoubtedly their return to the city found them poorer. Livia herself was still a woman of some substance – she probably inherited property not only from Marcus but also Alfidia, had the latter died by this stage. We do not know if her inheritance was adequate for the couple's needs. Roman law limited bequests to daughters. In addition, since, like Nero, Marcus had been proscribed, Livia shared his estate unequally with the Triumvirs. Also taking a slice out of the pie, we assume, was Livia's late-begotten 'brother', Marcus's adopted son, Marcus Livius Drusus Libo.

If a sense of relief was mixed with weariness on Livia's part in that summer of 39, it is hardly surprising. Financial constraints may have compromised the only way of life she knew; and her husband's distinctly uncertain political future apparently lay at the behest of a man to whom she attributed multiple wrongs – the death of her father, the loss of her fortune and three harrowing years of fear and danger. Seneca's Stoic

assessment that the happy life lay in 'peace of mind and lasting tranquillity'[3] provides grounds enough for Livia's certain unhappiness.

Help came to hand from a previously untried source, the same Marcus
Livius Drusus Libo with whom Livia now shared not only Marcus's
patrimony but a name. What form that help took we do not know, but
it is possible that Libo agreed to intervene on Nero and Livia's behalf
with Rome's new powers-that-be. The proposal may have come from
Nero or from Livia – or was perhaps Libo's own. The idea of Nero or
Livia requesting help from Octavian, their enemy and their victor, sits
oddly with that 'excessive haughtiness' or 'exceeding arrogance' which
Livy insisted on as a defining characteristic of the Claudii. Libo's intention – motivated by 'family' feeling? – may have been to initiate a dia-
logue which would result in the restitution of Nero's forfeited property.
In fact, in a dramatic outcome none could have anticipated, Libo's intervention (if such it was) resulted in further losses to Nero, on this occasion no less a prize than his wife.

Libo's loyalty, like Nero's, lay partly with Sextus Pompey, who at some
point became his brother-in-law. His connection with the Triumvirate,
however, was through his aunt Scribonia.[4] Scribonia had become a political tool at about the time Nero and Livia failed to find refuge with
Sextus on Sicily. Sextus's coolness towards the exiles was influenced by
a positive change in his relationship with Octavian. That change was
cemented when, in 40, Octavian married Scribonia and the two men
found themselves related. It must have seemed an easy matter to Libo
to ask his aunt to intervene with her powerful new husband on behalf
of his 'sister' and Nero. Scribonia was well placed to ask favours of her
new husband: shortly after her marriage to Octavian, she fell pregnant.
Given Nero's tarnished reputation, she could not, however, have anticipated much warmth in Octavian's likely response. She was magnificently
mistaken.

Octavian was twenty-four years old. Of uncertain health, he was nevertheless at the peak of his physical powers. For reasons not of love but
politics, he had married a woman ten years his senior whom Seneca
described uncosily as 'of the stern old type'.[5] The death of his great-uncle
Julius Caesar five years earlier had propelled Octavian unexpectedly to
the forefront of Roman politics. Heedless of the cautions of his mother

and stepfather, he had chosen to interpret that propulsion as the call of destiny. Perhaps the arrogance of youth made him reckless. It was a daunting inheritance for an eighteen-year-old boy with no experience of politics or warfare and the scantest family connections with Rome's governing hierarchy. Cicero's joke that Octavian 'must be praised, honoured – and must be removed' encapsulated senatorial Rome's misjudgement of the boy-heir as lightweight. It was not an assessment anyone thought to repeat in 39. At worst Octavian had achieved parity with his fellow Triumvir Mark Antony. Lepidus was scarcely thought of. The future of Rome, it was clear, now rested in one of two pairs of hands. For Octavian it was a heady prospect and one which may have raised to bursting point the pent-up feelings of five years of extreme physical and nervous exertion. His loveless marriage provided a leaky conduit for such emotions. He had reached the very state in which a man is apt to let slip his defences.

Cassius Dio's *Roman History* includes an account of the flight of the Claudii from Campania, following the fall of Naples and Lucius Antonius's surrender in January or February 40. It has a glib, pat quality to it. 'When Caesar's party got the upper hand, [Nero] set out with his wife Livia Drusilla and with his son Tiberius Claudius Nero. This episode illustrated remarkably the whimsicality of fate. This Livia who then fled from Caesar later on was married to him, and this Tiberius who then escaped with his parents succeeded him in the office of emperor.'[6] Events themselves were less clinical or neatly fore-ordained than Dio's account suggests. But within less than two years, the unexpected coda to Nero and Livia's flight was indeed a remarkable illustration of the whimsicality of fate.

It is a moot point what modern opinion would have made of Livia's appearance. Surviving portraits, of which Livia boasts a larger number than any other Roman woman,[7] depict a woman of rounded face with plump cheeks, a long straight nose and gently arching eyebrows. The most striking features of Livia's portrait busts are her tiny rosebud mouth and slightly prominent chin. Both nod towards a certain determination – a steeliness and strength of character denied by the smooth brow, open gaze and soft cheeks. The effect today is pleasantly arresting rather than beautiful, but such a reaction is at odds with contemporary responses. To her contemporaries, as we have seen, Livia's beauty was a watchword. It would prove an important facet of her history. Like the Cinderella princesses of fairytales, Livia was beautiful, intelligent and, after a period of travail, swept off her feet by Prince Charming. Ancient historians mistrusted that combination of good looks, shrewdness and influence over her husband. Some preferred, as time passed, to cast her in the role of wicked stepmother. Neither portrait can be trusted. In the heat of Rome's high summer, Livia's effect on Octavian was little short of electric.

The ancient sources are perfunctory in their treatment of Octavian falling in love with Livia. After an exposition of the history of 39, Dio offers simply, 'Besides these occurrences at the time Caesar married Livia.'[8] Octavian's emotional condition did not concern his first chroniclers: Livia became a figure of significance only insofar as she swayed Octavian's political judgement. Throughout the fifty-two years of their marriage, Octavian took pains to conceal that eventuality from any third party, especially the eye of history; his careful propaganda veiled the dynamics of his private life. Nevertheless, the sequence of events baldly recounted in the sources facilitates a number of inferences. Chief among them is the lightning speed of Octavian's love for Livia. Implicit within it is the likelihood of powerful feelings of sexual attraction. If Octavian's contemporary biographer Nicolaus of Damascus is to be believed, that attraction may have been on Livia's side as well as Octavian's. Nicolaus claimed that Octavian's good looks 'attracted many women'.[9]

Livia gave birth to her second child, a boy named Claudius Drusus Nero, known afterwards as Drusus, on 14 January 38 BC. Three days later she married Octavian. The birth was evidently easy since Livia was so quickly back on her feet. Its circumstances differed markedly from those of Drusus's conception, when Livia and Nero remained in exile, their lives clouded by uncertainty; its speed was characteristic of these early stages of Octavian and Livia's relationship. For Livia, uncertainty had passed by the time of Drusus's birth. She had agreed to divorce Nero and marry Octavian as long ago as late September or early October, when the couple's whirlwind engagement won the sophistical sanction of Rome's college of pontiffs. She had probably been Octavian's mistress since shortly after they met. At the time of that meeting, at the end of the previous summer, Livia was already pregnant with Drusus, her husband's child. But Octavian, himself the husband of a pregnant wife, was not deterred from asking Nero to divorce her in his favour. For the gossip-mongers of Rome who remembered Hortensius's pursuit of Marcia, it was a case of history repeating itself.

Whether Octavian was aware of or even inspired by that parallel we do not know. We can draw comfort on his behalf from the absence of censure of either Cato or Hortensius in surviving sources. Lucan, in his verse account of the Civil War, chose to interpret Cato's action as moral. He invoked Xenophon's evidence that the Spartans passed on fertile wives to their friends in order to create a bond between fathers and allow other men to sire heirs, an argument Asconius reiterated elsewhere in relation to Pompey and Marcus Aurelius Scaurus, whose solidarity he attributed to both fathering children by Mucia.[10] Although in Lucan's version it is Cato's part which deserves praise, no criticism attaches to Hortensius. Ditto, he must have hoped, Octavian. Cato's contemporaries, though intrigued, were apparently not shocked by the incident. What disturbed them was the fact of Marcia being pregnant at the time the deal was struck. Once again, ditto Octavian – with the added complication that Octavian's own wife was also pregnant. Unblinking, Octavian took a married woman as his mistress. He requested that her husband divorce her so that he in turn might marry her, having determined to divorce his own pregnant wife. But he balked at providing his detractors with unnecessary grounds for accusing him of impropriety. In his defence, he invoked the assistance of the college of pontiffs, asking the priests, as Tacitus recorded, 'the farcical question whether it was in order for [Livia] to marry –' that is, remarry '– while pregnant'.[11]

That learned fraternity obligingly ruled that so long as there was no doubt of the child's paternity – that Drusus was Nero's baby – no obstacles existed to Octavian and Livia's marriage. Cato-like, Nero himself erected no barriers and divorced his wife with every semblance of good grace. Brutally, Octavian ensured Scribonia's compliance: he divorced her the very day she gave birth. Her baby was a daughter, Julia, as it happened the only child Octavian would have. As a reward for the agonies of childbirth, Scribonia's treatment appears harsh. Octavian skimped on explanations. 'I could not bear the way she nagged at me,' he offered, in Suetonius's account.[12] Even in Rome, where divorce was an easy matter, his pretext was flimsy.

Octavian's unflinching assumption of another man's wife betrays the ruthless steadfastness of purpose that would afterwards win him leadership of the Roman world. At no point are his actions uncharacteristic, save in his spontaneous falling in love with the nineteen-year-old Livia. Even this is an inference on our part, though the inference of love is corroborated by the length and relative tranquillity of the marriage begun under such irregular circumstances. If, then, Octavian behaved in character, what of Livia? – what of Nero?

It is difficult to accept at face value Velleius Paterculus's assessment of Nero as 'a man of noble character and high intellectual training.'[13] The willingness with which Nero apparently ceded a beautiful, intelligent and previously loyal and faithful wife to the political opponent who had plundered his patrimony and only narrowly missed robbing him of his life surely stretches the broadest definition of nobility of character. Was Nero's concern with Livia's happiness? Had the experience of exile vanquished his Claudian pride and fighting spirit? Was he simply apathetic? Or, more probably, did Nero anticipate personal gain from Octavian's plan? If so, he demonstrated his customary flawed judgement, poor testament to that high intellectual training of Velleius's eulogy. With Marcus dead, it was Nero Octavian asked for Livia's hand. Symbolically, Nero played the father's role and gave Livia away at her wedding to Octavian, a formal re-enactment of a less elegant truth. Soon after Drusus's birth, in accordance with accepted practice, Octavian returned the newborn baby to Nero. He made an official record of his action and of the child's paternity. It was the only restitution of property Livia's second husband ever made to her first. The years following Livia's remarriage did not witness a revival in Nero's chequered career.

So what of Livia? How are we to explain her behaviour in embracing her proven enemy with such alacrity? Can we explain it? Did she act on the impulse of the moment, swayed by love or desire, or approach with calculation a premeditated goal? Perhaps she anticipated benefits from marriage to Octavian which outweighed both the unorthodoxy of her conduct and her nicer scruples. Although Octavian's position was still not assured, Livia could not have failed to recognize what form those benefits would take: material security, political sponsorship for her son Tiberius and restored prestige for the Claudii. Fifteen years later, the poet Horace published his first three books of Odes. He described Livia as '*unico gaudens . . . marito*' – 'rejoicing in her unparalleled husband'[14] – a neat compliment that lends itself to alternative construction: a wife whose very joy lies in her husband's distinction.

Characteristically, Tacitus suggested that Livia may have been a willing victim of Octavian's abduction. In Roman terms this was grounds for neither scandal nor blame. Cicero records the story of a woman called Tutia. Far from following where she was led, as in Livia's case, Tutia sought to exercise control over her private life and herself proposed to Cicero's son Quintus. Tutia was not only already married, though on the brink of divorce, but older than Quintus, who was twenty-two. In recording her conduct, Cicero imputes no disgrace or unseemliness to his son's pursuer, only interest in the unusual incident.[15] Tacitus's treatment of Livia is less benign. But Tacitus is not to be trusted where Livia is concerned. Or is he?

CHAPTER 9

'An eagle flew by'

Today tall pine trees flank one side of the remains of a villa that once belonged to Livia. They screen from view the encroaching suburb and the tarmac scar of a modern Italian motorway visible at the bottom of the steep hill. Underfoot, their resinous cones are stickily aromatic. Louder than the background murmur of the road is the all-pervasive chatter of cicadas. Little survives of Livia's villa above knee height. But its floor-plan, clearly discernible, remains impressive.

Here is the site of a small garden, partly embraced by the house. Beyond, traces of a grand terrace once formally planted have fallen victim to the farming methods of succeeding centuries. Despite losses, both areas have yielded up to excavation earthenware pots punctured with holes for drainage. The *ollae perforatae* were used by Roman gardeners for bringing on specimens prior to planting out. Here, in just such pots, Livia grew laurel bushes. Here too she raised broods of white chickens from which, two thousand years ago, the villa took its name. Pliny called Livia's villa Ad Gallinas, 'The Poultry'. It stood close to the ninth stone marker on the Via Flaminia, the road that led northwest from Rome to the Adriatic.[1] In the vicinity of the ancient Etrurian city of Veii, it once enjoyed long views across the Tiber valley. Today it is within sight of the unlovely Roman satellite town of Prima Porta.

It was more than a love of husbandry that guided Livia's hand in the matter of laurels and chicken-keeping. We have no reason to attribute to her the countrywoman's instinct for tending and growing. Although she would later be noted for her fondness for gardening and commissioned for the summer dining room of her villa a garden-inspired mural that remains one of the highlights of Roman art, her childhood – typical of ancient Rome – had been essentially urban.

At Ad Gallinas, both chickens and laurels were the result of a portent, one of those uncanny, apparently 'natural' signs used by Romans to take the temperature of the times. Suetonius places the portent at the beginning of Livia's marriage to Octavian: 'As Livia was returning to her home at Veii . . . an eagle flew by and dropped into her lap a white pullet which it had just pounced upon. Noticing a laurel twig in its beak, she decided to keep the pullet for breeding and to plant the twig.'[2]

Evidently this unusual windfall did not frighten Livia, who recognized it, Cassius Dio tells us unsurprisingly, as 'a sign of no small moment'.[3] She understood it as a promise of good fortune and took steps to harness the promised boon. The twig took root. So luxuriant was its growth that in years to come five successive emperors of Rome – the entire Julio-Claudian dynasty of rulers – cut from The Poultry's laurels the stems they wore twisted into triumphal wreaths. In defiance of a Roman belief that white chickens were sterile[4] – the grounds for Juvenal's description of fortune's favourite as 'the son of a white hen' – the plummeting portent produced a brood of pale chicks.

We must decide for ourselves the truth of this curious incident. Ancient writers accepted its veracity and, like Livia, interpreted it positively. If it did happen, it must have been a source of comfort to Livia. At the time of her wedding to Octavian, the omens had been less benign. Fire destroyed the hut of Romulus, one of Rome's most sacred sites. Across the city reports circulated of the anger of the Great Mother, that deity whose statue Claudia Quinta had miraculously liberated from the sandbanks of Ostia. Dio notes that olive oil sprouted from the banks of the Tiber. In the Forum, palm trees sprang up from nowhere.[5] As superstitious as her new husband – to whom Suetonius attributed 'absolute faith in . . . premonitory signs'[6] – and, like him, conscious of the singular circumstances of their marriage, Livia gave credence to such 'ominous' happenings. Better by half that this youthful aristocratic wife and mother should cultivate laurel groves and white poultry, symbols of rulership and good luck.

*

Livia was sixteen when she gave birth to her first child in November 42 BC. Her pregnancy had been marked by a degree of anxiety concerning the baby's sex. We do not know Nero's thoughts in the matter. Suetonius tells us that 'Livia had tried various means of foretelling whether her child would be male or female.'[7] There is no suggestion that she did this at Nero's prompting. Presumably the anxiety was her own. She had taken too much to heart the lessons of an aristocratic childhood, with its emphasis on the discrepancy in the relative values of male and female. Whether she had learnt this from Marcus and Alfidia, from the all-male cult of the atria's *armaria* or from precepts of Claudian history – the memory of Clodia and her incestuous sisters shamefully recent – we will never know. If Livia had surmised that the interests of a family were better served by sons, few under the Republic would have challenged her. Roman history furnished examples of sons inspired and exalted by their noble mothers' lofty birth. Plutarch records that Livia's contemporary, Lucius Cornelius Sulla, son of Sulla the dictator, was honoured as a child by his playmates not on account of his father's repute but the prestige of his mother, the aristocratic Caecilia Metella.[8] Such instances offered pause for thought to the scion of a famously proud family on the brink of motherhood.

Livia need not have worried. Her fate, like Lady Macbeth's, was to bring forth boy children only. She took an egg from the nest of a broody hen. Depending on the source consulted, she warmed the egg in her hands or against her breast. Either way, she was assiduous in her efforts not to let the egg cool, passing it among her slaves and waiting women. In this way she succeeded in hatching the egg. The chick was a cock, complete with a handsome comb.[9] Clearly – and correctly – the portent foretold a healthy baby boy. Livia's reaction to Tiberius's birth is not recorded. In the light of her desire for a male heir of the Claudii so strong that it drove her to primitive acts of clairvoyance, we may draw our own conclusions.

Among Livia's contemporaries, maternal ambition would occupy a central place in her mythology. Rome's curtailment of female aspiration was stringent. Public life presented few roles for women. The historian Livy quoted a senatorial debate in which a tribune called Valerius claimed that, in compensation for the glittering prizes women might not possess, they were permitted purple and gold fabrics and splendid embroidery.[10] Elsewhere Livy attributed female ostentation in the matter of dress to their exclusion from male sources of prestige: political offices, priesthoods, triumphs and spoils of war.[11] With caveats, society was happy to sanction a patrician mother's legitimate ambition for her son.

In Livia's case, it is possible that motherhood unleashed latent ambitions which were simply a facet of her Claudian inheritance. In the light of subsequent events – or the version of events the sources bequeath us, which we should approach with caution – her concern over the sex of her first child looks like an early warning sign. A woman's son can become his stepfather's principal heir without skulduggery on the part of his mother. When the prize is as great as the throne of Rome, only a mother of exemplary virtue would not dare to dream. Over time, her determined championing of Tiberius notwithstanding, official propaganda would seek to present Livia as just such a mother.

In 42 BC the Roman Republic had not yet been dismantled. A determined mother might plan the consulship, even in exceptional circumstances a dictatorship, for her son, but no further. No evidence survives to suggest that Livia was unhappy with her lot at that time. Married to the husband of her father's choice, a man who shared her own family distinction, she would soon give birth to that son whose sex she had taken pains to divine. At the same time, Nero, like Marcus before him, won election to the praetorship.

This was the life foretold for Livia not in any hatched egg or falling pullet but the accretions of family exempla displayed in Marcus's atrium. So much can change in three years. By the time of Livia's return to Rome in the summer of 39, Nero was no longer realistically a vehicle for his wife's hopes. Henceforth her ambition must fasten on Tiberius – just as Cornelia, celebrated mother of the Gracchi, and Julius Caesar's mother Aurelia had channelled their hopes through their sons. If Nero's poor record blighted Tiberius's prospects, Livia must look elsewhere for the champion her son required. The man who had killed her father and robbed her of the resources that ought to have been hers by inheritance and marriage was an unlikely guardian angel. But in 39 BC, Livia could lift her eyes no higher than Octavian.

*

Octavian pursued his quarry with ardour. The speed of his assault on both Livia's affections and her marriage inspired a sardonic response in his fellow Triumvir Mark Antony. It may also have provided the grounds for Tacitus's subsequent assertion that Livia's removal from Nero's house took the form of an 'abduction'. Inevitably, given Octavian's prominence, his breakneck courtship spilled over into the public arena. For the remainder of their married lives, Octavian and Livia would work hard to kick over the traces of so noisy a beginning. It was not by accident that Livia later came to acquire the honorary status of *univira*, the Roman 'one-man woman'. Official amnesia in relation to her first marriage effectively denied the possibility of youthful improprieties. In the short term, Octavian and Livia were preoccupied with the consummation – on a number of levels – of their desire. Before her marriage on 17 January 38 BC it is likely that Livia had already become Octavian's mistress. In this capacity, setting the pattern for the remainder of their lives together, she appears to have exerted an influence over him that was more than physical. A disgruntled Scribonia certainly thought so.

Octavian celebrated his twenty-fourth birthday on 23 September 39 BC. He marked the month of his birthday (if not the date itself) with a lavish celebration. Dio tells us that he held a 'magnificent entertainment' for friends, and at the same time ordered 'at public expense' a festival for the citizens of Rome.[12] The occasion for this munificence was not in fact his birthday but a traditional Roman rite of passage.

Roman portraiture of the late Republic includes almost no examples of likenesses of young men.[13] The Republic accorded social and political significance to age, and art reflected this bent. Minimum-age qualifications applied to the magistracies of state: thirty for the quaestorship, forty-two for the consulship. One result of this career clockwatching was the emphasis placed on young men's progress towards political eligibility. The final stage on that journey was a ritualized first shave, in which the beard clippings were dedicated either to one of the gods or to an ancestor (distinctions between the two frequently blurring in the minds of young Roman noblemen). It was known as the '*depositio barbae*'. Although individual celebrations varied, the *depositio* usually took place around the time of a man's twentieth birthday. The epitaph of Laetilius

Gallus, a decurion's son, who lived 'twenty years, seven months and seven days', explicitly states, 'I bore an unshaven beard when I met my death.'[14] Clearly, the celebration had been in Gallus's contemplation. His failure to attain this last condition of official maturity adds to the poignancy of his early death.

In Octavian's case, postponement arose from preoccupation with affairs of state. He spent the months preceding his twentieth birthday locked in deadly combat with Mark Antony's troops at Mutina. Within weeks of his birthday, recent hostilities briefly consigned to history, Octavian found himself joint ruler of Rome. Given his extreme youth, his membership of the Triumvirate overturned Republican regulations on the proper age for political office. As a marker of readiness for a senatorial career, the *depositio barbae* had become irrelevant to the leapfrogging Octavian. Postponement had the further happy outcome of allowing what by all accounts was a somewhat weedy, yellowish beard additional time to grow. The change in Octavian's status between the ages of twenty and twenty-four also enabled him to translate a conventional rite of passage into a city-wide spectacle. His purpose, according to rumour, was to impress Livia.

He probably succeeded. Livia cannot have been long returned to Rome. She was wrestling with adjustment to her new downgraded status in the city of her birth and weary after three years of struggle and danger. Ill at ease in her marriage to Nero, she was also beginning to feel her pregnancy. If she was impressed, it was not by the ceremony of Octavian's shaving or the consecration of the shorn beard in a decorative casket. It was the underlying statement of status and power embodied in the scale of the accompanying celebrations which must have struck Livia forcibly. Octavian, too, was pleased with the outcome of this particular piece of theatre. He did not allow his beard to re-grow but, according to Dio, 'kept his chin smooth afterwards . . . for he was already beginning to be enamoured of Livia.'[15] Livia may have been five years younger than her would-be lover, but Octavian recognized that in order to succeed, his suit required the appearance of maturity. This was an acknowledgement not simply of Livia's status as a married woman with children, but presumably of her intelligence and gravitas.

Public opinion applauded Octavian's gift of a festival for the people.

If we can trust the satirist Juvenal, writing a century later, it may also at this point have extended a partial amnesty to Octavian for the brutalities of his rise to power. Juvenal tells us that the *depositio barbae* traditionally drew a line under former misdeeds.[16] On the brink of abducting another man's pregnant wife, Octavian surely appreciated this measure of whitewash. The amnesty would be of short duration.

Mark Antony's malignity is the likeliest cause for a private fancy-dress dinner party becoming public knowledge. Despite Octavian having married his favourite sister to his colleague in 40 BC, relations between the two leading Triumvirs were less than happy. Neither Mark Antony nor his wife Octavia would attend Livia's wedding in January 38. Rivals for pre-eminence in Rome, Mark Antony and Octavian were locked into a cycle of point-scoring. Octavian's misguided 'Feast of the Divine Twelve' was too striking an error of judgement for his colleague to ignore.

As with so much of our evidence, doubts attach to this banquet in which, at a time of food shortages in Rome, six male and six female guests each dressed the part of a god or goddess. It may have taken place in 39, 38 or 36. The Treaty of Misenum notwithstanding, in each year outbreaks of famine plagued the capital. Suetonius records that, on the following morning, taunts of 'The Gods have gobbled all the grain!' showed the way the popular winds were blowing.[17] An anonymous lampoon circulated. Antony wrote 'a spiteful letter', now lost, naming all twelve participants. Octavian took the part of Apollo and was castigated as 'impious' for his pains, while all twelve guests were rumoured to have indulged in injudicious-sounding 'novel adulteries of the gods'.[18] Livia was almost certainly present. She may have played Juno to Nero's Jupiter. The banquet may or may not have taken place following the *depositio barbae*: Apollo was traditionally depicted as clean-shaven. In 36, as Dio notes, the Senate voted Octavian the right to hold an annual banquet in the Temple of Capitoline Jupiter. It is this which probably explains the final flourish of the lampoon quoted by Suetonius: 'Jupiter himself had flown from his golden throne.'[19]

The poet Martial commended a slave called Glaucia. 'Not an ordinary household slave nor a child of the profit-making slave market', Glaucia was a 'pet' or 'darling', a decorative, talkative child slave whose role was partly ornamental, partly for amusement – 'prattling boys, such as the women keep about them for their amusement', as Cassius Dio describes them.[20] The Romans called such slaves '*deliciae*'.[21] *Deliciae* occupied a special place in the household and in their owners' affections. Frequently naked, they were prized for their beauty and wit. Glaucia, Martial tells us, 'died to the grief of all Rome, the short-lived delight of his loving patron'.[22] Livia kept *deliciae*, as did Octavian. At a dinner party described by Dio as Livia and Octavian's marriage feast, a pert *delicia* upbraided Livia for reclining beside Octavian when her 'husband' – indicating Nero, who was also present – reclined on a different couch.

Dio's account is proof of the extent to which Nero was involved in Livia's remarriage, present not only at the wedding itself but at the celebrations attached to it. Hot on the heels of the scandal of the Feast of the Divine Twelve, it may also offer some explanation for Livia's subsequent resolution to present herself as a model of rectitude. The beginning of her relationship with Octavian was marred by censure and scandal. This was not the prominence her Claudian pride demanded. Perhaps Livia made a decision that marriage to Octavian justified these short-term slights. In the long term, her determination to confound her detractors by espousing an unassailable appearance of virtue would become one of the defining impulses of her marriage.

Happily for Livia, her path would traverse the smooth as well as the rough. For Octavian, Suetonius tells us, she 'remained the one woman whom he truly loved until his death'.[23] She repaid that love by careful tending of the grove of laurels at her villa near Veii, sign and substance of imperial kingship. All Octavian's heirs wore Livia's laurel garlands. All, unexpectedly, traced their right to rule from Livia.

CHAPTER 10

The price of comfort

The marble colonnades of the Forum of Augustus sheltered the story of Rome. Portrait busts of the city's heroes – winners of military triumphs from Aeneas to the present day – lined their covered walkways. Among them were the men Octavian counted as family.

These were not the Octavii. The portraits commemorated the Julians, Octavian's family by adoption. They included the deified Julius Caesar, those kings of Alba Longa whose calf-length crimson leather boots Caesar had worn on ceremonial occasions, and Rome's legendary founders Romulus and Aeneas. Their presence provided a counterweight to the busts of eminent Republicans, each mounted and inscribed with his achievements, with whom Octavian could not claim kinship.

Twenty years before building began, Octavian had vowed to construct a temple to Mars Ultor, Rome's avenging god of war. The occasion was the battle of Philippi, killing fields of the Roman Republic. Two decades later, after acquiring a suitable site at the cost of 100 million sesterces, Octavian fulfilled his promise. The new temple stood at the heart of a forum which celebrated antecedents of the same Republican nobles vanquished in the wake of Octavian's vow. By commemorating under a single roof Republican and Julian heroes, Octavian sought in marble and bronze to align himself with Rome's oldest aristocracy and that system of government he had chosen to reject.

There was no truth in the association. Nobility in Rome was a technical measure, conferred by attainment of senatorial rank. Technically Octavian was of noble stock, since his father, Gaius Octavius, had risen to the praetorship. Just as a summer demands more than a single swallow, an aristocratic atrium could not be furnished with only one ancestor mask. Beneath the surface lay a different story. The visual propaganda of the Forum of Augustus, grandiloquent and misleading, demonstrates the desire felt by the most powerful man in the world to shrug off the outsider status of his birth. The Roman 'family' of the Forum's busts was an exercise in historical revisionism, Octavian's attempted truce with the nobles of the Republic and with Rome's past. Throughout the early years of his pre-eminence, Octavian struggled to win acceptance by the former ruling class. This was surely in his mind when, in 38 BC, he married one of them. In the same year, the appointment to the consulship of Livia's fellow Claudian, Appius Claudius Pulcher, confirmed that at least one aristocratic family of the Republic was prepared to do business with Octavian's upstart regime.

Love-match or otherwise, the marriage of Octavian and Livia was a bargain to which both contributed and from which both anticipated returns. The price Livia paid for comfort and security was symbolic. To Octavian's present, she contributed a family history described by Velleius as 'most noble', and a past, as we have seen, of notable distinction. As Marcus had discovered, five hundred years of Claudian and Livii Drusan office-holders were insufficient to quash the parvenu Octavian. In embracing her father's killer, Livia lent his regime authority and status. As when Julia married Marius, gratitude was Octavian's part. He was Napoleon, of unknown Corsican stock, to Livia's Habsburg Marie Louise. It is impossible that either overlooked this aspect of their marriage, even if it was not their primary motivation, which in both cases is questionable. In 33 BC, alongside Livia's son Tiberius, they sponsored funeral games in honour of Nero, who had recently died; also celebrated in the games was Livia's father Marcus. It was Octavian who benefited from what looks like an act of atonement but was also a parade of Livia's Republican nobility. He broadcast his connection by marriage to a political force which, though in theory defeated, unnerved him through its continuing influence over the people of Rome and its mistrust of his own constitutionally innovatory rule.

'Those who contemplate marriage,' Musonius Rufus wrote, the following century, 'ought to have regard neither for family, whether one be of high-born parents, nor for wealth, whether on either side there be great possessions, nor for physical traits, whether one or the other have beauty. For neither wealth, nor beauty, nor high birth is effective in promoting partnership of interest or sympathy . . .'[1] The philosopher had overlooked the recent example of Rome's first couple.

In 70 BC a wealthy equestrian from a town called Velitrae was elected to the quaestorship and became the first member of his family to join the Senate. Velleius Paterculus described him as 'a dignified person, of upright and blameless life, and extremely rich'. [2] His name was Gaius Octavius. He was a Roman citizen, though not of Roman origin. His son would become Rome's first emperor; his father was a provincial moneylender.

Like Livia's maternal grandparents, the Octavii enjoyed a degree of local prominence, presumably on account of their wealth. There can be no other explanation for Gaius's second marriage. At about the time of his first magistracy, Gaius divorced his wife, a local woman called Ancharia, and engaged himself to another local woman. On this occasion, his choice fell on a bride of unassailably patrician maternal connections. Atia was the daughter of Marcus Atius Balbus, like Gaius a man of uncertain origin, whom Mark Antony would later dismiss as the son of an African baker and perfume-maker. This possibility notwithstanding, Atia's mother was none other than Julius Caesar's sister, Julia, an illustrious connection which endowed Atia with all the attractions she needed in Gaius's eyes. Julia herself may not have embraced this choice of son-in-law. Perhaps Balbus took pity on the *novus homo* and urged the virtue of his splendid bank account. By dint of determination and usury's full coffers, Gaius Octavius progressed from middle class provincialism to office-holding Roman nobility with elevated family connections. His two children by Atia, Octavian and his elder sister Octavia, found themselves before their twentieth birthdays great-nephew and great-niece of Rome's first deified dictator.

Gaius Octavius the younger, known as Octavian, was born early in the morning of 23 September 63 BC, a little more than four years before his future wife Livia. Like Livia, he was born in Rome on the Palatine Hill, in a house which Suetonius calls Ox Heads. Just as Livia travelled between Rome, Fundi and Pisenum, Octavian spent much of his childhood at the house of his Velitraean grandfather on the edge of the Alban Hills southeast of Rome. The house would later become an early tourist attraction. Suetonius records within it 'a small room, not unlike a butler's pantry ... still shown and described as Augustus's nursery';[3] he also notes a shrine in Rome that marked the site of Octavian's birth. By Suetonius's time, at the beginning of the second century AD, both had become destinations for pilgrims. In truth, Octavian's childhood lacked the distinction of Livia's aristocratic upbringing.

This was not the fault of the busy and opportunistic Gaius Octavius. Before his death in 58, Octavian's father had held both the position of praetor and a provincial governorship. If senatorial status was new to the Octavii, Gaius treated his immediate family to a lucrative baptism by fire. On his death, his four-year-old son went to live with his maternal grandmother, Julia – the point at which Rome's two future autocrats may first have met. Eight years later, promoting the connection of which his father had been so proud as well as demonstrating a degree of statesmanlike precocity, Octavian delivered Julia's funeral oration. Through Atia's remarriage, the same period witnessed the accession to the consulship, Rome's grandest office, of Octavian's new stepfather Philippus, a vacillating and over-cautious aristocrat descended from the Macedonian royal family. Six years after Philippus, Octavia's husband Gaius Claudius Marcellus also held the consulship and devoted himself to opposition to his wife's great-uncle, Caesar. As consuls, both men were rewarded with what St John Chrysostom later described as 'the splendid trappings ... the cheers ... in the city, the acclamations in the Hippodrome and the flatteries of the spectators',[4] not to mention the public attendance by *lictors* each carrying the fasces of office – outward manifestations of rank which must have thrilled a teenager of Rome's profoundly hierarchical society. Despite the paucity of *imagines* in Gaius Octavius's atrium, his son acquired early on a close personal acquaintance with the workings of the Roman state. Octavian saw at first hand the power and allure of high office and the complex allegiances of the Senate House.

Octavian's childhood, like Livia's, took place against a background of political instability. As his great-uncle would demonstrate in revolutionary fashion, it was an age of possibilities. By the time Octavian and Caesar met again, around Octavian's fifteenth birthday, the young man from nowhere was old enough to understand in part the extent of those possibilities, even if Caesar's ultimate goal remained hidden. By then it must also have been obvious to Octavian that success in Rome demanded more than political acumen and intelligence. In his memoirs, Suetonius tells us, 'he merely [recorded] that he came of a rich old equestrian family, and that his father had been the first Octavian to enter the Senate.'[5] We do not know when Octavian learnt that this was not enough.

Livia was not the twenty-four-year-old Octavian's first wife. On the contrary, he had been engaged three times previously and married at least once. Livia's predecessors had each commended themselves to his bosom not through claims of love or attraction but for motives that were explicitly political. Not for Octavian Tennyson's 'A simple maiden in her flower is worth a hundred coats-of-arms.'

Servilia was the daughter of Publius Servilius Vatia Isauricus. Eminent by birth, connected by marriage to several of Caesar's assassins, she nevertheless exercised a fleeting hold over Octavian. Within months their engagement lapsed. In Servilia's place, Octavian made his first alliance with the Claudii. He engaged himself to Claudia, the daughter of Publius Clodius Pulcher, that patrician-plebeian crowd-pleaser whose boisterous exploits enflamed Rome during Livia's infancy. Briefly disentangled from the arms of his high-living sisters, Clodius had married Fulvia, a battleaxe of a woman who may not have deserved the criticism ancient historians heaped upon her. Out of the frying pan into the fire, Fulvia married Mark Antony. Octavian's match with Claudia, Fulvia's daughter and Mark Antony's stepdaughter, sealed the alliance of the two leading Triumvirs in 43 BC. Neither alliance nor betrothal lasted. Claudia's extreme youth prevented consummation in the short term, while Fulvia's overt hostility to her would-be son-in-law, witnessed in the siege of Perusia, did little to commend the virtue of waiting. In the meantime, Octavian's priorities changed. By the year 40 BC his fears focused on Sextus Pompey, all-powerful on nearby Sicily. He disentangled himself from the still virgin Claudia and married Sextus's aunt Scribonia, a veteran of two previous marriages and a woman who understood unrosily the political aspect of upper-class marriage in Rome. After Scribonia, Livia.

There is no reason to doubt Octavian's love for Livia. Cassius Dio attributes to him an endorsement of marriage which presupposes happiness on Octavian's part. 'For is there anything better than a wife who is chaste, domestic, a good housekeeper, a rearer of children; one to gladden you in health, to tend you in sickness; to be your partner in good fortune, to console you in misfortune; to restrain the mad passion of youth and to temper the unseasonable harshness of old age?'[6] It is also the case, however, that Octavian's track record suggests he would have married Livia without love or physical attraction. Where his father led, Octavian followed, repeatedly exploiting the family connections marriage created in order to enhance his status and bolster the political alliance of the moment. It was simply the Roman way. Why else would Musonius Rufus counsel against marriage for worldly ends, other than the prevalence of exactly this sort of marriage? Happily, Octavian's final victim was not a blushing ingénue. Even at nineteen, Livia understood as clearly as her new husband the philosophy of their union. It need not preclude love, happiness or fulfilment.

Julius Caesar's will, in which he named Octavian as his principal heir, gives striking evidence of the immensity of his wealth. Plutarch, in his life of Caesar, states that 'he had given every Roman citizen a considerable gift'[7] – a bequest of 300 sesterces. Of the residue of his estate, following what may have amounted to 300,000 such payments, two beneficiaries each received an eighth. Finally, three-quarters of what still remained passed to Octavian,[8] a sum estimated at sixty-six million sesterces. To this Octavian added the fortunes of his father and grandfather, large in scale whether or not we choose to believe their origins in moneylending. Octavian owned in addition a number of houses and villas, including property at Lanuvium, Palestrina and Tivoli. Over time his wealth increased exponentially. Cassius Dio claimed that he received more than a billion sesterces in legacies from friends, and bequeathed to his own heirs a sum in the region of 150 million sesterces.[9] Such was the scale of Octavian's personal fortune that, on four occasions, he may have made payments to the state treasury from the imperial privy purse.[10]

*

This was the settlement for which Livia traded complicity with her father's killer. To Octavian she gave the political blessing of her unrivalled Republican ancestry. To Nero, in accordance with Roman divorce custom, she gave her children. Tiberius was three years old, Drusus a matter of days, when both returned to live in their father's house. Even if we believe the sources' appraisal of the austerity of Livia's nature, it was a high price for a mother to pay.

Octavian was short in stature. Erring on the side of flattery, his freedman, Julius Marathus, estimated his height at five feet seven inches. Despite this, Suetonius records him as handsomely proportioned, to the extent that only the proximity of someone taller exposed his shortness. His complexion was somewhere between dark and fair and his hair yellowish in colour and slightly curly. Like many naturally good looking people, he was careless of his appearance. He was, however, proud of his eyes. Although Pliny the Elder claimed that his eyes were like those of a horse and that he became irritated if people stared at them too closely,[11] Suetonius offers a different account. 'Augustus's eyes were clear and bright, and he liked to believe that they shone with a sort of divine radiance: it gave him profound pleasure if anyone at whom he glanced keenly dropped his head as though dazzled by looking into the sun.'[12]

Livia was not dazzled by that divine radiance, not in the summer of 39 BC nor through the fifty-two years of her marriage to Octavian. A woman of intelligence and education, she did not imbue with god-like powers the man responsible for the death of her father, the fugitive discomforts of her marriage to Nero and her surrender of her children. That would happen later, when Octavian was dead and the stability of Livia's position required his deification. Then she willingly gave a reward of a million sesterces to Numerius Atticus, the senator and former praetor who claimed to have witnessed the emperor's ascent to heaven 'in the same way, as tradition has it, as occurred in the case of Proculus and Romulus', as Cassius Dio records.[13] At the end of her life, Livia would find herself the priestess of her deified husband's cult. Even then, we should be wary of assuming that she believed in the rites she professed. She had lived too long in Rome and understood too well the machinations of the city's politics. It was knowledge she acquired early, probably during her marriage to Nero, with its unexpected reversals and vicissitudes. Livia did not drop her head before Octavian's glance. She recognized the value of his suit as surely as she apprehended her own value to him. For an instant, footsore in Rome, her parents dead, her husband's future uncertain, she was perhaps bewitched.

CHAPTER 11

'No magic chant will make you a mother'

It was not lead poisoning which brought about the fall of the Roman Empire. Scientists have disproved dinosaur-extinction-style theories, popular in some quarters, that lead pipes in aqueducts weakened Rome's lifeblood or that the measures taken by Romans to sweeten and preserve wine led to a diminished sperm count in men and a rise in premature and stillbirths among women. Up to a point Romans recognized lead's hazards. In Livia's lifetime, Vitruvius cautioned against the dangers of lead piping. 'Water conducted through [terracotta] pipes is more wholesome than that through lead; indeed that conveyed in lead must be injurious, because from it white lead is obtained, and this is said to be injurious to the human system ... Water therefore should on no account be conducted in leaden pipes if we are desirous that it should be wholesome.'[1] Pliny is among several authors who describe reducing unfermented grape juice in lead or lead-lined vessels in order to create a sugar-rich must to add to wine either as a preservative or to mask sourness. Since Romans drank wine diluted with water, it seems improbable that the quantities of lead leached in the reducing process, when imbibed, would prove sufficient to contribute to widespread poisoning or a decline in the birthrate.

At the time of her marriage to Octavian, Livia was weeks short of her twentieth birthday and the mother of two healthy children. The timing of her marriage ceremony three days after Drusus's birth places an upper limit on Livia's required recovery period after labour, at least in that instance. It is reasonable to infer that, at this point in her life, Livia gave

birth easily, despite the physical rigours of the early months of her pregnancy, which overlapped with the close of her period of exile, and the
heightened emotions of her burgeoning affair with Octavian. For his
part, Octavian, less than five years his new wife's senior, had recently
become a father for the first time with the birth in 39 of his daughter
Julia. In both cases the couple's youth and proven fertility were grounds
for hope that together they would shortly have more children. This surely
was the meaning of the Prima Porta portent months after their marriage: that 'sterile' white chicken had not only confounded Roman cer-
tainties by producing its brood of white chicks, but the twig of laurel
held in its beak clearly symbolized the future authority of the couple's
offspring.

The likelihood of children must have coloured the thoughts of both
Livia and Octavian; in Octavian's case, it is impossible to state with accuracy the point at which his plans for Rome became explicitly dynastic.
Livia and Octavian's marriage predates Octavian's assumption of absolute
power. Since he had probably been contemplating sovereignty of this
nature for some time, it is likely that he had considered its long-term
implications and requirements, notably an heir. But Livia would conceive only once in the fifty-two years of her second marriage. That pregnancy terminated in stillbirth.

Livia's failure to have children by Octavian is central to her history.
Her reputation for scheming, ambition and ultimately murder all pivot
on the manner in which she discharged her role as mother. Did she
overstep acceptable boundaries? In the absence of children from her
second marriage, Livia's maternal ambitions – which, as we have seen,
Rome was prepared to consider a legitimate outlet for female aspiration
– focused on her sons by her marriage to Nero, Tiberius and Drusus.
But Octavian's covert decision in essence to create a hereditary monarchy
would theoretically exclude his stepsons. First in the line of succession
were Octavian's biological heirs. At a stroke Livia's legitimate grounds
for ambition vanished. Only Julia's children, or those of Livia's sister-
in-law Octavia, could inherit Octavian's position on the basis of blood
kinship. Livia's hopes were unfounded – not motherlove but her own
lust for power. That one of Livia's sons did indeed succeed her husband
was all the proof of Livia's guilt a writer like Tacitus needed. Livia had

exceeded herself: she had employed treachery, deceit and possibly worse to achieve her ends. In Tacitus's hands Livia is above all mother and stepmother, a mother whose perverse nature defiles that relationship of purity and trust, a stepmother of fairytale malevolence. In each case, the ultimate victim was Rome. 'Livia the mother was a curse to the state; Livia the stepmother was a curse to the house of the Caesars.'[2]

Virtually all the surviving sources postdate Tiberius's accession. The ancient writers work backwards from that fact to arrange arguably unrelated events in Livia's life and that of Octavian's family into a neat narrative of maternal scheming. This retrospective reading eventually provides the source of Robert Graves's Livia, villainess of *I, Claudius*, and Sian Phillips's powerful television portrayal of 1976. Through misuse of hindsight, ancient historians bequeathed to posterity not the image of a goddess of the Roman pantheon, to which Livia was entitled, but a caricature of feminine ruthlessness which remains current despite repeated debunking by classicists and scholars. Cassius Dio described the Prima Porta portent as one which gave pleasure to Livia and proved that she 'was destined to hold in her lap even Caesar's power and to dominate him in everything'. The statement is one calculated to strike a chill into Roman readers' hearts. 'Other people,' he hastens to explain, did not share her pleasure, but 'were greatly disturbed ... by this.'[3] He does not, of course, provide a source for his assertion either of Livia's pleasure or the displeasure of those nameless other people. It is enough that he has cast doubt on Livia's good intentions.

Children were central to the Roman concept of marriage. A second-century funerary inscription to a 'Lady Panthia', discovered in Pergamum, commends a wife for the bearing and rearing of children: 'You bore me children completely like myself; you cared for your bridegroom and your children; you guided straight the runner of life in our home.'[4] We have seen that men like Hortensius chose wives with a proven track record of successful childbearing – as indeed Octavian may have done. Childlessness in marriage, by contrast, was a potential source of acrimony. In an extreme example, when Scipio Aemilianus was unexpectedly discovered dead in 129 BC, contemporaries suspected suicide or the dark hand of his wife – 'Sempronia ... who was not loved by him because she was ugly and barren,' as Appian recorded.⁵ If Appian is trustworthy, Scipio paid a high price for his insensitivity over Sempronia's failure to conceive.

Romans assumed as a matter of course that the responsibility for infertility lay with the wife. This is the explanation for a document known as the 'laudatio Turiae', probably from the early Christian period of the Empire.⁶ The funeral oration of a husband for his wife, it records the wife's certainty that she is to blame for the couple's childlessness, and her subsequent sacrifice.

> You did not believe you could be fertile and were disconsolate to see me without children; you did not wish me by continuing my marriage to you to give up hope of having children, and to be on that account unhappy, so you proposed divorce, so that you would vacate the house and turn it over to a woman more fertile . . . and that you would henceforth render me the services and devotion of a sister or mother-in-law.⁷

In Turia's case, this selfless offer enrages her devoted husband, who refuses to countenance it. A husband who took a different line, though apparently without animosity, was the dictator Sulla. In the generation before Livia's birth, Plutarch tells us, Sulla divorced his third wife Cloelia for her failure to bear children, but did so 'honourably and with words of praise, to which he added gifts'.⁸ Within days Sulla married for a fourth time. His new bride was the high-born Caecilia Metella, widow of the leader of the Senate Aemilius Scaurus, a union clearly for political ends. The speed of his remarriage, we read, notwithstanding his professed reasons for divorce, led to suspicions that he had accused Cloelia unfairly – further lustre for the blameless divorcee's posterity.

There are no reports of Octavian contemplating divorce from Livia, although there is strong evidence to doubt his fidelity to her. He apparently resisted apportioning to her blame for their childlessness – on the Turia principle – and did not, like Sulla, use that misfortune as a pretext to enter a more convenient marriage. Nor do we learn that, like Scipio Aemilianus and Sempronia, Octavian and Livia's failure to have children created ill feeling between them, even though we know, apparently from Livia herself, that Octavian felt little fondness for Tiberius and adopted him as his heir only with reluctance. Their marriage was of even tenor and long duration. If it arose from pragmatism, such considerations clearly became a habit that suited both well.

We cannot unravel the degree of Livia's regret over her childlessness with Octavian. No details survive concerning the unsuccessful outcome of her third pregnancy save its happening, recorded by Suetonius and Pliny. Today the effects of miscarriage and stillbirth are recognized as emotional as well as physical. In marrying Octavian, Livia had accepted the inevitability of surrendering her existing children for the duration of their father's life. That she was prepared to make this sacrifice need not indicate that she was a woman of hardened sensibilities who would not have suffered as a result of an unsuccessful pregnancy: marriage with Octavian left her no other choice. There may have been serious physical consequences attaching to this pregnancy – the likeliest explanation for Livia's failure to conceive again – but we can assume from the sources' silence that these were not recognized at the time. This suggests that any complications which did arise were internal and therefore not apparent to contemporary doctors or, presumably, to Livia and Octavian.

Hindsight sharpens our appreciation of how different Livia's reputation might have been had Octavian's successor not been his stepson Tiberius. Had Livia given birth to Octavian's son, she would at least have escaped the stereotype of the wicked stepmother, prevalent in Greek and Roman theatre and literature, which, as we will see, proved grist to her detractors' mills. But it is dangerous to assume that Livia's sinister reputation for ambition, scheming and murder rests solely on the tenuous kinship of Octavian and Tiberius. Republican sentiments survived in imperial Rome, particularly among the educated classes who supplied the empire with its annalists and historians. Such men opposed as a matter of course the principle of hereditary monarchy which Octavian evolved. Their dislike of Livia arose in part from her position as wife of one emperor and mother of a second. It encompassed mistrust of any connection between women and the exercise of 'male' power. Livia enjoyed through two generations proximity to the centre of power, with all the potential influence that entailed. That the second emperor was not the son of the first hardly mattered. It merely provided historians with another negative tag with which to taunt Livia – that of stepmother, since the price of Tiberius's victory was the demise of Octavian's adopted sons and heirs, Livia's stepchildren. Criticized for his curmudgeonliness towards his mother following his accession, Tiberius, himself of Republican birth through both his parents, perhaps understood the Roman mentality too well. His refusal to allow the Senate to add to his titles that of 'Son of Julia', as Livia was then known, may have been intended in part to spare his mother as much as himself. Public admissions of Livia's influence were to the benefit of neither Livia herself nor the institution into which her family had evolved.

The Romans inherited Greek thought on human conception. As early as the beginning of the fifth century BC, the Greek philosopher Alcmaeon of Croton had suggested possible explanations for the mechanisms of new life.[9] Alcmaeon's theory that both parents produced semen, itself formed from blood, was challenged by Aristotle in the following century: Aristotle ascribed semen to the father, menstrual fluid to the mother. In the last century of the Roman Republic, the poet Lucretius offered a synthesis of current debate. His 'two-seed' theory, by which the semen of both mother and father mingled in the newborn child, kept faith with Alcmaeon's. Lucretius's chief interest was the transmission of hereditary characteristics, a suitably Roman concern given patrician conviction of the importance of high birth and family history.[10] 'It may seem strange that female offspring is engendered from the father's seed, and the mother's body gives birth to males. The fact is that the embryo is always composed of atoms from both sources, only it derives more than half from the parent which it more closely resembles. This is noticeable in either case, whether the child's origin is predominantly male or female.'[11] What the poet failed to offer women like Livia, Cloelia or Sempronia was practical information on how to optimize chances of conception. The curious puzzle of how a female body gives birth to a male child – if she ever thought of it – may have struck Livia as insignificant in the years following the stillbirth of her baby. It is more likely that she reached a conclusion like that of Pliny, whose *Natural History* is one of our sources for Livia's stillbirth. Pliny cited Livia and Octavian as an example of a couple who, despite producing children from other unions, are sterile together.[12] It was simply a biological anomaly, proof of the extent to which science remained unfathomable.

Suetonius tells us that once Octavian had achieved mastery of Rome, his domestic policy included reviving 'certain obsolescent rites and appointments: the augury of the Goddess Safety, the office of Flamen Dialis [a priesthood of Jupiter], the Lupercalian Festival, the Secular Games and the Cross-Roads Festival'.[13]

The 'Lupercalian Festival' had not long been in abeyance. It was at the Lupercalia of 44 BC, one month before the Ides of March, that Julius Caesar, to the acclamation of large crowds, twice refused Mark Antony's offer of a royal diadem.

Of ancient origin, the festival consisted of a race through the streets of Rome. The competitors were two colleges of priests, the Luperci Quintilii and the Fabii. Both made sacrifices in the Lupercal cave at the south-west corner of the Palatine Hill, a sacred enclosure described by Dionysius of Halicarnassus as overarched by a grove of oak trees and watered by springs that welled up between the rocks.[14] The competing teams made a circuit of the Palatine then returned to the Lupercal. Naked save for loincloths, they carried goatskin thongs with which they struck out at bystanders. Women were their chosen target.

This baffling exercise, which enjoyed notable popularity with the man on the street, operated on a number of levels. It was concerned with the purification of the community of Rome; it became a rite of passage for young men; and, as Ovid outlines in the *Fasti*, it was connected with female fertility.[15] Women struck by the thongs of the Luperci would become mothers in the tenth month after the festival; those already pregnant, at the touch of the priests' lash, were guaranteed a safe and easy labour. 'Bride, what do you wait for? No potent drugs, no prayers,/ No magic chant will make you a mother./ Endure the lash of the fertile hand; your father-in-law/ Will soon have the grandsire's name he covets.'[16]

We cannot specify the attraction of the Lupercalia for Octavian. It is likely that he responded to its association with Rome's legendary founders, Romulus and Remus. Perhaps he hoped to remind Romans of the refusal by his adopted father Caesar of a royal crown weeks before his assassination. In his domestic policy Octavian repeatedly took measures to increase the birthrate, particularly among the upper classes. Possibly, the man whose superstitions extended to carrying an amulet of seal-skin to ward off thunder felt that in endorsing this sacred celebration of fertility, he would win the gods' favour for Livia. It was not to be.

In the mind of Romilius Pollio, the lead-lined pans used for reducing grape juice to must carried no health hazards. The centenarian, a con-temporary of Livia and Octavian unknown in the sources save on account of his remarkable age, attributed his health and survival to *mulsum* (wine sweetened with honey) and olive oil: '*intus mulso, foris olio*', honeyed wine within, oil without.[17] A tombstone in the Roman harbour town of Ostia offers baths, wine and love as a recipe for longevity.[18] Livia's own prescription, shared at the end of her long life, echoes the formula.[19] Pliny records her daily indulgence in Pucine wine. This little-known red wine from Istria – a region also noted by the ancients for the excellence of its olive oil – grew on a hilly promontory between Aquilea and Tergeste at the head of the Adriatic, 'not far from Mount Timavus'.[20] Sea breezes buffeted the vineyard, resulting in small, highly prized harvests and, presumably, costly vintages. But Livia was a wealthy woman. Although she was denied the child Octavian craved as his successor, her life was otherwise richly endowed. According to Pliny, 'there is not a wine that is deemed superior to this for medicinal purposes'. Livia 'never drank any other'.[21] Long life and health became part of her legend. One by one she outlived her enemies. Three times she survived the rigours of preg-nancy, twice giving birth to healthy sons who between them achieved an exemplary record of service to the state. She survived flight from the armies of the Triumvirs, famine in Rome, scandal . . . and the hidden perils of Roman viticulture and sanitation.

CHAPTER 12

By the side of the goddess

In the Temple of Venus Genetrix, at the centre of the Forum Julium, Julius Caesar had honoured two goddesses with statues. To the first he attributed victory over Pompey the Great at the Battle of Pharsalus. The second was his mistress.

Caesar claimed the first goddess, Venus Genetrix herself, as an ancestress of the Julian clan. He had promised her this temple in return for victory in Thessaly in 48 BC. His mistress was not a mythical figure, although in her home country she enjoyed divine status and sacred attributes. She was associated with the Nile goddess Isis, whom Roman religion in turn affiliated with Venus Genetrix. She was the last Queen of Egypt, Cleopatra VII.

Caesar, Appian tells us, in furnishing the new temple, 'placed a beautiful image of Cleopatra by the side of the goddess'.[1] He spent a million gold pieces on building the forum, complete with marble temple and rostra – the spoils of victory in Gaul.[2] Part of that sum was evidently earmarked for Cleopatra's statue. It was made of gilded bronze, and must certainly have eclipsed its more venerable neighbour.

How Cleopatra responded to this conspicuous compliment we do not know. There is every chance that she saw the statue. At the time, she was living in Rome with her husband Ptolemy, who was also her brother, and her infant son Caesarion, Caesar's child, born the previous summer.[3] The Ptolemaic court had taken up residence in a house belonging to Caesar on the banks of the Tiber probably towards the end of 46 BC. It was not an arrangement which would be seen to reflect credit upon

either party. As Cassius Dio recorded, Caesar 'incurred the greatest censure from all because of his passion for Cleopatra – not now the passion he had displayed in Egypt (for that was a matter of hearsay), but
that which was displayed in Rome itself. For she had come to the city
with her husband and settled in Caesar's own house, so that he too
derived an ill repute on account of both of them.'[4] Caesar's worship of
his earthly goddess, perfunctory as all his dealings with women, was
less sacred than profane.

Dio's account was written more than two centuries after the events
it describes. Its portrait of Roman disapproval of Cleopatra represents
an attitude towards the Egyptian queen that was neither Dio's invention
nor simple reportage: it was a fiction devised by Octavian. Octavian
later exploited for his own purposes memories of the bold impact of
Cleopatra's presence in Rome in 46 BC: her exotic appearance, splendidly dressed, heavily jewelled, her hair elaborately unRoman,[5] her olive
skin expertly enhanced by cosmetics; the oily deference of her attendant eunuchs and maid-servants; her incestuous, effete co-sovereign husband. Octavian transformed Roman perceptions of Cleopatra into a
figure far removed from his 'father's' golden goddess. That he did so
changed the course of Livia's life. His actions were motivated by desire
for political conquest.

It came about like this.

Once upon a time, three men met on an island. The time was 43 BC, as
we have seen, and the men's purpose was power. Together they had
decided to rule the Roman world. They may or may not have recognized the pitfalls of joint rule. Did each of them long for sole power?
Possibly. In 36 BC the three became two, when Marcus Aemilius Lepidus played into the hands of his colleagues by attempting to conquer
Sicily. His punishment was expulsion from the Triumvirate, which had
three years left to run; he retained until his death the title of Pontifex
Maximus. In practical terms Lepidus's banishment did little to clarify
the relative positions of his survivors: Mark Antony retained control of
Rome's eastern provinces; Octavian the west, including Rome itself. The
men shared little beyond a common enemy in the Parthians, fearsome
on their eastern borders, and the affection of Octavia, fourth wife of the

former, elder sister of the latter. It would not be easy for Octavian to compress two into one and govern Rome outright. He required a careful stratagem.

Romans had been at war with Romans on and off for more than half a century – since Livia's adoptive grandfather Marcus Livius Drusus was killed with that artisan's knife in the atrium of his house on the Palatine. The victims of battle were Rome's upper classes as much as her foot soldiers. Twice Proscriptions had depleted aristocratic wealth and power. Fallout from the Ides of March was cruel, bloody and expensive, with fighting at Pharsalus, Thapsus, Munda, Philippi and Perusia throughout the late 40s.[6] By the time of Lepidus's disgrace in 36 BC there were few in Rome who welcomed the prospect of further civil war. In the north of Italy, 170,000 veterans clamoured for their promised settlements of land.[7] If Octavian wanted rid of Mark Antony – and he did, despite the emollient intermediary role played by Octavia – he needed a scapegoat to galvanize both military and grass-roots support. He could not otherwise eliminate the man whose popularity at this point eclipsed his own. To little avail the Triumvirs hastened to disparage one another in front of the Senate and the people of Rome, squabbling for pre-eminence. 'By frequent denunciations before the people Caesar [Octavian] tried to inflame the multitude against Antony. Antony, too, kept sending counter-accusations against Caesar,' Plutarch records.[8] The two Triumvirs had reached gridlock. Both sought a way out. Octavian found his *casus belli* carved from gold in his 'father's' temple of Venus Genetrix.

The weapon with which Octavian defeated Mark Antony was Cleopatra, one-time paramour of Julius Caesar, Mark Antony's mistress, mother of three of his children and later his wife. Without Cleopatra, Octavian might never have ruled Rome. Without Cleopatra, Octavian could not have concealed self-interest behind a masquerade of patriotism. Without Cleopatra, Livia would not have achieved the public persona imperial propaganda devised for her and which she in turn embraced with rigour. Cleopatra provided the catalyst in Octavian's bid for absolute power and, by unwitting contrast, in Octavian's propaganda, a template of virtuous womanly behaviour to which Livia would adhere lifelong. That Cleopatra did this, of course, was not her own but Octavian's doing. Cleopatra became Octavian's fallguy, as she has in part remained throughout history.

In his lengthy treatise *Institutio Oratoria*, published at the end of the first century AD, the rhetorician Quintilian indicated an important facet of the Roman character. 'If the Greeks bear away the palm for moral precepts, Rome can produce more striking examples of moral performance, which is a far greater thing.'[9]

The Romans were a practical, empiricist people. They preferred concrete examples to abstract precepts and attacked problems head-on rather than employing cunning or guile.[10] Cicero understood this. We have already seen him elaborate the popular taste for magnificence through the sorry example of that cheese-paring quaestor Quintus Tubero. Octavian understood it too. Since he could not admit publicly his ambition for absolute power, he found concrete grounds for 'reasonable' opposition to Mark Antony. Cleopatra provided those grounds.

'When Caesar had made sufficient preparations,' Plutarch tells us, 'a vote was passed to wage war against Cleopatra, and to take away from Antony the authority which he had surrendered to a woman.'[11] It was Cleopatra, not Mark Antony, who became the enemy of Octavian and Rome. In Octavian's version of events, Mark Antony – despite prolonged vilification by his fellow Triumvir – would eventually be incidental. Cleopatra, who had usurped his power and assumed his authority, presented the real danger. At the beginning of 32 BC, she played directly into her adversary's hands, when it became clear that she meant to accompany Mark Antony on his campaign against Octavian and take a full role in the events she generously subsidized.[12] Mark Antony's failure to force her to return to Egypt appeared to prove the points her opponent had repeatedly made against the couple. For years Octavian had manipulated Cleopatra's 'other' status: her foreignness; her sex; her exoticism, witnessed by Romans during her romantic sojourn in Caesar's villa a decade earlier; her fertility, which could so easily be made to resemble promiscuity. By these means he had fashioned a personification of 'anti-Rome' tangible even to the most practically minded Roman. 'Caesar said in addition ... that the Romans were carrying on war with Mardion the eunuch, and Potheinus, Iras [Cleopatra's hairdresser] and

Charmian her waiting woman, by whom the principal affairs of the government were managed.'[13] It was an image that contrasted powerfully with Octavian's leadership, rooted, as it sought to present itself, in Republican traditions of martial vigour and political collectivism, Rome's favourite quality of male-focused *virtus*. In Octavian's regime, Livia officially stood outside the arena of power; no waiting women, hairdressers or eunuchs influenced the counsels of state. The very distinctness of Cleopatra's petticoats government was her enemy's proof of its badness.

It was a policy that reaped dividends for Octavian. But its shilling-shocker sensationalism also made demands on Livia. If Cleopatra's villainy consisted in large measure of her sex, what then of Livia, who shared that sex? Octavian's careful branding of Cleopatra necessitated an equally considered reappraisal of Livia's role and reputation. It was essential that in the eyes of Rome clear blue water separated the two women. But Livia, like Cleopatra, had recently performed the role of mistress. The circumstances of her marriage, as we have seen, were hardly exemplary. We can surmise – although the people of Rome may not have been able to – Claudian hauteur on Livia's part as powerful as the regal arrogance which had so irked Cicero in Cleopatra. Both were women of education and intelligence. For Cleopatra, the exercise of power was intrinsic to her position as monarch; Livia had been brought up in the dog days of the Republic, when patrician women like Fulvia and Sempronia, though calumniated for their pains, took an increasingly active interest in public affairs. To muddy the waters further, it seems that Octavian himself had not been faithful to Livia since their hasty marriage. No wonder Mark Antony was initially baffled by Octavian's approach. 'What's come over you?' he wrote to his belligerent colleague. 'Is it because I go to bed with the queen? But she isn't my wife, is she? And it isn't as if it's something new, is it? Haven't I been doing it for nine years now? And what about you, is Livia the only woman you go to bed with? I congratulate you, if at the time you read this letter you haven't also had Tertulla or Terentilla or Rufilla or Salvia Titisenia or the whole lot of them. Does it really matter where you get a stand or who the woman is?'[14]

The answer was for Livia – inescapably female – to exemplify an assertively Roman concept of womanliness and womanly goodness. The means Octavian chose was portraiture. Beginning in the 30s, Livia sat for a number of official likenesses. Each shares the same streamlined iconography – idealized images that imbue Livia with an appearance of virtue, seriousness and lack of affectation, and a serene, unruffled beauty ultimately derived from historic representations of Greek goddesses.[15]

In place of Cleopatra's elaborate eastern hairstyle that kept Iras so busy, Livia wears a simple, lozenge-shaped bun known as the *nodus*. It sits above her forehead on her hairline. Beneath and behind it, the hair is neatly drawn back into a smaller bun at the nape of the neck. Ovid commended the *nodus* in his erotic poem *Ars Amatoria* as flattering female beauty, particularly that of women with rounded faces.[16] Although Livia would appear a casebook example of the round-faced woman whom the *nodus* benefited, the style also recommended itself for more sober reasons. Current since before Livia's birth, the *nodus* had strongly Republican connotations. It survives in the carved imagery of Republican tomb reliefs, a visual source of unassailable gravitas.[17] It was old-fashioned rather than unfashionable, a political statement as much as a grooming choice.[18] It became the principal decorative element of Livia's early portraits. At the same time, it allied Livia with her sister-in-law Octavia, the first public figure to adopt the *nodus* – and, on account of her husband's infidelity, like Livia, Cleopatra's adversary.

The appearance of virtue alone was not enough. Where Cleopatra was extravagant, Livia must espouse restraint. Lucan's description written in the first century encapsulates the challenge of Cleopatra for Livia: '. . . the queen, her dangerous beauty heightened by cosmetics, . . . was decked out in the spoils of the Red Sea. Her head and neck felt the weight of her jewels.'[19] Livia wears no jewellery in her early marble portraits; her features do not suggest cosmetic enhancement; details are pared down to a minimum; signs of danger are absent. In his *Natural History*, Pliny records a later incident in which Livia dedicated a crystal on the Capitoline Hill. The crystal in question was no ordinary lapidary shard but the biggest example of its sort ever seen – a gift presumably to Livia in her capacity as Empress of Rome.[20] By then the habit of self-denial, acquired in tacit rebuke to Octavian's Cleopatra, was deeply ingrained. Instead of accepting the gift, Livia arranged for its display on the Capitoline, where every Roman might see it. Public asceticism had become a presiding virtue of Octavian's premiership. 'I detest the Persian style/ Of elaboration,' Horace asserted.

Garlands bore me
Laced up with lime-bark. Don't run a mile
To find the last rose of summer for me.
None of your fussy attempts to refine
On simple myrtle. Myrtle suits both
You pouring, me drinking, wine
Under the trellised vine's thick growth.[21]

The poet might as easily have substituted 'Egyptian' for Persian. The luxury of the Ptolemies was a byword of the ancient world. Accounts like Lucan's description of a royal banquet in Alexandria provided a gaudy foil for Livia and Octavian's assiduously published restraint: 'The entrance hall was panelled in ivory, and its doors inlaid with tinted tortoise-shell, the dark patches concealed by emeralds. There were jewel-studded couches, rows of yellow jasper wine-cups on the tables, bright coverlets spread over the sofas.'[22] By contrast, Suetonius records the modesty of Octavian's domestic environment as preserved during the historian's lifetime: 'the frugality of his household equipment and furniture is still visible even now from the surviving couches and tables, which are scarcely of a quality for private life.'[23]

Did Livia protest against this enforced persona? Her subsequent behaviour suggests that she understood all too clearly the importance of appearance to oppose Octavian in an initiative from which both stood to gain so much. Developments which we view from a distance of two thousand years as smooth, coherent and even teleological were likely more fitful and less obvious at the time. Neither Octavian nor Livia invented overnight the 'Livia' we inherit today, just as the former's caricature of Cleopatra evolved over time. It is almost certainly the case that that 'Livia' is a fiction grounded in fact, the public virtues ascribed to the figurehead an exaggeration and enhancement of her natural qualities. Continence was the key to the public Livia, moderate in her actions and inclinations, steadfast in her affections. The ordinariness of Livia's public persona reflected both the truth and, it has been argued, a long tradition of ascribing to female rulers and consorts the virtues 'of ordinary women writ large; chaste and fertile, pious and generous, modest but able to speak out at need, emphatically not pursuing an independent policy or building a powerbase.'[24]

Livia had been brought up in a family with long experience of the demands made by the state on its servants. She understood, too, like the majority of Roman women – Sempronia and Fulvia were exceptions – the disparity between husband and wife. It was in her own interest that Octavian vanquish Mark Antony. In 36 BC, with Lepidus expelled from Sicily, Augustus's empire remained no more than a possibility. No source records regret on Livia's part that the sacrifice the gods demanded for victory was Cleopatra. Octavian had set his sights on glittering prizes. Perhaps Livia placed her trust in that laurel sprig which fell to earth at her villa at Prima Porta. Already it had put forth roots and branches.

'Her beauty, they say, was not, in and of itself, entirely incomparable, nor was it the sort that would amaze those who saw her,' Plutarch wrote of Cleopatra more than a century after her death. 'But interaction with her was captivating, and her appearance, along with her persuasiveness in discussion and her character that accompanied all interaction, was stimulating. Her voice was also a source of pleasure.'[25] If Plutarch is to be believed, it was to Octavian's advantage that Cleopatra's charms revealed themselves only at close quarters. Even during her residence on the banks of the Tiber late in 46 BC, the Egyptian queen can have had few opportunities of casting her spell over the ordinary Roman. Livia, by contrast, was universally acknowledged to be beautiful, Velleius Paterculus's 'most eminent of Roman women . . . in beauty'.

At a certain point, Romans received the chance to decide for themselves. Historians have suggested that Octavian continued his adopted father's work of beautifying the Temple of Venus Genetrix at the heart of the Forum Julium. Beside Caesar's golden statue of Cleopatra, Octavian erected images of his own.[26] In order to do so he issued an edict that revolutionized the position of certain women in Rome. The temple images – bust portraits carved from life – represented Livia and Octavia. Octavian's edict legalizing such portraits transformed their lives for ever.

*

Neither history nor Octavian forgot Cleopatra's dramatic suicide in 30 BC. Two years later, in 28 BC, Octavian took measures to forbid the building of temples within Rome's city boundaries. The proscription was not universal. It applied only to temples to the goddess Isis. The Egyptian deity so closely associated with Cleopatra, who dressed as Isis and mined the goddess's iconography in her official portraiture, had latterly become an object of popular worship across the Greek-speaking world and even in Rome itself.[27]

Among Romans, Isis's cult was chiefly confined to women, possibly as a result of its association with childbirth. Octavian felt no sympathy on that account. Venus Genetrix, progenitor of the Julii, was also associated with childbirth. Her worship had not been tainted by Cleopatra. Nor did it encompass the sentiments Diodorus Siculus attributed to followers of Isis: that queens were more honoured than kings and that wives ruled husbands. In Oxyrhynchus in Egypt in the second century, a hymn to Isis went a step further, praising the goddess who 'made the power of women equal to that of men'.[28] Had he lived to hear it, it would have been a step too far for Octavian. When seven years had passed, he extended his ban into the country surrounding Rome. Cleopatra's conqueror was determined to stamp out every expression of her cult. On the surface, equal power for women would play no part in Livia's long and happy second marriage.

CHAPTER 13

Sacrosanct

Cato the Censor did not seek to curry favour with women. In 195 BC he expressed his unwavering support for an unpopular Punic War era decree which restricted women's finery, including their allowance of gold jewellery, measured by weight. A movement was afoot in Rome for reform of the Oppian Law. The impetus came not solely from senatorial ranks, but from women themselves. 'Will you give the reins to their intractable nature, and then expect that they themselves should set bounds to their licentiousness, and without your interference?' Cato demanded of the Senate in a well-known speech preserved by Livy. 'Recollect all the institutions respecting the sex, by which our forefathers restrained their profligacy and subjected them to their husbands; and yet, even with the help of all these restrictions, they can scarcely be kept within bounds.'[1]

Extreme to modern ears, Cato's was an orthodox Roman outlook, although not on that occasion the prevailing view: the Oppian Law was repealed in 195, despite the vigour of Cato's rhetoric. Cato opposed on principle every intrusion of women into Roman public life and in this he espoused majority thinking. 'What sort of practice is this, of running out into public, besetting the streets, and addressing other women's husbands?' he suggested asking the woman who clamoured for the law's repeal. 'Could not each have made the same request to her husband at home? ... Although if females would let their modesty confine them within the limits of their own rights, it did not become you, even at home, to concern yourselves about any laws that might be passed or repealed here.'[2]

It is not to be expected that Cato would embrace the suggestion of public commemoration for women. Indeed Pliny notes, 'There are still extant some declamations by Cato, during his censorship, against the practice of erecting statues of women in the Roman provinces.'[3] As with repeal of the Oppian Law, however, Cato found himself confronted by significant opposition. In spite of his 'declamations', Pliny tells us, 'he could not prevent these statues being erected.' Unfortunately for Cato, in time women's statues would despoil not only the provinces but even Rome.

In the Temple of Semo Sancus on the Quirinal Hill survived a bronze image that probably depicted the early-sixth-century Roman consort, Tanaquil. Sources mention an equestrian statue of Cloelia, an escapee hostage to Lars Porsenna at the birth of the Republic. The actions of Claudia Quinta at Ostium were also rewarded with a statue, as we have seen.[4] But only on one occasion in the history of the Republic do the sources record a public statue in Rome being formally voted to a woman. The woman in question was Cornelia of the Gracchi and the commission originated not with the Senate but with the people of Rome.[5] Once completed, the seated bronze figure conformed to Roman prejudices. Its inscription – 'Cornelia, daughter of Africanus, mother of the Gracchi' – asserted Cornelia's status as an appendage of great men.[6] In a symbolic gesture, Livia's husband afterwards restored Cornelia's statue. He also moved it. Its new resting place was a portico built by his sister Octavia, where it was displayed among images of ideal mothers.[7] Hereafter its context fixed its meaning, while Octavian hijacked for Octavia the virtuous associations of Cornelia's posterity.

Throughout his domestic policy-making, Octavian took pains to emphasize the importance of family and family roles. Social legislation, aimed at Rome's moral regeneration, afterwards formed a cornerstone of his premiership. It was one of which he was sufficiently proud to list it prominently in the *Res Gestae Divi Augusti* ('The Acts of the Divine Augustus'), that record of his achievements he bequeathed to be engraved on bronze tablets outside his mausoleum.[8]

The object of Augustus's moral regeneration was a return to a rosy-hued Republican past of rectitude and exemplary female behaviour. Octavian incorporated Cornelia of the Gracchi, a Republican popular heroine, within his vision of virtuous Roman womanhood, and expected from Livia lifelong lip service to the same vision. Conveniently Octavian overlooked rumours of Cornelia's involvement alongside her daughter Sempronia in the murder of the latter's unsympathetic husband Scipio Aemilianus – just as his propagandists would be encouraged to overlook aspects of Livia's history, notably her first marriage and hasty divorce. It may be significant that Pliny's only comments on the restored statue are to reiterate Cornelia's relationship to her father and sons, and to state without elaboration, 'She is represented in a sitting position, and the statue is remarkable for having no straps to the shoes.'[9] It was not the only time in history when footwear was a safer topic than murder.

Over the next half-century, Octavian repeatedly exploited visual imagery to convey political philosophy. In 35 BC, Cassius Dio tells us, he evolved a proposal concerning his wife and sister. It was a revolutionary innovation for Rome, as startling as the commission of a statue of Cornelia once had been. Livia and Octavia were to receive tribunician sacrosanctity. This legal protection had previously been reserved for elected officials, the Tribunes of the People, and was potentially more powerful even than that usually restricted to Rome's highest-ranking women, the Vestal Virgins.[10] The implications of that award were far-reaching, as we shall see. It was accompanied by a grant of honours. Included in those honours was the right – unique among Roman women both before and after – to be represented in public statues.

Whether by triumviral edict or vote of the Senate, the grant was made law. Close on its heels, Octavian displayed in the Temple of Venus Genetrix new marble images of his wife and sister. A decade had passed since Caesar's installation of Cleopatra's golden statue. The trio of female portraits, representing the best-known women of the contemporary Roman world, existed in curious juxtaposition. The Triumvirs' battle for mastery of Rome was waged even in sacred precincts.

From the moment Mark Antony and Octavia set sail for Greece in 39 BC, missing Livia and Octavian's wedding the following January, Livia found herself in effect married to Rome's first citizen. Octavian was not, as he would later become, formally first among Rome's equals. He shared for the moment triumviral status with Mark Antony and Lepidus, both his senior in years and, in the political life of the Republic, in experience too. But it was Octavian, overlord of the western provinces and of Rome itself, and resident in Rome full time, who became the visible face of the triple dictatorship. Mark Antony would never return to the city again. Whatever the future held, Livia must have seen clearly that she was allying herself with a man of singular prominence.

She may well have anticipated influence from her new position. Although Rome excluded women from its political life, it muddied distinctions between public and private spheres. Both overlapped in the morning *salutatio*, which, as we have seen, took place behind open aristocratic doors; and at senatorial dinner parties, at which in Rome, unlike in Greece, women were present and active participants. A daughter of Rome's ruling class, Livia would have understood by instinct as well as precedent the opportunities for interesting herself in Octavian's public life presented by these incursions into her domestic realm. The role she conceived must have been of a behind-the-scenes variety – she was surely too shrewd to aspire to the impropriety of Fulvia or Sempronia – but such hidden influence amounted nevertheless to an approximation to power. The power in question, as Livia also understood, derived exclusively from her marriage to Octavian. It did not take account of her birth status as a scion of the Claudii.

It is impossible to know whether Livia was always ambitious or if her ambition grew incrementally with Octavian's success. Her concern that her first child by Nero be a boy may indicate that she had always expected to participate in politics, albeit indirectly. Up to a point Rome condoned just such a concealed, ancillary role for its patrician matrons. That role would materialize only in the event that Nero, Tiberius or both achieved high senatorial office. Access to this ill-defined possibility was arguably Livia's true patrimony, the legacy of her family background and of the nature of the marriage her father arranged for her to a fellow Claudian and a politician. Livia cannot have anticipated any independent part in Roman public life. Perhaps the wilderness years with Nero strengthened latent resolve. Certainly she appeared to perceive readily the implications for herself of Octavian's rising star and, over time, his unprecedented authority. If she welcomed such a prospect, as we reasonably assume she did, she also glimpsed from the outset the overwhelming importance of remaining married to Octavian.

By 35 BC, when Octavian decided to confer sacrosanctity within his family, he had been married to Livia for three years. Initially, his decision concerned only his sister Octavia and excluded Livia. Octavia was doubly bound to Octavian: not only was she his sister, an indivisible connection, she was married to his fellow Triumvir Mark Antony and, as a consequence, was an important tool in Octavian's power-broking. The foundations of Livia's position, by contrast, were less solid. Only love and a keen appreciation of her Republican credentials bound Octavian to Livia. Both ties were soluble. Octavian's track record of broken engagements yielded stony ground for hope that love would survive long term; there were other daughters of the nobility whose fathers would countenance so advantageous a match. Livia needed a means of insuring her marriage. A child was the obvious answer. So far she had either failed to conceive or given birth only to a stillborn baby. She needed to prove her indispensability to Octavian.

If the sources are correct, the events of 35 BC demonstrate Livia's shrewdness and mettle. Octavian's decision to bestow sacrosanctity on Octavia was motivated by a desire to provide himself with formal grounds for war against Mark Antony. Direct benefits to Octavia were only indirectly her brother's purpose. With Octavia sacred, indignities committed against her by her errant husband in the course of a flaunting relationship with Cleopatra became attacks on the Roman state. At a stroke the decree of Octavia's sacredness transformed the fact of Mark Antony's infidelity, and each child arising from that infidelity, into a transgression against Rome and Octavian's Government. Such transgressions might justly be punishable through war. [11] By elevating Octavia, Octavian created the means of eliminating his fellow Triumvir and a route to absolute power. He did so, apparently, constitutionally.

The outcome would prove entirely satisfactory to Octavian. It bestowed on Octavia, too, a degree of public prominence and independence unheard of in the Republic. But for Livia it promised cold comfort – until she suggested that Octavian also include her in the grant. Dio, our only source here, is unclear about how it became law; nor does he speculate on the process by which a policy devised for Octavia came to include Livia.

Octavian made his move at a moment of strength, in the aftermath of victory in Pannonia, south of the Danube. In Dio's account, he deferred the military triumph voted to him, 'but granted to Octavia and Livia statues, the right of administering their own affairs without a guardian, and the same security and inviolability as the tribunes enjoyed'.[12] Dio's order is probably significant: Octavia first, then Livia; the grant of statues more startling than financial independence or official protection.

In the long term it was Livia who would reap greater benefits from the events of 35 BC. Octavian's award of sacrosanctity thrust both women into the public arena. Public representation implied a public role, sacredness suggested a step towards more than human status, and the freedom to administer their affairs facilitated a degree of private wealth that was in itself a form of independence and a public platform. Sacrosanctity became the pedestal on which Livia elevated herself above the ordinary status of political wife. Irrespective of Octavian's short-term intentions, it gave a green light to Livia's ambitions. It sowed the first seeds of her later deification and removed barriers to her amassing a fortune which would come to rival those of Hellenistic consorts, even Cleopatra herself. Before Octavian was declared emperor, his wife took her first steps towards becoming empress.

It is clear that Octavian's aims were practical and propagandist. Octavia was popular and widely admired. Octavian had enabled her – without provocative action on the part of either brother or sister – to provide him with cause for war against Mark Antony. In addition, since he recognized that awards to the wives of the tribunes would be interpreted as a celebration specifically of their wifely virtues – the only form of public celebration save motherhood available to women – Octavian was able to embark by stealth on that policy of moral reform he would later pursue so doggedly. For the remainder of their lives, Octavia and especially Livia existed in the public arena as personifications of an Octavian concept of exemplary womanhood. Their good behaviour, celebrated in Rome's streets and temples, contrasted with the conduct of Cleopatra, for whom sexual loyalty had resembled a question of political necessity.

It also offered an ongoing rebuke to Mark Antony, in the face of whose affronts Octavia remained serene and apparently devoted, upheld by the love of her brother and the comfort of the sister-in-law whose portrait stood alongside her own.[13]

At the beginning of the third century AD, the ancient Church writer Tertullian turned his thoughts to women's hairdressing. 'All these wasted pains on arranging your hair – what contribution can this make to your salvation? Why can you not give your hair a rest? One minute you are building it up, the next you are letting it down – raising it one moment, stretching it the next.'[14] Two centuries before Tertullian, Livia grasped clearly the surprising contribution a hairstyle could make.

The conclusion was one suggested to her by her sister-in-law. Octavia, as we have seen, adopted the *nodus* hairstyle before Livia. Her face, was longer than Livia's, so it is unlikely that her inspiration was Ovid, with his frivolous advocacy of the *nodus* as a corrective to rounded features. If Octavia's choice was influenced by poetry, it was by default – Ovid's very failure to find a classical precedent for the *nodus* was perhaps the deciding factor.[15] The absence of earlier Hellenistic *nodi* meant the hairstyle could be branded as native, distinctively Roman. Octavia's choice – apparently a simple, private matter of how to dress her hair – became a statement of nationalism flung in the face of Cleopatra. As such, it could not be ignored by Livia.

There remains the possibility that it was Octavian who 'discovered' the Republican *nodus*. It is inconceivable that, having bestowed upon his sister and wife the unprecedented right to public statues, Octavian then took no interest in the form of those statues. Octavian idealized the Republic even as he overturned it. He also idealized his sister Octavia, to whom he remained devoted until her death in 11 BC. There were persuasive reasons for Octavia and Livia to share this unfussy, Roman hairstyle that contrasted so powerfully with the towering, jewel-studded, melon-shaped styles sported by Cleopatra. In seeming to resemble Octavia physically, was it not possible that Livia would acquire in the eye of the viewer something of Octavia's character and her blameless reputation? Resemblances between the two women could only benefit Livia. They suggested a closer kinship between the sisters-in-law, which appealed to the dynastically-minded Octavian. In due course, he may have wished for an heir of his own body to succeed him. Livia's failure to conceive denied him that possibility. But if Livia and Octavia were as closely related as their similarly coiffed portraits suggested, a child of Octavia's became the next best thing. Did the choice of a hairstyle let Livia off the hook? The politics of survival is seldom so simple, but the point should not be discounted. It liberated Livia to prove her indispensability to Octavian through means other than procreation.

CHAPTER 14

'A charming view with minimal expense'

The old man of Corycia described by Virgil in the fourth book of the *Georgics* as 'happy as a king' owns 'a few poor acres/Of land once derelict, useless for arable,/ No good for grazing, unfit for the cultivation of vines'.[1] In this unpromising plot the old man lays out a miraculous kitchen garden. He does not neglect flowers, sowing 'white lilies, verbena, small-seeded poppy'. He keeps bees. Poetically he is not restricted by the plot's small compass or the factors underlying its unsuitability for cereal crops, grass or vines. He grows pine trees, lime trees and elms. Pears and black-thorn fruit for him. 'His is the first rose of spring, the earliest apples of autumn'.[2] Hyacinths brighten his winter. His few poor acres are a paradise, an idyllic enclosure of nature perfected as the ancient Persians understood the term, a precursor of Eden.

Nature occupied Livia's thoughts in the aftermath of Octavian's defeat of Mark Antony and Cleopatra. In September 31 BC, close to Octavian's thirty-second birthday, Mark Antony surrendered to his fellow Triumvir. The occasion was a naval battle – at Actium on the coast of northwest Greece, a quiet pearl-fishing centre in the grip of tall mountains. Octavian's fleet was commanded by Marcus Agrippa, the friend of his boyhood and foremost among his generals. It was Octavian, not Agrippa, who was the real victor, supreme at last. In its wake, his victory brought lasting peace to Rome.

Mark Antony committed suicide. Cleopatra followed suit. In an interview with Octavian, she had struggled to save herself. The sources' reports vary; so, too, do their writers' interpretations. Possibly the vanquished queen girded herself for one final seduction of a ruler of Rome: first Caesar, then Mark Antony, but not, as it happened, Caesar's heir, who resisted her practised charms. Depending on the source consulted, Cleopatra may have invoked Livia's intervention on her behalf. Possibly she sought to placate Octavian with precious jewels from the royal treasury earmarked for Livia and Octavia. All in vain. She died, famously, from the poison of an asp. Hindsight, in the form of familiarity with the Book of Genesis, shapes our perception of that painful detail as akin to the enemy within another idyllic garden, itself a parallel of Virgil's few poor acres.

Livia was planning decorations at that villa near Veii which Suetonius describes as 'hers'.[3] Among the schemes she had in mind was a treatment as unprecedented as Octavian's youthful ascent to power or that grant of sacrosanctity which gave Livia the freedom to administer her own estates without male guardianship. Her plans focused on a partly subterranean room usually considered to have functioned as a summer dining room or *triclinium*. It was housed in a classical pavilion close to the peristyle of the main villa complex. The long rectangular room was lit by high windows at either end of a barrel-vaulted roof. Cool in summer on account of its underground position, it would be decorated with a single, continuous mural in which spring, summer and autumn merged in a vision of natural bounty. Like Virgil's lilies, verbena and poppies, everything in Livia's summer dining room flowers and fruits together. It is an impossible, perfect moment in nature and, at the same time, with its serene palette of aquamarine and beryl, a direct refutation of Seneca's later assertion that 'the place where one lives . . . can contribute little towards tranquillity'.[4] The effect of that blue-green stage-cloth, even today, after removal to a museum in the cacophonous centre of twenty-first-century Rome, is astonishing, impressive and undeniably tranquil.

Livia had already espoused a hairstyle and a moral code inspired by opposition to Cleopatra. Now her vision of nature offered a further verdant contrast. In place of Cleopatra's deadly serpent, Livia's mural depicted nature at its most generous and life-giving. It was surely a metaphor for Octavian's rule in Rome and perhaps, even at this stage, given Livia's relative youth, a prayer that she too might bring forth fruit in the form of children.

It was the work of an artist probably called Studius, like Octavian an innovator. We know almost nothing about Studius – even his name is disputed – beyond a passage in Pliny's *Natural History* in which the author credits him with the invention of landscape painting in Rome.

> It was he who first instituted that most delightful technique of painting walls with representations of villas, porticoes and landscape gardens, woods, groves, hills, pools, channels, rivers, coastline – in fact, every sort of thing which one might want, and also various representations of people within them walking or sailing, or, back on land, arriving at villas on ass-back or in carriages, and also fishing, fowling or hunting or even harvesting the wine-grapes. There are also specimens among his pictures of notable villas which are accessible only through marshy ground, and of women who . . . are carried on the shoulders of men who totter along beneath the restless burdens which are being carried, and many other lively subjects of this sort indicative of a sharp wit. This artist also began the practice of painting representations of sea-side towns on the walls of open galleries, thus producing a charming view with minimal expense.[5]

The charming view in the case of Livia's summer dining room at Prima Porta did not exercise Studius's 'sharp wit'. It falls into Pliny's earlier category of 'landscape gardens, woods, groves'. All four walls are decorated in identical fashion. Behind a low lattice cane fence in the foreground, an area of neatly tended grass is contained within a similarly low, decorative stone wall. At regular intervals this smooth sward is punctuated by tall trees, accommodated by recesses in the wall, and isolated specimens of low, shrubby plants. Beyond the wall arises a dense grove of further trees and plants, their details crisp against a shadowy backdrop of generalized foliage. Branches bend under the weight of fruit, stems arch with flowers. Everywhere birds perch and flutter, unable to believe their luck in finding themselves in this multi-season gastronomical extravaganza. Only the fence and the wall, and a single large, domed birdcage containing a captive nightingale, indicate a human presence, felt but not seen. The painting does not include figures. Nor does it incorporate the sort of architectural element more typical of Roman mural painting of gardens: columns and pilasters. We surmise that the foreground area is a garden on account of its neatness; there are no urns or fountains as we might expect. Real beauty is rooted not in the garden but in the borrowed landscape beyond. Expansive in its fecundity, it will surely overwhelm the thin green line of lawn. Birds dart, injecting a note of movement. The cerulean blue of the painted background has grown chalky and patchy over two thousand years, suggesting the clouds that certainly never marred this smiling sky.

The effect must have been startling on Livia's guests. The room was almost certainly restricted to seasonal use. Gentle breezes cool the villa's hilltop site, but the Italian sun is pellucid to the point of harshness. Here, below a steep flight of steps, an oasis of tranquillity masquerades as nature. Such gardens may not have been unusual in the fertile valley of the Tiber, but none could manage to screen out the heat of the season, nor to induce quince trees to bear fruit while oleander and myrtle blossom. In her sculpted portraits after 35 BC, Livia combined native and classical elements. The *nodus* hairstyle formed one component of an idealized, ageless vision remote from the often harsh verism of Republican portraiture, more akin to an earlier style of Classical goddess portrait. In her country villa, Livia introduced a decorative scheme of a sort which Pliny states was new to Rome. To date, archaeological evidence indicates it had no exact parallels. But it is possible that such large-scale scenographic mural painting echoes scenographies of the Hellenistic period and depictions of those eastern pleasure gardens known as *paradeisa*. Like Livia's statuary, her summer dining room is a characteristic example of the innovatory manner in which Octavian's visual culture at this date combined moving forwards with looking backwards, radicalism with reassurance.

We must reach our own conclusion on Pliny's statement that Studius's 'charming views' could be had for 'minimal expense'. Vitruvius, in his *De Architectura*, provides instructions on the preparation of plastered and stuccoed wall surfaces preliminary to fresco painting. He also offers information on the laborious and arcane processes employed in deriving colours, as well as the steps necessary to safeguard the results. These include rubbing passages of vermilion 'with a hard brush charged with Punic wax melted and tempered with oil'.[6] There is nothing half-hearted in Vitruvius's directions. Undoubtedly Livia's domestic commission was less extensive than schemes intended for public porticoes or colonnades, but the room is large and largely covered by Studius's work. Studius was presumably assisted by a team of assistants, perhaps including that painter subsequently granted his freedom who is attested among the slaves in Livia's *columbarium*.[7] Both the preparation and the work itself must have been time-consuming and costly.

Such is the quality of that work and the accuracy of its details that it is still possible to identify species of trees, plants and birds. A botanical analysis made in 2003 pointed to the strawberry tree, bay laurel, oleander, holm oak, English oak, Cornelian cherry, myrtle, hart's-tongue fern, early dog violet, crown daisy, stinking chamomile, Italian cypress, quince, stone pine, opium poppy, pomegranate, cabbage rose and date palm.[8] Other authorities have identified box, viburnum, periwinkles, chrysanthemums, ivy, iris and acanthus, alongside birds including pigeons, quails, blackbirds, thrushes, orioles, warblers, jays, magpies, buntings and sparrows – as well as the nightingale confined within its cage.[9]

At the centre of Livia's peristyle garden, archaeologists have discovered what they believe to be the base of a fountain.[10] Its reflected light, sound and movement would have animated a small formal enclosure of box-edged paths, statues and aromatic Mediterranean shrubs. Marble Ionic columns supported a sheltered walkway paved with elegant mosaics; surviving black and white marble tesserae preserve fragments of lost figure motifs. Further from the house was the larger garden terrace where, as we have seen, the remains of terracotta pots testify to ancient methods of propagation. It may also be the case that the villa gardens included additionally a hanging garden, irrigated by an aqueduct which extended from a hilltop north of the villa. Remains of the previously unknown aqueduct were revealed during excavation of a modern road tunnel.[11]

These varied and extensive gardens at Livia's villa provide the context for Studius's murals. It is likely that the scheme developed as more than a purely decorative treatment. The plants and trees featured include indigenous species alongside varieties already within garden cultivation, suggesting the possibility that the painter worked in part from life, using as models cuttings found close to hand in the villa gardens. Ancient authors point to Livia's enjoyment of horticulture. Her decision to plant the laurel sprig dropped by the white pullet known afterwards as the Prima Porta portent may not have been inspired solely by superstition or ambition. Pliny describes the laurel as 'remarkably ornamental to houses',[12] indicating an established tradition of its domestic cultivation. In addition, at some point in her life, Livia is credited with developing a variety of autumn-ripening fig afterwards known as the 'Liviana'. The description by the third-century Greek writer Athenaeus, of Liviana figs growing near to Rome may point to the villa near Veii.[13]

Why then did Livia choose to decorate this room – designed, from its scale, for public entertaining – with images of trees, birds and flowers arranged in a format that appeared wholly new in contemporary Rome? The dynamic was more than a delight in novelty. The choice, we may assume, was Livia's own, although it is impossible to rule out Octavian's influence. In his grant of sacrosanctity of 35 BC, Octavian had bestowed on Livia authority over her own property. As with the related grant of public statuary, it is likely that he anticipated nevertheless a continuing interest for himself. From Suetonius, we know that the Prima Porta villa was regarded as belonging to Livia in her own right. Archaeologists date its first structures to around 50 BC.[14] As there is no record of Livia's purchase, this may indicate that the villa and its gardens originally belonged to her father Marcus and were a present to Livia before her wedding to Nero or as part of her dowry on that occasion – which, by Roman custom, Nero would have returned to her on their divorce. An early donation on Marcus's part would explain the property having escaped the forfeiture of the Proscriptions.

In 29 BC, after seven years writing, Virgil published the four books of his *Georgics*, and Roman readers discovered for the first time the old man of Corycia, 'happy as a king' in his abundant garden, as we have seen. The poem may have been written under the patronage of Maecenas, Octavian's friend and *arbiter elegantiarium*. Maecenas was the principal patron of Octavian's court, a friend not only of Virgil but famously of Horace too. Works enjoying Maecenas's sponsorship would almost certainly have been known to Livia. Given the impossibility of stipulating an exact date for the decoration of her summer *triclinium*, we cannot know if she was influenced in her choice by Virgil's poem, with its idealization of that old man remote from worldly concerns, who defeats the seasons to pluck hyacinths in winter and even cocks a snook at nature by successfully transplanting mature trees. It is enough that Livia broadcast to a small invited coterie her love of gardening, proclaimed in vibrant shades of blue and green.

Perhaps she hoped to associate herself with husbandry, fertility or regeneration; perhaps she intended the compliment not for herself but for Octavian and his fledgling regime. Alternatively, the scheme may have been intended as a celebration of the lush fecundity of the estate itself, as forecast in that portent of the falling pullet with its sprig of laurel. Livia may have acted disingenuously to suggest that she, too, like the old man of Virgil's poem, stood outside politics, remote from Rome's all-male centre of power. Did she mean to assert, through the unassuming medium of floriferous fresco, her claim to be a woman without ambition, domestic in her focus, no threat to the status quo of a city rent by change, and happy in her garden on a hilltop close by the Via Flaminia?

If so, Livia was not as clever as she thought. From a love of gardening derives knowledge of plants, a knowledge traditionally associated with women. Plants in early societies held a key to life, the ingredients of simple medicine. Misapplied, however, plants had the power to harm as well as heal. It is a short step from gardener to poisoner. The proud boast of Livia's summer dining room – one of the great enduring achievements of Roman art – would return to haunt its patron. Then the cost of its charming view appeared anything but minimal.

CHAPTER 15

'A man and his family
should live together as partners'

In August AD 14 Livia's elder son Tiberius, dressed in grey, delivered a funeral oration on the rostra of the Temple of Divus Julius in the Forum. The subject of the eulogy was his adopted father Octavian, the recently deceased Emperor Augustus. It was not the first time Tiberius had spoken publicly at the funeral of his 'father'. The previous occasion had been almost half a century earlier when Tiberius was only nine years old.

Livia's first husband, Tiberius Claudius Nero, died in 33 or 32 BC, at most six years after bestowing his wife on Octavian. He left behind him the two children of his marriage to Livia, Tiberius and Drusus, and a reputation for political ineptitude. It is not to be wondered that, as Dio tells us, he entrusted his sons' guardianship to Octavian. The bequest reunited the boys with their mother and offered them the chance of an upbringing in the household of the most prominent man in Rome. At the eleventh hour, the hapless Nero had finally backed a winner.

Characteristically, the decision posed a dilemma in the short term. In AD 14, the tone of Augustus's eulogy was unashamedly celebratory. 'Who does not realize that not all mankind assembled together could worthily sound his praises?' Tiberius asked the mourning people of Rome.[1] Nero's career required more careful handling. As we have seen, he had devoted considerable energy to opposing the man he now entrusted with Tiberius and Drusus's future. If Nero's quicksilver loyalty lay anywhere, it was with Mark Antony. In 33 BC the second five-year term of the Triumvirate expired and was not renewed. Mark Antony and Octavian locked horns in enmity. With Nero's funeral meats scarcely cold, Octavian would decisively vanquish Nero's former champion. The mentors of the nine-year-old Tiberius needed to tread cautiously in composing his father's eulogy. They would have been wise to focus on the early years of the dead man's career, his naval victory at Alexandria in 48 BC and subsequent foundation of veterans' colonies in southern Gaul.[2] Both were safely unambiguous achievements in the service of Octavian's adopted father Julius Caesar.

Livia had been separated from her younger son Drusus since the first week of his life. Tiberius had last lived with his mother when he was three years old. The sources do not record Livia's reaction to being reunited with her children, but there is no reason to assume her response differed from that of any mother in so extraordinary a situation. In Rome, it has been argued, the bond between a mother and her son superseded in loyalty every conceivable relationship, including that of husband and wife.[3] Livia's future behaviour would demonstrate the depth of her maternal instinct and the strength of that bond, restored after a caesura of six years.

Despite enjoying the patronage of Octavia, Vitruvius, in his treatise *De Architectura* written in the years after Actium, is occasionally out of sympathy with Octavian. The writer delineated a correspondence between status and accommodation, a principle of the house reflecting its owner's role in society.

> Houses for moneylenders and tax collectors must be spacious and attractive and safe from ambush; for lawyers and rhetoricians they must be stylish and sufficiently large to hold meetings; but for gentlemen who must perform their duties to the citizenry by holding offices and magistracies, great grand halls must be made, courtyards and very large peristyles, woodlands and wide open walks, all finished off as an ornament to their noble status.[4]

It was not a theory to which Octavian allowed himself to subscribe. The house which became Tiberius and Drusus's home after 32 BC deliberately gave the lie to the pre-eminence of their stepfather's position. Neither its architecture nor the manner of its furnishing or painted decoration trumpeted wealth and power. It was a policy Octavian had espoused from the outset. His first house, Suetonius tells us, had previously belonged to Catullus's friend, the poet and orator Gaius Licinius Calvus; it was close to the Roman Forum, at the top of the Ringmakers' Stairs. If we trust Suetonius's account – and at least one author has suggested persuasive grounds for caution[5] – Octavian afterwards moved to another house which had recently belonged to an orator, 'Hortensius's house on the Palatine Hill'. 'Oddly enough,' we read, 'his new palace was neither larger nor more elegant than the first; the courts being supported by squat columns of peperino stone, and the living rooms innocent of marble or elaborately tessellated floors.' Within this relatively unadorned space, we know, Octavian chose furniture to match. 'How simply [Octavian's] palace was furnished may be deduced by examining the couches and tables still preserved, many of which would now hardly be considered fit for a private citizen. He is said to have always slept on a low bed, with a very ordinary coverlet.'[6] The rooms were modest in size; simple mosaics covered the floors; the walls were handsomely painted, often in rich shades of cinnabar red, viridian and ochre, but without extravagance by contemporary standards.[7] If it was true, as had been rumoured, that Octavian acquired a taste for Corinthian bronze during the Proscriptions, he clearly took pains to cure himself of this weakness. Overnight Tiberius and Drusus found themselves at the epicentre of the Roman world. If Suetonius is correct, they did not inherit a lifestyle of unbridled luxury.

Livia did not long share Octavian's house near the Forum. Two years after their marriage, the couple travelled uphill, away from Rome's commercial and political centre, to return to the Palatine, the district in which we assume both had been born. The house into which they moved – if it was indeed Hortensius's house – may have belonged to Octavian for as long as six years, since the change of ownership came about not through conventional sale but as a result of confiscation during the Proscriptions of 42.[8] Suetonius's assessment notwithstanding, it was evidently a covetable dwelling: Cicero told Atticus that the consul Lentulus hoped to win the villa as a prize from Pompey as early as 49 BC.[9] Velleius

Paterculus records that in 36 BC Octavian 'made the announcement that he meant to set apart for public use certain houses which he had secured by purchase through his agents in order that there might be a free area about his own residence'.[10] Octavian intended to declare part of his home accessible to the Roman people: he had bought a number of neighbouring houses to that end. He also planned to enlarge the existing house, an undertaking which would have enhanced its desirability further. We are forced to question, at least in part, Velleius's statement that Octavian's house was 'noteworthy neither for size nor for decoration'. Octavian lived there apparently happily for more than forty years, close to that sacred Lupercalian cave we have already visited. As time passed, he gathered round him more of his own building projects, among them a splendid solid marble temple of Apollo, built, it would seem, where in 36 BC lightning struck an earlier structure. Such was the house in which Livia passed the years of her marriage and in which, after Nero's death, she brought up their sons.

Octavian matched his behaviour to his surroundings. Pliny records that it was Julius Caesar who, for the first time, served four different kinds of wine at a Roman dinner party, treating his guests at a feast during his third consulship to Falernian, Chian, Lesbian and Mamertine vintages; at a banquet recorded by Macrobius, Caesar enjoyed sea urchins, sea anemones, oysters, mussels, clams, 'thrushes under a patch of asparagus', roe deer, wild boar, hares, ducks, udder and 'fowls forcefed on wheatmeal'.[11] Octavian's tastes were simpler: three courses at dinner and 'no great extravagance', according to the sources.[12] 'He did not, if he could help it, leave or enter any city or town except in the evening or at night, to avoid disturbing anyone by the obligation of ceremony', Suetonius relates. 'In his consulship he commonly went through the streets on foot ... His morning receptions were open to all, including ordinary people, and he met the requests of those who approached him with great affability, jocosely reproving one man because he presented a petition to him with as much hesitation "as he would a penny to an elephant".[13] He expected a similar disdain for extravagance and lack of affectation in those around him, including Livia and his stepsons. Unlike Marcus's Palatine house, with its atrium and *alae* richly decorated with ancestor masks and trophies of past greatness, Octavian's domestic environment did not aim at fostering family pride. In the case of his daughter Julia and his stepson Tiberius, it was a policy that largely failed. Interior decoration notwithstanding, Julia grew up acutely conscious of her position as the only child of Rome's first emperor. Tiberius was never less than the scion of his ancient Claudian forebears. The extent of Octavian's culpability is questionable.

It was a youthful household. In 32 BC Octavian was thirty-one years old, Livia twenty-six. Octavia was six years her brother's senior. Octavian's closest confidants, Agrippa and Maecenas, were thirty-one and thirty-eight respectively. The Republic's emphasis on age and experience was among many casualties of Octavian's Roman revolution. Portraits of Livia, Octavia and Octavian after 35 BC present images of unflinching youth – as they would continue to do until their sitters' deaths, in Livia's case a period of more than half a century in which time magically stood still. In youth lay hope and promise, the natural regeneration of Virgil's garden and Studius's frescoes. It was not a staid or intimidating environment for two small boys to find themselves in.

Nor were Tiberius and Drusus alone. Octavian's daughter Julia had lived with her father and stepmother from birth. She was three years younger than Tiberius, months older than Drusus. In Octavia's care were not only her own children by two marriages, but those of her second husband, the five-times-married Mark Antony. It is possible that through their mother's second marriage, and thanks to Octavia's magnanimity, Livia's sons grew up among a large extended family of step-cousins:[14] Marcellus and his two sisters, both called Claudia Marcella, Octavia's children by her first marriage; Octavia's two daughters by Mark Antony, both Antonia; Mark Antony's son by Fulvia, Iullus Antonius; and the younger children of his liaison with Cleopatra, twins Alexander Helios and Cleopatra Selene, born in 40 BC, equidistant in age between Tiberius and Drusus, and Ptolemy Philadelphus. This loose kinship of a dozen children shared parents and step-parents; the still point at the centre of the circle was Octavian. Over time, as the latter's thoughts became increasingly dynastic, the nature of the children's relationships with one another and with Octavian would gain increasing significance. In the short term, Octavian appears to have taken pleasure in his cumbersome family. Plutarch records that his affection and esteem for Mark Antony's son

Iullus Antonius was second only to his feelings for Livia's sons and those of Agrippa.[15] Despite his paternity, Antonius would afterwards become consul; later he served as proconsul of Asia.

Although imperial propaganda subsequently sought to emphasize Livia's role as a mother figure, her part initially was secondary to that of her husband. It was the complexities of imperial succession which cast light on Livia's maternal role, most notably in Tacitus's account. In his revisionist history, Livia was guilty of manifold transgressions, predominantly in her capacity as an overbearing mother and wicked stepmother.[16] Tacitus overlooked the fact that, in the conventional sense, Livia had only one stepchild, her stepdaughter Julia, whose upbringing was devised not by Livia but her father Octavian. Livia's ambition focused on her elder son Tiberius. The only 'crime' Tacitus brought with certaintly to bear against her was Tiberius's accession in AD 14 as second *princeps* of Rome.

It is a challenge to discover the legacy of a happy childhood in the adult Tiberius. But the sources' virtual silence on Tiberius's boyhood in Octavian's house provide no foundation for the difficult man into whom he was to grow. Octavian, by all accounts, relished family life. 'My ideal,' he told his fellow Romans in Cassius Dio's rendering, 'is that we may have lawful homes to dwell in and houses full of descendants, that we may approach the gods together with our wives and children, that a man and his family should live together as partners who risk all their fortunes in equal measure, and likewise reap pleasure from the hopes they rest upon one another.'[17] Certainly, Octavian and Livia seem to have given Tiberius their full support when, in the aftermath of Nero's death, he decided, though still a child, to stage gladiatorial contests in memory of Nero and his grandfather Drusus. 'The first took place in the Forum, the second in the amphitheatre,' Suetonius reports. '[Tiberius] persuaded some retired gladiators to appear with the rest, by paying them 1,000 gold pieces each.'[18] Further to enhance the posthumous celebrations, Octavian and Livia funded lavish theatrical performances which Tiberius, perhaps on account of his age, did not attend.

His transfer to his mother's care and the guardianship of Octavian would prove among the most important events not only of Tiberius's life but of Livia's too. More than forty years later, Tiberius inherited from Octavian rulership of Rome. The succession was not elected but dynastic. Yet Tiberius and Octavian shared no blood ties. Their connection came through Livia. Four decades spent in Octavian's house – the result of Nero's death – strengthened that connection until, Octavian having exhausted alternative avenues, Tiberius appeared as his only successor within his loose-knit family. The extent of Livia's involvement in that development has occupied posterity for two thousand years. It is reasonable to assume that the likelihood of Octavian's choice would have been significantly less had Nero not entrusted Tiberius to his care nor Livia brought up her children in the household of the victor of Actium.

The late 30s proved momentous years for Tiberius. Hot on the heels of his father's death, discounting mourning obsequies, he found himself engaged. This happened before March 32 BC, when Tiberius was still only nine years old.[19] His bride-to-be had recently celebrated her first birthday. She was Vipsania Agrippina, the daughter of Octavian's closest friend, Marcus Agrippa. We do not know if Tiberius himself was consulted, though this seems unlikely. Nor is Livia's role in the match clear. On her father's side, Vipsania was the daughter of a *novus homo*, without patrician blood; her mother's family could boast only equestrian rank. Elements of Vipsania's family shared the Republican politics of Livia's father and first husband – her maternal grandfather Atticus was that correspondent of Cicero who had negotiated the latter's purchase of Marcus's property in Rome in 50 BC; like Marcus, Cicero had fallen victim to the Triumvirs' Proscriptions. The point was a tenuous one, however, and possibly insufficient to slake Claudian pride. If, on the surface, Agrippa gained more than Livia from the match, Livia had the consolation of Tiberius marrying within Octavian's inner circle. Perhaps at this stage her sights were not set on Julia, Tiberius's stepsister, as a bride for her elder son. Like Vipsania, Octavian's daughter had been engaged from earliest infancy – if Mark Antony is to be believed, first to his own son Antyllus (whom Octavian later executed), subsequently to a client king in modern-day Romania, Cotiso of the Getae.[20]

We cannot know the nature of Livia's involvement in her sons' education. It is probable that Tiberius had begun formal learning two years before his father's death, and would have continued a similar programme following his removal to Octavian's house. At some point, the sources disclose, Octavia employed the philosopher Nestor of Tarsus, also described as Nestor the Stoic.[21] Octavia's immediate focus was her son, Marcellus. Since Marcellus was only six months older than Tiberius, the boys probably took their lessons together; Velleius Paterculus describes Tiberius as 'nurtured by the teaching of eminent praeceptors'.[22] In fact, Tiberius may have enjoyed the greater benefits of Nestor's teaching: in 25 BC, 'then hardly more than a child' as Suetonius describes him, Marcellus married his twice-engaged cousin Julia and presumably put the schoolroom behind him.[23] We do not know if, in turn, Drusus inherited the services of Nestor.

Livia's ambitions for her sons at this stage are matter for speculation. At Nero's death, Mark Antony remained ruler of half the Roman Empire. Octavian could not guarantee victory over his erstwhile fellow Triumvir nor, in the event of such a victory, could he formulate with any certainty the likely aspect of his continuing political position in Rome. It would be curious if Livia had not taken pleasure in her lot – the dramatic change in her life since her divorce from the ill-starred Nero. But the unresolved nature of her second husband's power gave her no room to anticipate more than wealth and influence for her sons. There was no question at this stage of an inheritance for Tiberius or Drusus that consisted of more than financial resources or clients. For the time being their Claudian name – the bequest of Livia and Nero – remained among their principal advantages.

Suetonius describes Octavian's involvement in the education of his daughter Julia and, afterwards, that of his granddaughters. 'He taught [them] that they should be accustomed even to work with wool, and he forbade them to say or do anything that could not be reported with complete honesty . . .'[24] Such proscriptiveness leaves little room for doubt that Octavian involved himself in the education of all his stepchildren, or for assuming that his influence was anything but rigorous. In all aspects of his life, Octavian inclined to the exercise of control. Like most educated Romans, Livia included, he spoke and read both Latin and

Greek, although his Greek, despite tutors, was never wholly proficient. Suetonius describes him scanning the works of authors in both languages 'for precepts and examples instructive to the public or to individuals'[25] – an intriguing insight into Octavian's character and the private life of Rome's first couple. The two languages must have played a central role in Tiberius and Drusus's education from the age of seven onwards. The boys' bilingualism would have benefited from the prevalence of spoken Greek around them. The common language of the East, Greek was widely used by the many foreign slaves who worked in Roman households. Suetonius states that, unlike Octavian, Tiberius spoke the language fluently; he also wrote Greek verses modelled on the style of his favourite Alexandrian poets, Euphorion, Rhianus and Parthenius. There is no indication that he inherited such recondite inclinations from Livia, or that she encouraged him in such pursuits. Even given the paucity of surviving sources, the picture of Livia we inherit is remarkably unbookish. Her mastery of the Roman ideal was too assured to trespass on intellectual preserves Rome considered essentially masculine. In this, however, she may have been at odds with the other women of Octavian's household. Macrobius later describes Julia's 'love of letters and great erudition, not hard to come by in her house'.[26] The husband provided for Cleopatra Selene was King Juba of Mauretania, scholarly and learned, the author of works in both Latin and Greek, repeatedly referenced in Pliny's *Natural History*. It is significant that when Livia built a portico in Rome, she lined its walls with paintings. By contrast, Octavia's portico contained a library.

The return of her children to her care offered Livia both emotional fulfilment and a form of occupation. Until the establishment of Octavian's principate in 27 BC, Livia confronted a role that was confusingly amorphous and essentially restricted. She enjoyed prominence without direction. Tiberius and Drusus supplied in large measure the purpose which may have been lacking since her marriage to Octavian six years earlier. Inevitably they would continue to occupy her thoughts. The form those thoughts took – strongly contested by historians – is the basis of Livia's legend.

CHAPTER 16

'They compelled him, as it seemed,
to accept autocratic powers'

The year 23 BC was one of omens and plagues. In Rome, the Tiber flooded. Its rising waters swept away a wooden bridge, the Pons Sulpicius. The same storms destroyed buildings and others fell casualty to fire. Elsewhere in the city a wolf was caught, a highly symbolic entrapment given the role of the suckling she-wolf in the story of Romulus and Remus. The sources do not hazard an interpretation. Where fire and storm failed, plague returned to the capital. It was probably typhoid fever: its victims included great as well as small. Among the former were Octavian and his nephew Marcellus, that classmate of Tiberius. One recovered, the other died. Octavian was the lucky one, responding to a shock treatment of cold baths and cold potions.[1] The skill of his physician Antonius Musa was handsomely rewarded both by Octavian and the Senate, but failed to effect a similar cure for Marcellus. Marcellus died in the autumn of 23 BC, triumphant, according to Cassius Dio, after '[making] a brilliant success of the games which he was supervising as aedile.'[2] Poets lamented his untimely death. 'What profit did he get from birth, courage, or the best of mothers, from being embraced at Caesar's hearth? Or, a moment ago, the waving awnings in the crowded theatre, and everything fondled by his mother's hands?' asked the elegist Propertius in gloomy vein. 'He is dead, and his twentieth year left ruined: so bright a day confined in so small a circle.'[3]

Marcellus's death changed Livia's life for both better and worse. It provided the first occasion when she stood accused of those crimes which shadow her posthumous reputation; at the same time, with the benefit of hindsight, we can see that it brought Tiberius a small step closer to inheriting Octavian's mantle. Cassius Dio describes its aftermath. 'At the time the accusation was current that Livia had had a hand in the death of Marcellus . . . This suspicion was much disputed because of the climatic nature both of that year and of the one that followed, which proved so unhealthy that there was a high rate of mortality in both.'[4] The accusation was one of poisoning. As Dio indicates, it was mostly discounted – so much so that no other surviving source preserves the rumour. Marcellus almost certainly died of the same fever that threatened Octavian and countless others in Rome that year. Livia, of course, had no interest in her husband's death. But the rumour machine found concrete grounds for her desire to eliminate Marcellus: 'he had been preferred for the succession before her sons.'[5] Poison was a woman's weapon, invisible but potentially fatal; children were a woman's motive. The smear was one which has clung to Livia.

Four years earlier, not only Livia's world but that of the whole Roman people had changed dramatically. On 13 January 27 BC Octavian – granted the prefix 'imperator' since his victory over Mark Antony at Actium – received at a meeting of the Senate the title he would retain until his death: 'Augustus', 'revered one'. The change of name was symbolic.

Did Octavian discuss with Livia the speech he made at the Senate House that day? Prior to Livia's remarriage, Scribonia had complained of the excessive power she exercised over Octavian in her role of mistress: her protest was couched in language suggestive of political rather than erotic or amatory influence.[6] Scribonia's disdain for a rival notwithstanding, this seems to point to a habit on Livia's part of expressing her opinions freely to Octavian and, on the latter's part, of listening to and absorbing those opinions. There is no reason to assume that marriage dulled this habit or that Livia's viewpoint declined in cogency or forcefulness. Surely Livia knew something of what was in her husband's mind on that epoch-making January day. It was an undertaking of considerable daring.

Careful to assert the strength of his position, Octavian confounded his listeners by rejecting the very building blocks on which that strength rested. Cassius Dio offers a lengthy transcript of this oratorical master-stroke. 'The fact that it is in my power to rule over you for life is evident to you all. Every one of the rival factions has been justly tried and extinguished ... the disposition both of yourselves and of the people leaves no doubt that you wish to have me at your head. Yet for all that I shall lead you no longer, and nobody will be able to say that all the actions of my career to date have been undertaken for the sake of winning supreme power. On the contrary, I lay down my office in its entirety and return to you all authority absolutely.'[7] Despite inspiring mixed feelings among his listeners, this nimble piece of casuistry stimulated the very response we assume Octavian wanted. 'They frequently broke in with shouts, pleading for monarchical government and bringing forward every argument in its favour, until finally they compelled him, as it seemed, to accept autocratic powers.'[8]

A grateful Senate gave back with interest the authority Octavian had returned to it. Octavian found himself still consul of Rome, an appointment he shared in 27 with Marcus Agrippa. In addition, he received for ten years a large overseas province that consisted of Gaul, Spain, Syria, Egypt, Cilicia and Cyprus. This in turn guaranteed his power militarily, since these were the countries in which most of Rome's legions were stationed. As well as the name Augustus, he adopted the resolutely unmonarchical-sounding title of 'leading citizen', 'princeps'. The designation had formerly been used by Pompey and Crassus, those members of the First Triumvirate to whom, at the time of Livia's birth, Marcus gave his support. As if on cue, the Tiber burst its banks. Flooding in Rome's low-lying districts enabled small boats to navigate precincts of the city. On this occasion, the soothsayers maintained, the portent was positive, portending power to the new princeps.

Octavian made much of his 'restoration' of the Republic, with its ziggurat of magistracies, each assiduously defined as to its duties, stepping-stones to the coveted consulship. But there could no longer be any doubt that, after nearly five centuries, the Republic was dead. Married to its slayer was the daughter of two families who had distinguished themselves throughout its history by the consistency of their service: Livia of the Claudii, granddaughter by adoption of Marcus Livius Drusus. Her father had died in the name of the Republic, her husband forfeited his wealth and position. We will never know whether Livia's pride in Octavian's achievement contained traces of ambivalence. Perhaps as a child she had dreamed of marrying a man as distinguished as the ancestors whose wax images lined her father's atrium, those myriad Claudian consuls, dictators and censors, recipients of triumphs and ovations. She had done exactly that, though not in a manner either she or Marcus could have foretold. Octavian had overarched them all, with no thought of their dutiful examples. 'With universal consent I was in complete control of affairs,' he recorded in his funerary inscription. 'After this time I excelled all in authority.'⁹ Vaunting in tone, it was no less than the truth.

Over time, Octavian's changed status would affect every member of his extended family. Republican politics, as we have seen, struggled to separate public and private spheres of interest, the politician from the individual. In 27 BC, alongside increased authority and a new name, the Senate voted smaller, symbolic awards to Octavian. The doorposts of his Palatine house were wreathed with bay leaves and a civic crown was set above his door. Such signs brought the public world of the Senate House, with its hierarchy of offices, into Octavian's private realm. Octavian's doorposts were Livia's doorposts; she, too, passed daily beneath the civic crown. What did such symbols mean to her? On the surface, she shared neither Octavian's change of name nor a feminized equivalent of his 'princeps' title. Senatorial decrees in this respect took no account of Livia. She had been the wife of the Triumvir Octavian, and was now the wife of the princeps Augustus. Since constitutionally her position did not exist, that position continued unchanged.

It was not the Senate but Augustus who in time made Livia Empress. Augustus's domestic agenda aimed at no less than a moral revolution in Rome. Ultimately unpopular and unsuccessful, it was a policy which required exempla. Augustus provided them from within his own family. Wife and mother, Livia became an archetype. Imperial propaganda emphasized her fulfilment of the twin roles. She was outstanding in her virtue, fidelity and love, the feminine attributes of *pietas*, *fides* and *concordia*. That very outstandingness constituted her public persona; it required no bay-leaf garland or symbolic crown.

On that January day in 27 BC Augustus concealed from the Senate, though perhaps not from Livia, aspects of his long-term philosophy. In private, the settlement probably served to coalesce plans he had nurtured for several years. He owed his position, he recognized, in part to his relationship to Julius Caesar. In the wake of the Ides of March, as an eighteen-year-old virtual *novus homo* without authority, he had been forced to capitalize on his status as son of the deified dictator – the provocation for a taunt of Mark Antony's about the boy who owed everything to a name. Latterly he had ceased to assert this once critical relationship. In order to lend credence to his claim of 'restoring' the Republic, Augustus needed to distance himself from his adopted father. Caesar's ambitions for an eastern-style monarchy in Rome were too recent, too well known and still too contentious. But experience had shown Augustus the value of Julian blood – the loyalty that persisted among the people, the army and Caesarian clients – and the potential of such an inheritance. After 27 BC Augustus's position consisted of legal powers, honorific grants and personal authority. As contained within the umbrella term *princeps*, all were specific to him and the immediate circumstances of their award; they lacked the constitutional precedents by which such a package could be transmitted intact to a second generation. Undaunted, Augustus began to consider the possibility of perpetuating his principate. His thoughts, more circumspect than those of Caesar, moved closer to the creation of a dynasty. Such schemes could not fail to implicate Livia, his wife.

To date, Livia's second marriage had lasted more than a decade. Except on one occasion it had failed to result in conception. Although both Livia and Augustus were still of childbearing age, the likelihood of them producing a male heir together must have appeared increasingly slight. Augustus faced two alternatives: either he must divorce Livia in favour of a wife who could provide the heirs she had failed to provide, or he must fall back on that pool of cousins and stepcousins who thronged his Palatine house in the care of his wife and sister. The sources, we know, show no evidence of Augustus contemplating the first course, perhaps our strongest proof of his love for Livia. He approached the second alternative with decision. His choice fell on Marcellus.

In Velleius's account of Marcellus's death, written fifty years after the event, Augustus's intentions towards his nephew were widely under-stood. 'People thought,' he tells us, 'that, if anything should happen to Caesar, Marcellus would be his successor in power ... He was, we are told, a young man of noble qualities, cheerful in mind and disposition, and equal to the station for which he was being reared.'[10] Velleius does not examine in what way the inexperienced Marcellus was equal to Augustus's recently elevated station, but is clear that this was indeed the role for which he was being prepared. In fact his qualification for the principate consisted chiefly of his kinship with his uncle and their shared blood link to Julius Caesar, Marcellus's great-great-uncle through his mother Octavia. Alone it was enough. By 23 BC Augustus had shown Marcellus repeated clear indications of his favour. The Senate, too, had begun to work on Marcellus's behalf, including among honours voted to Augustus the previous year a waiving in the young man's case of the age qualifications for senatorial office.[11] The process had started as long ago as the beginning of the decade, when Marcellus was thirteen.

If Roman loyalty depended on public magnificence – Juvenal's bread and circuses – 29 BC must have proved a happy year. Octavian (as he still was) celebrated a triple triumph. The triumph was Rome's grandest public spectacle, a carefully choreographed parade through the city's streets of the spoils of Roman victory. It was a demonstration of mili-tarism and nationhood, of conquest and rejoicing, of the relationship between an expansionist people and their warlike gods, of the winning maleness of Rome. The triumph pitted the glitter of booty against the pathos of Rome's prisoners. Its route began on the broad expanse of the Campus Martius.

In 29 BC Octavian's triple triumph, held over three days, wore the aspect of a family affair. At least five of that youthful Palatine house-hold wound their way through the Velabrum into the Forum, up the steep curves of the Sacra Via to the Temple of Jupiter Optimus Max-imus.[12] Two were children of Mark Antony and Cleopatra. The twins Alexander Helios and Cleopatra Selene, splendidly named after the sun and the moon, found themselves exposed to Roman gaze in the third triumph, a celebration of the conquest of Egypt described by Dio as surpassing all 'in costliness and magnificence'.[13] For public edification, they walked in the train of 'an effigy of the dead Cleopatra upon a couch', a brutal but undoubtedly powerful piece of street theatre. A more enviable fate belonged to the two Roman boys who rode the trace horses of Octavian's chariot. They were Marcellus and Tiberius, respectively his nephew and elder stepson. Together they shared Octavian's glory.

Their presence invited more than one interpretation. To those among the crowd who recognized the proud teenagers, Octavian's choice was a memorable introduction of the younger generation of his family into Rome's public arena. In the absence of sons of his own, the conquering Triumvir had chosen to accompany him these two from the gaggle of boys in his house. Their mothers must have read alternative meanings into this parade of family solidarity. For Livia, pleasure at Tiberius's inclusion, in the absence of direct kinship with Octavian, was tempered by the knowledge that it was Marcellus, Octavian's nearest male descendant, who occupied the place of greater honour: it was Marcellus who rode the right-hand trace-horse; Tiberius took the left. Given Rome's emphasis on ties of blood and descent through a common male ancestor – so-called agnatic kinship – there was no surprise in this. Octavian's triumph was also Octavia's triumph. Widowed, she avoided marginalization through her relationships with her brother and now her son. It was perhaps a challenge to Claudian pride.

Even Dio's account does not suggest that Livia had conceived a desire for Tiberius to succeed Octavian as early as 29 BC. Had she done so, she would have committed herself to a lengthy waiting game. In the event that Octavian had discussed with her his plans for succession, she deliberately – and uncharacteristically – set herself in opposition to his wishes. But there is no evidence of such a course on Livia's part. Despite the vainglory of his triple triumph – laurels for Illyria, Actium and Egypt – Octavian had yet to achieve formalized mastery of Rome. That came in 27 BC, two years after he proclaimed on Roman streets the order of preference of his youthful family – Marcellus first, then Tiberius. In 29 BC Livia understood the implication; she may even have been involved with Octavian in his preparations for the triumph. Octavia understood it too. It was not Tiberius who, at the triumph's climax, stood alongside Octavian in the new Senate House commissioned by Julius Caesar. There

Octavian dedicated a statue of Victory looted at Tarentum, heaped with the spoils of Rome's conquest of Egypt. Octavia's triumph, unlike her brother's, would be of short duration.

Marcellus, Seneca claimed afterwards, possessed 'the certain hope of becoming emperor'.[14] That hope is traceable to Octavian's public preferment in the triumphs of 29 BC. It was kindled not only in the breast of Marcellus himself but that of his mother and, if Velleius's carefully imprecise account can be trusted, in the minds of any number of Roman onlookers. Clearly Octavia the peace-maker, a model of wifely virtue, did not lack ambition for her son. Her response to Marcellus's death, six years after Octavian's symbolic declaration, was extreme. It enables us to contextualize that maternal ambition for which Livia was subsequently so robustly scorned – but of which we have so little real evidence – and offers proof of the degree of Octavia's desire for a crown for her only son. It also invites questions. Was power for her son the ultimate aim of every patrician Roman mother? Does a throne invite ambitious scheming? 'Throughout her entire life she never ceased to weep and sigh,' Seneca relates, '[nor even allowed] herself to be distracted; concentrating on one thing alone, with her whole mind fixed on it, she remained all her life as she was at his funeral ... regarding any cessation in weeping as a second bereavement. She refused to have a single portrait of her darling son and would not permit any mention of him.'[15] Seneca claims that in the heat of her bereavement Octavia conceived a hatred for all other mothers. The chief focus of that loathing, we are to believe, was Livia – 'as the good fortune once held out to [Octavia] seemed to have passed to [Livia's] son'.[16] Perhaps it was Seneca's account which in turn shaped that of Cassius Dio. Both men wrote after the events they describe. Or perhaps Dio was influenced, as Seneca may have been, by the fact of Tiberius's eventual succession to look backwards and find false conclusions. More than two hundred years had passed when the Greek historian recorded a rumour that Livia murdered Marcellus as a result of his preferment 'for the succession before her sons'. It was not a rumour known to Tacitus, whose strongly anti-Livia account is more nearly contemporary.

Propertius's lament for Marcellus places his death at the smart seaside resort of Baiae, at the western end of the Bay of Naples, where convalescents enjoyed sulphur baths in the natural hot springs and the Roman *ton* exploited the distance from the city to allow themselves a relaxation of the capital's moral code.[17] 'Where the sea, barred from shadowy Lake Avernus, plays by Baiae's steamy pools of water; where Misenus, trumpeter of Troy, lies in the sand, and the road built by Hercules's effort sounds; there, where the cymbals clashed for the Theban god when he sought to favour the cities of men – but now, Baiae, hateful with this great crime, what hostile god exists in your waters? – there, burdened, Marcellus sank his head beneath Stygian waves, and now his spirit haunts your lake.'[18]

Temporarily, tragedy cast its blight over the easygoing seaside resort described by Martial as the 'golden shore of happy Venus, pleasant gift of proud Nature'.[19] Hedonism or simply the passage of time restored its customary indolence to the cluster of sea-facing hills. Gentle breezes stirred the leaves of the myrtle groves, spotted with luxury villas like the hills around Fundi. The sources do not record a visit by Livia to Baiae in the autumn of 23 BC, although outbreaks of plague in Rome and a series of troubling omens made this a sensible year to travel. They do not record her whereabouts at all. But there was something in the air in that year of portents and tragedy. A friend of Augustus, the *novus homo* Lucius Nonius Asprenas, stood trial in the *princeps*'s presence. The indictment brought against him was poisoning. Asprenas had given a lavish banquet for a hundred and thirty friends. All perished. In the event the accused was acquitted, although he forfeited his chances of the consulship.[20]

CHAPTER 17

'Born of his sacred blood'

Intermittently Livia disappears from the sources. We know relatively little of her life in the years immediately following Augustus's settlement of 27 BC. His goal achieved, Augustus chose to leave Rome. His depart-ure – in Dio Cassius's account prompted by plans to invade Britain[1] – took him first to Gaul and afterwards to Spain, a round trip that kept Augustus away from Rome for three years. Disturbing reports told of revolts by Cantabrian and Asturian tribes in Spain's 'impregnable' north-western plains and the foothills of the Pyrenees.[2] Augustus enjoyed lim-ited success in subduing them. On this the final occasion when he acted as his own military commander, he took with him in his train his trace-horse riders of 29 BC, Marcellus and Tiberius.

There is no record of Livia travelling with Augustus that year – nor any denial in the sources that she did so. Under the Republic, wives had traditionally remained in Rome to watch over the interests of their absent husbands, a custom with which Augustus was largely in sympathy. Later, he required that those legates whom he himself appointed to the provinces confined time spent with their wives exclusively to the period outside the campaigning season, but Augustus was capable of making excep-tions in his own case. On this occasion, he entrusted care of his affairs to his fellow consul and oldest friend, Marcus Agrippa, who stayed behind in the capital. With Augustus on campaign, Tiberius at his side, and Agrippa at the helm in Rome, Livia would have been right to consider that, Drusus excepted, all her interests lay for the moment in the provinces.

Unlike Octavia, Livia's maternal role was small in scale. She was responsible for her younger son Drusus, then twelve years old, and her step-daughter Julia, Drusus's exact contemporary. Since both children probably remained in the schoolroom full-time, Livia's was not an onerous burden, nor sufficient in responsibility to justify separating husband and wife for the whole of Augustus's three-year absence. It is reasonable to conclude, as a recent biographer has done, that the assertion fifty years later by one of Livia's grandsons that she had accompanied Augustus on journeys 'to the West and to the East' encompasses this journey westwards to Spain at the outset of Augustus's principate.[3] A detail may corroborate this contention. In 11 BC Octavia died. Her funeral, following a period of public mourning, was an event of some grandeur. For the first time in Rome there were two orations.[4] The second was a private eulogy delivered by Augustus in the Temple of Divus Julius. The first, spoken as tradition demanded from the rostra in the Forum, was given by Octavia's nephew Drusus. His prominence in the ceremony points to a relationship between Livia's younger son and his aunt. This may have developed during the period Livia spent in the provinces with Augustus in the years after 27. At the time Drusus was still a child. Temporarily without father, mother or brother, he must have welcomed the affection of his kind and motherly aunt.

There were potent incentives for Livia's presence in Spain. Not only did Tiberius make repeated forays into the political arena during his absence from Rome – including successfully addressing Augustus on behalf of Archelaus of Cappadocia, a client king whom Tiberius may have inherited from his father Nero – but Augustus himself fell ill. Although the nature of his illness is unclear, it appears to have been of considerable duration, lasting perhaps as long as a year. Augustus used the opportunity offered by a protracted convalescence in the Spanish coastal town of Tarraco to write his autobiography.[5] Subsequently lost, on publication in 22 BC it extended to thirteen volumes.[6] We do not know Augustus's motives, but it is possible to interpret the writing of autobiography as a valedictory undertaking. Perhaps Livia heard alarm bells ringing. Aside from love, she did not overlook her entire dependence on Augustus's survival.

On 24 April 27 BC, months before Augustus's departure for Gaul, Tiberius had undergone one of those rites of passage, like the *depositio barbae*, by which Romans charted a young man's progress towards eligibility for senatorial office. Accompanied by Augustus, his legal guardian, Tiberius formally exchanged the *toga praetexta* worn by children for the uniform of Roman manhood. The appropriately named *toga virilis* was an entirely white garment of some complexity, which Augustus would afterwards take measures to promote. The ceremony took place in the Forum, at the very centre of Rome, and involved the recording of Tiberius's name on the rollcall of citizens. It was potentially an intimidating initiation into Roman public life, and an emotional one too for the young man's mother. As babies, aristocratic Roman children received a gold amulet or *bulla*, which they wore around their necks. Before his departure for the Forum, Tiberius dedicated his *bulla* at an altar in the atrium, accompanying the surrender with an act of sacrifice. The objects of his piety were those spirits of dead ancestors, the *lares*, who in the case of Claudians were so numerous. For Livia the day combined pride with sadness, an ending and a beginning.

Seneca offers a clearcut explanation for Octavia's later dislike of Livia. He does not discuss that rivalry between the sisters-in-law in the matter of their children's marriages of which we will discover more, or suggest that antipathy was anything but recent, arising from the single factor of Marcellus's death. Livia after all had modelled her portraiture and even her appearance on those of her sister-in-law. What then were her feelings in April 27 BC, witnessing Tiberius complete the initiation ceremony Marcellus had presumably only recently undergone? Livia, we know, had longed to become a mother of sons as early as 42 BC, warming an egg in her hands and cradling it against her breast. Brought up in the intensely political environment of the late-Republican aristocracy, she may have dreamt of bearing sons who attained high office, but she could not have conceived of the inheritance Augustus appeared to extend to Marcellus. Did she experience jealousy on Tiberius's part? Was her disaffection directed against Octavia, whose son enjoyed the preferment Tiberius's parternity denied him – or against Marcellus himself? Was she angered by her own inability to conceive an heir for her husband? Or did Augustus's settlement, conferred by the Senate at the beginning of the year, serve to stimulate that maternal ambition we have assumed as part of Livia's make-up? Were Augustus's unconstitutional dreams of hereditary authority matched from the outset by Livia's? It seems probable. Livia as well as Augustus benefited from his election to the principate. It was in both their interests to perpetuate the revolutionary settlement. With Tiberius's symbolic discarding of the *toga praetexta*, Livia was free at last to give rein to any aspirations she harboured for her first-born son. Always a step ahead, giving the lie to her plans, was her nephew by marriage, Marcellus.

Livia understood her husband's purpose in taking Marcellus and Tiberius with him to the provinces. Some historians have suggested that Augustus sought to test the two boys and select whichever fared better as his heir. But two years previously, in the most splendid public spectacle of the decade, Augustus had made clear that it was Marcellus to whom he accorded higher rank. The sources record no intervening event which could have provided grounds for altering that precedence. We know nothing of Marcellus's achievements, only the record of Tiberius's political initiation, 'his defence, against various charges, of the Jewish King Archelaus, also the Trallians and the Thessalians, at a court presided over by Augustus', as Suetonius reports.[7] The sources' relative silence concerning Marcellus may not amount to a commendation, but it appears to rule out the possibility of disgrace.

Augustus's purpose in Spain was to introduce both boys to the legions whose loyalty underpinned imperial power. To make sure of his aim, he sponsored games for the soldiers, 'a number of spectacles to be held within the military camps, and these were organized by Tiberius and Marcellus', according to Dio.[8] Augustus ensured that the legions recognized the authorship of their entertainment.

In 25 BC, at a ceremony in Rome at which he himself was not present, Augustus gave incontrovertible proof that the dispositions of the Egyptian triumph had not been altered. The *princeps* married his only daughter Julia to Marcellus.

In itself this did not amount to a public nomination of Marcellus as his uncle's successor – Augustus recognized the impossibility of so explicit a gesture. To his intimates, however, it offered a clear statement of Augustus's considered priorities in an heir. Through Octavia Marcellus shared Augustus's paternity. Children of the marriage would thus be doubly related to the *princeps*. They would also share his kinship with Julius Caesar, the importance of which must have become clear to Tiberius as well as Marcellus during their time spent among the legions in Spain. We have seen that, latterly, Augustus had soft-pedalled his relationship with Rome's last dictator, his purpose in part to disguise his own monarchical intentions. But he had not renounced Caesar's legacy outright. He continued to derive benefits from his great-uncle's extensive client base, his fortune and the loyalty the Caesarian name inspired among Rome's soldiers. More than this, Augustus recognized the benefits, albeit largely intangible, of his association with Caesar's divinity – as Virgil would express it, 'Born from a god, himself to godhead born: His sire already signs him for the skies.' [9] During his lifetime, Caesar had asserted divine forebears for the Julians, the same Venus Genetrix to whom he erected a temple and whose maternity he invoked in his oration at the funeral of his aunt Julia. After his death, he himself became a god, a nomination ratified by the Senate. Symbolically Augustus reiterated Caesar's highfalutin claims, placing busts of Octavia and Livia alongside the statue of the goddess in the Temple of Venus Genetrix. In his chosen successor, he wanted a man of his own family. For the secure perpetuation of the settlement of 27 BC, he preferred a candidate who shared with him that intimation of divinity other Romans could not claim. Fifty years later, Julia's youngest daughter Agrippina berated Tiberius. She discovered the then emperor sacrificing to the deceased Augustus, himself also by then a god. 'The man who offers victims to the deified Augustus,' she said, 'ought not to persecute his descendants. It is not in mute statues that Augustus's divine spirit has lodged – I, born of his sacred blood, am its incarnation!' [10] Agrippina's consciousness of divinity is an attitude which arose later in the principate. It is not wholly removed from Augustus's own philosophy.

If Livia's ambition for Tiberius already at this point fixated on his succeeding as *princeps* – and such a supposition is wholly conjectural – the marriage of Marcellus and Julia must have been a bitter pill. Theirs was not, insofar as the contemporary accounts record, an engagement of longstanding. Julia, we have seen, despite being only fourteen, had been engaged twice before – to a son of Mark Antony and a foreign client king. Both were politically motivated alliances. In marrying his daughter to Marcellus, Augustus gave equal weighting to politics and genetics. Although a similar attitude in 39 BC may have accounted for Livia's own attraction in Augustus's eyes – her embodiment of the patrician and Republican connections of the Claudii and Livii Drusi – it was not an argument calculated to appease her more than a decade later. Genetics was quantifiable and inarguable. It left no room for Livia's plans for Tiberius. No matter that Tiberius had been engaged since 32 BC to Agrippa's daughter Vipsania Agrippina. Engagements, as both Augustus and Julia had proven, were easily broken, and Vipsania was still only a child. Neither Livia nor Tiberius gained from Julia's marriage to Marcellus. It was cold comfort indeed that Agrippa had improved his position in the seven years since his daughter's engagement, having won victory at Naulochus and Actium and afterwards shared Augustus's consulships of 28 and 27. Agrippa found himself at the very heart of Augustus's regime. Such achievements did not compensate the '*superbissimi*' Claudii.

In his account of Marcellus's death, Velleius Paterculus pinpoints tensions within Augustus's inner circle.

> People thought that, if anything should happen to Caesar, Marcellus would be his successor in power, at the same time believing, however, that this would not fall to his lot without opposition from Marcus Agrippa . . . After his death Agrippa, who had set out for Asia on the pretext of commissions from the emperor, but who, according to current gossip, had withdrawn, for the time being, on account of his secret animosity for Marcellus, now returned from Asia . . .[11]

It is impossible to state with certainty the architect of Tiberius's engagement to Vipsania. Livia's wounded pride notwithstanding, the alliance promised benefits to Augustus. If we believe Velleius, Agrippa's resentment of Marcellus's promotion was well founded. Agrippa was responsible for almost every major victory by which Octavian defeated Mark Antony to become Augustus. His loyalty demanded recompense. Augustus denied him the possibility of challenging either his own authority or, hypothetically, that of Marcellus by binding Agrippa to his own family through ties of marriage. Tiberius was his chosen instrument; Livia bore the cost.

In 20 BC Tiberius married the thirteen-year-old Vipsania. Eight years previously, at Augustus's request, Agrippa himself had married the *princeps*'s niece Marcella, a daughter of Octavia. Livia's thoughts on a political marriage for her elder son motivated by the need to placate an army commander of unknown family are not known. Perhaps she drew comfort from the double guaranteee of protection for Tiberius which his marriage surely earned him – from Augustus, but from Agrippa too, trusting in that love between fathers and sons-in-law with which Catullus upbraided Lesbia: 'I loved you then not only as the common sort love a mistress, but as a father loves his sons and sons-in-law.'[12] She is likely to have discounted the argument propounded by the contemporary historian Cornelius Nepos, that Tiberius and Vipsania's engagement cemented the friendship of Augustus and Agrippa's father-in-law, Atticus.[13] Livia was not so sentimental as to rate Augustus's friendships above her ambitions for her sons.

In 25 BC, in a gesture perhaps intended to silence rumours of a rift, it was Agrippa who gave Julia away at her marriage to Marcellus. Ill health detained Augustus in the provinces – that, and it was suggested, fear of explaining himself to Livia.[14] From a distance Augustus and Agrippa clearly reached an understanding that restored former amicability. When, later, Agrippa's house on the Palatine burnt down, Augustus invited his friend to share his own house. Agrippa's future son-in-law Tiberius lived under the same roof.

Another year passed before Augustus was sufficiently recovered to undertake the journey back to Rome. His homecoming was marked by further privileges granted by the Senate. Among them, Dio tells us, 'Marcellus was given the right to sit in the Senate among the former praetors, and the right to stand for the consulship ten years earlier than the normal age, and Tiberius the right to stand for each office five years before the normal age; the former was at once elected aedile and the latter quaestor.'[15] Riding Augustus's coat-tails, both young men had achieved concessions unthinkable in the ordinary course of Republican politics. As Livia would undoubtedly have been aware, the discrepancy between the twin awards inclined heavily in Marcellus's favour. Her protest, if any, was in vain.

In the years since Livia's marriage, the stakes had risen significantly. Octavian the triumvir had emerged as sole ruler of Rome in the aftermath of victory over Mark Antony and Cleopatra in 31 BC. Four years later, his unprecedented power was formalized. He was Augustus, emperor, even if he chose to call himself 'first citizen' and to think of himself as such. Within this timespan, the possible scope of Livia's ambitions not only for her sons but for herself increased exponentially in a manner neither she nor anyone else could have predicted. Rome, the historians tell us, was reborn. 'Agriculture returned to the fields, respect to religion, to mankind freedom from anxiety, and to each citizen his property rights were now assured; old laws were usefully amended, and new laws passed for the general good.'[16] Velleius Paterculus found himself defeated by the business of panegyric: 'the enthusiasm of Augustus's reception by men of all classes, ages, and ranks, and the magnificence of his triumphs and of the spectacles which he gave – all this it would be impossible adequately to describe even within the compass of a formal history, to say nothing of a work so circumscribed as this.'[17]

Excluded for the most part from the public celebrations of Augustus's success, Livia could not fail to be touched by the prevailing mood of euphoria. It was a short step to desiring that euphoria for one of her sons. No precedent existed for Augustus's 'revolution', nor for the expectations it imposed upon members of his family. In its early stages the principate was a constantly evolving entity. In 29 BC provincials in Asia and Bithynia received permission to build temples to the deified Julius Caesar and to Roma, Rome's presiding goddess. Greek provincials followed suit. They consecrated not temples but precincts to Roma – and, in a development new in Roman history, to Augustus.[18] There were lofty implications in such acts of piety and commemoration offered to a living politician. The most ambitious mother could scarcely have aimed so high.

CHAPTER 18

'Her sacred office'

In Ancient Egypt a geographer called Ptolemy drew a map of India. He included among its features 'the Sardonyx Mountains'. Sardonyx is an agate sport prized for its lustrous striations of brownish-red and white. Egyptians, Greeks, Romans and Sumerians once coveted the stone. In Rome cameo carvers carefully manipulated its striped contrasts. In their painstaking gewgaws, rich red-brown provides a foil for opaque or translucent elements of snow-white and cream.

In the Kunsthistorisches Museum in Vienna there is an example of a sardonyx cameo from Livia's lifetime. An exquisite *objet de vertu* probably intended for private circulation, it depicts Livia in the years after the death of Augustus. Gazing right to left, she contemplates a bust of her deified husband. She too is invested with elements of divine iconography. A posy of wheat ears affiliates her to Ceres, goddess of agriculture, earthly plenty, nurture and marriage, the favourite deity of Augustus's programme of moral legislation, with its emphasis on encouraging the birthrate. She wears the crown of Fortuna, the Roman personification of luck; and on her shield are visible the lions of Cybele, that atavistic figure of the Earth Mother whose image – beached on the sandbanks of Ostia – a woman of the Claudii once miraculously dragged to shore.[1]

Following Augustus's death, the Senate took action quickly. Cassius Dio records that it 'declared Augustus to be immortal, assigned to him sacred rites and priests to perform them, and appointed Livia ... to be his priestess. They also authorized her to be attended by a lictor whenever she exercised her sacred office.'[2] Readers whose perception of Livia is shaped by Robert Graves's villainess of *I, Claudius* may be surprised by her promotion to the priesthood. By the time of Augustus's death, Livia's association with Rome's religious life spanned half a century. It was a connection her contemporaries applauded, and became a cornerstone of her exalted reputation within her lifetime. Despite his propensity for hyperbole, Tiberius's apologist Velleius Paterculus caught the popular feeling when he described Livia as 'a woman pre-eminent among women ... who in all things resembled the gods more than mankind'.[3] Livia garnered rewards from her long years of visible piety.

In 90 BC a woman of the upper classes brought peace to Rome in the form of an end to the Social War. Caecilia Metella had a dream. It concerned a temple in the Forum Holitorium dedicated to Juno Sospita, Rome's warlike patron goddess. The temple had fallen into misuse. At the foot of a statue of the goddess, a bitch gave birth to her litter in a basket. Women abused the temple – either as a haunt for prostitutes or a public lavatory, the sources do not specify.[4] Unsurprisingly, given Roman gods' predisposition towards anger and their disinterest in any gospel of redemption, the goddess asserted that, in her displeasure, she had decided to abandon both the temple and Rome itself. In her wake she forecast disasters for the godless city. But Caecilia successfully implored her not to leave.[5] In response to the dream, depending on the source consulted, the temple was restored by Caecilia herself or, on the instructions of the Senate, the consul for the year. Thereafter the fortunes of war, we are told, again favoured Rome.

The incident illustrates the role of women – earthly and divine – in Rome's wellbeing. At a time of crisis, the Senate accepted the veracity of Caecilia's dream and acted promptly. With the temple restored by the intervention of an aristocratic Roman matron, the goddess remained in situ. She exercised her extraterrestrial powers to safeguard the state. Caecilia played the heroine's part. Renewed piety, in the form of the restored temple, brought about a reinvigoration of Roman power and military victory. A woman's dream successfully upheld Rome's masculine vigour.

We do not know if Livia was familiar with the example of Caecilia

Metella, though it is possible. Among the causes of the outbreak of the Social War of 90 BC was the murder of the same Marcus Livius Drusus who adopted Livia's father. Livia, like Augustus, restored a number of shrines and temples in Rome. Although her benefactions did not rival Augustus's impressive tally of eighty-two temples renovated or rebuilt, it was a task she embraced early on. Even before Augustus's settlement of 27 BC, Livia had restored the shrines of Patrician and Plebeian Chastity.[6] For the remainder of her public life she would continue to favour religious sites associated with women. Among them were the Temples of Fortuna Muliebris ('womanly virtue') and Bona Dea Subsaxana (the 'good goddess Subsaxana'), that cult whose all-female rites Livia's kinsman Clodius had violated at the time of Livia's birth in pursuit of an illicit assignation with Caesar's wife.

Caecilia Metella is proof of the extent to which, even under the Republic, aspects of Rome's religious life were considered an appropriate sphere for women's interest. Roman religion was a crowded pantheon. Some of its deities personified abstractions, others were epic heroes and heroines on the grandest scale; several, like Fortuna Muliebris, specifically addressed concerns of one sex. Rome applauded religious observance, which had an active omnipresence in the city's life on account of the daily practice of animal sacrifice – an offering of spilt blood and baked meats – common in many households. Religion permeated every aspect of the state's life. Priesthoods, no less than magistracies, were offices for politicians. Many were male appointments, sacrifice being a man's business. But prominent women won praise for their involvement with respectable Roman cults. Just as Caecilia Metella had 'rescued' the cult of Juno Sospita, so Augustus and Livia recognized in religion an aspect of Roman public life in which Livia could involve herself with impunity and even praise, to the ultimate benefit of her husband. That their instinct was correct appears to be proved by the record of Livia's religious activities preserved in Ovid's *Fasti*, the poet's unfinished treatment of Roman legends structured around the religious festivals of the year. Far from attesting disapprobation, the *Fasti* applauds Livia's efforts.[7] Although the poem adopts an adulatory tone towards Augustus's family, this does not negate its value as a source. That Ovid felt able to commend Livia's religious activities within such a context indicates the extent to which they were considered both appropriate and laudable.

Livia benefited from Rome's confusion of gods and family. In the aristocratic atrium, as we have seen, an altar served the *lares* – those divine spirits who represented a family's ancestors and watched over their daily lives. In sacrificing to the *lares*, Romans made a show of *pietas*, a virtue understood in its broadest sense as respect not simply for the gods but also for the family itself.[8] Roman women may have been responsible for overseeing the religious lives of their husbands' houses. A new bride asserted her status as mistress of the house in an act of dedication to her husband's household gods the morning after her wedding. Although women were prevented from taking part in religious sacrifices – they were forbidden either to slaughter the sacrificial victim or to prepare the spelt flour which ceremoniously was sprinkled over it[9] – it was a small step to transpose dutiful domestic religious observance into the public arena.

In Livia's case, as with so much of her life, her actions complemented those of Augustus. Augustus cherished a lifelong ambition of moral renewal in Rome. His assessment of the decay in Roman standards was a textbook example of Rome's rosy view of its own past. Sallust had attributed the defeat of Carthage in the mid-second century BC to Roman love of luxury: 'Lust for money grew, then lust for power; these were the foundations of all evils.'[10] For his part, Augustus found in modern laxity and luxury foundations of a plethora of social ills, including the falling birthrate among the upper classes, the prevalence of divorce, 'easy' adultery of the sort encapsulated in the poetry of Catullus and Propertius, and the reluctance among men of senatorial rank to marry and produce children.[11] For Augustus these were not the signifiers of a sophisticated, affluent and socially relaxed society, but of a world given up to corruption and self-gratification, the vices, as Cleopatra had fulsomely demonstrated, of non-Romans – like Sallust's Carthaginians.

His thoughts probably turned to possible remedies as early as 28 BC. That year he dedicated the Temple of Apollo adjoining his Palatine house. Its lavishness contrasted with the simpler decoration of the dwelling place next door, a trio of statues by the distinguished Greek sculptors Scopas, Cephisodotus and Timoteus proof of the earnestness of Augustus's

piety.[12] He would return to the fray a decade later, with a legislative programme that criminalized adultery and sought to enforce through pro-
scriptive measures glaring double standards of sexual probity for men
and women. Though his efforts proved largely unsuccessful in practice,
the *princeps* claimed long-term victory. His legislation, as we shall see,
established a hypothetical blueprint of patrician virtue. Its principal focus
was female chastity. Rhetoric exploited the example of virtuous women
of Rome's past in addition to religious and mythological exempla. It was
a policy that could not fail to have implications for Livia.

What Augustus did in the Senate House, Livia echoed in the city's
temples. Ovid states explicitly that Livia's restoration of the Temple of
Bona Dea Subsaxana was undertaken in imitation of her husband: 'The
heiress of the ancient name of the Crassi dedicated this, who with her
virgin body had submitted to no man; Livia restored it so that she might
not fail to imitate her husband and in every way follow him.'[13] Denied
an official role, she worked to reinforce by visible precept the spirit of
Augustus's schemes. It was surely not by accident that in the year in
which Augustus first made concrete plans to set his moral revolution
in motion, Livia restored two shrines dedicated to female chastity. Since
one of Augustus's targets was women's immorality, he needed to provide Roman women of all ranks with a focus for chaster aspirations. By
entrusting the task of restoration to Livia, Augustus offered Romans a
visible example to follow. The cults of Patrician and Plebeian Chastity
applied only to women: Augustus could not himself embody either. Livia
not only did what Augustus was prevented from doing, she reaped the
benefits of association with so virtuous a cult, which was essential to
the success of her husband's programme of reform. She did so exactly
a decade after her second marriage. By sharing in Augustus's political
life in this manner, Livia took a significant step towards expunging the
scandal of 39 BC. That such a step was possible suggests the extent to
which Livia's good behaviour of the intervening period had erased the
smirch of former indiscretions. She had learnt important lessons.

Her reward was a public platform that did not exist in the constitution or by custom; that platform, inevitably, brought with it an increased
degree of prominence. Livia's built legacy is small compared with
Augustus's, although it outstrips that of successive imperial spouses,

rivalled only by the contribution to Rome's cityscape of her sister-in-law Octavia. It enacts on a larger scale the pattern of patronage and benefaction expected of patrician women. In this respect – although it could not be acknowledged as such – Livia's behaviour conformed to that tradionally advocated for female consorts: her actions were those of any prominent Roman woman writ large.[14] All that differed were Livia's motives: on the one hand, a calculation of how to benefit Augustus without asserting an unorthodox role for herself, on the other – perhaps – the deliberate creation of just such a role, independent and remote from Republican strictures on women's position.

Augustus's principate witnessed a revival of religious cults. Many were concerned with female deities, feminine virtues and women's spheres of interest. Annual festivals celebrated Ceres, Flora, Vesta and Juno Lucina, goddesses whose associations comprehensively embraced the feminine arena of fertility, childbirth, maternal love and the home.[15] In the religious acts of these festivals, it was women who served as celebrants. Such developments did not increase the personal freedoms of Roman women – on the contrary, they reinforced concepts of an 'appropriate', compartmentalized female sphere. But in the cases of Rome's most prominent women, Livia above all, they facilitated an association with aspects of divinity which, skilfully exploited, could become an approach to power. We do not know how far Livia involved herself in these celebrations and the sources are mostly silent on her religious life. But in 7 BC, six months after Livia and Tiberius jointly dedicated the covered public walkway known as the Porticus of Livia, Livia separately dedicated a shrine within that portico. It was the Shrine of August Concord, celebrating the harmony Augustus had brought to Rome and the political life of the city and, more obliquely, the harmony of Augustus and Livia's marriage. It was, at one level, Livia's celebration of herself, a public statement of virtue and achievement, an assertion in the public arena of private life and personal fulfilment. It became, on a purely visual level, one of the great sites of Rome. 'If . . . as you go to the ancient Forum, you should see the others set parallel to it one after the other, and the basilicas and the temples, and you should also see the Capitoline and the art works there and on the Palatine and in the portico of Livia, you would easily forget about anything existing anywhere else,' wrote Livia's contemporary, the Greek historian and geographer Strabo. 'This, then, is Rome.'[16] Strabo's vision was of a new Rome. With circumspection and discretion, Livia became one of its builders.

On the sardonyx cameo housed in Vienna's Kunst historisches Museum, Livia holds a bust of Augustus outstretched in her right hand. Wife and deceased husband both display attributes of the gods. In Augustus's case, following posthumous deification in AD 14, divine attributes are his by right; Livia's divinity at this point is associative. It arose from long involvement with carefully chosen religious cults and further benefited from a document written on 3 April AD 13. Augustus adopted Livia in his will. After his death she became his daughter, renamed Julia Augusta.

That startling action, through testamentary paternity, imbued the *princeps*'s widow-daughter with a spark of his divinity and drew her closer to her own eventual deification. But the image of the sardonyx, in which a mortal Livia dwarfs her immortal husband, is misleading. Livia's achievements – in the religious sphere and elsewhere – do not challenge those of Augustus. The towering scale of Augustus's public contribution is not rivalled by those ancillary undertakings Rome thought fit to permit its women. The relative sizes of Livia and Augustus in the Vienna sardonyx reverse the mirror of history. Like her divinity, Livia's achievements too were associative, arising from opportunities created by her status as Augustus's wife. Her influence was that of Shakespeare's Volumnia, the mother of the wayward hero Coriolanus, who exploits her family relationship to attain results: 'Thou shalt no sooner march to assault thy country than to tread ... on thy mother's womb that brought thee to this world.' Volumnia's aim was nothing less than the preservation of Rome, against which Coriolanus planned to march at the head of an enemy Volscian army. Her success was commemorated in the building of a temple. 'O my mother, mother, O! You have won a happy victory to Rome ... you deserve to have a temple built you: all the swords in Italy, and her confederate arms, could not have made this peace.'[17] The temple in question was that of Fortuna Muliebris, restored by Livia.[18] To its associations of womanly virtue was added the gloss of patriotic duty. Five hundred years after Coriolanus's death, it was an appropriate combination for association with the wife of Rome's first citizen.

Livia exploited the limited possibilities safely available to her to create a public persona sufficient in magnitude to inspire images like this richly coloured agate cameo. The origin of the deception at the centre of that image can be traced to Livia's skilful involvement in Roman public life, which began in 28 BC with the restoration of the shrines of Pudicitia Patricia and Pudicitia Plebeia. Her continuing involvement, spanning her lifetime, would prove unprecedented among Roman women.

CHAPTER 19

'If you come to any harm...
that is the end of me too'

There is a surprise in Augustus's longevity. At the time of his death the *princeps* was weeks short of his seventy-seventh birthday, an age significantly in excess of that of the average contemporary Roman. It was a record unrivalled by any in his family save Livia. Livia enjoyed robust health. Throughout her nine decades, the sources record only one bout of serious illness and that in extreme old age. Augustus's health, however, was less certain, less predictable; it could not, like that of his wife, be guaranteed by daily draughts of Pucine wine. Suetonius outlines 'seasonal disorders' which plagued Augustus all his adult life: 'in early spring a tightness of the diaphragm; and when the sirocco blew, catarrh. These so weakened his constitution that either hot or cold weather caused him great distress.'[1] His skin was marked by hard, dry patches that resembled ringworm. In his left hip, thigh and leg he experienced an unspecified 'weakness' which resulted in something approximating to a limp; 'sometimes the forefinger of his right hand would be so numbed by cold that it could hardly serve to guide a pen, even when strengthened with a long horn finger-stall':[2] later he suffered from rheumatism. In winter, he shrouded himself in layers of woollen clothes; in summer, he hid from the sun's glare beneath a broad-brimmed hat. It was unsettling for Livia. Only when she had secured the principate for Tiberius was her position safe against Augustus's ailments and the threat of his death. Until that moment, she must bend all her energies on his survival. Cassius Dio attributes to Livia a speech in which she outlines to Augustus her dependence upon him. In Dio's account, Livia's motive is personal gratification – her desire, through Augustus, to exercise power in Rome. The historian does not indicate the source of his evidence. Possibly the statement is one of many in which the ancient commentators demonized Livia through insinuation. A fabrication or otherwise, it explains Livia's position neatly: 'I have an equal share in whatever happens to you, good or bad: so long as you are safe, I also take my part in reigning, while if you come to any harm, which heaven forbid, that is the end of me too.'[3]

On this account, as we have seen, the year 23 BC was an anxious one for Livia. Only recently recovered from that illness which had detained him in Spain for over a year – a period he devoted, as if prey to intimations of mortality, to the composition of a lengthy autobiography – Augustus fell ill again. This time his illness was not less but more serious, the worst, the sources agree, of the 'several dangerous' afflictions by which Augustus's life was sporadically threatened. Suetonius attributes his suffering to abscesses on the liver. It was not a condition contemporary medicine could be expected to treat with accuracy or indeed efficacy.

There are signs, however, that Suetonius's diagnosis fell wide of the mark, not least the patient's recovery in the hands of Antonius Musa. Musa, as we have seen, successfully advocated a course of cold baths and cold fomentations. This treatment reversed conventional medical thinking, with its studious avoidance of anything cold – 'for nothing is more harmful to the liver,' as the Roman encyclopaedist Celsus asserted in his first-century treatise, *On Medicine*.[4] Perhaps the sickly *princeps* was suffering from smallpox, scarlet fever, influenza or tyhoid fever: all were recorded by contemporary writers as the cause of the plague then devastating Rome. Against this is the fact that Augustus does not appear to have infected any of his immediate circle with his illness, perhaps a point in Suetonius's favour.

Clearly Augustus's condition was grave. Livia's response to this latest health scare is not recorded, but it is probable that she experienced genuine fear on her husband's behalf. He had returned to Rome only a year before, previously detained in the provinces, as we have seen, by afflictions sufficiently severe to summon Livia to his side. We cannot know how fully his volatile health had recovered before this second collapse. In this instance, Augustus himself appears to have doubted his recovery. 'He arranged all his affairs as if he were at the point of death,' Dio tells us, 'and gathered around him the officers of state and the most prominent senators and knights.'[5] At this moment of crisis he symbolically renounced his leadership of Rome. The recipient of his vast inheritance came as a surprise to some of those gathered in the house on the Palatine. 'People thought that if anything should happen to Caesar, Marcellus would be his successor in power,' Velleius Paterculus tells us.[6] Livia may have thought the same, following Marcellus's marriage to Julia and almost a decade's conspicuous preferment. But it was not his son-in-law to whom Augustus handed his signet ring carved with the head of Alexander the Great. Marcus Agrippa, Augustus's true right-hand man and the husband of his niece Marcella, received the imperial seal. At the same time, a memorandum of the State's financial and military resources was entrusted to the *princeps*'s fellow consul for the year, Gnaeus Calpurnius Piso.[7]

It is reasonable to assume that Livia shared the general surprise at this turn of events. The signs are that Augustus was too unwell to summon the strength to discuss his plans with her prior to taking action. If despite being, as Dio says, on the brink of death, he paused to consider the alternatives from Livia's point of view, he may well have concluded that neither course touched her closely. If anything, inheritance by Agrippa was preferable to Livia than that Marcellus should assume Rome's throne. Tiberius's longstanding engagement to Vipsania would make Livia's son the new *princeps*'s son-in-law, Livia a fellow parent-in-law alongside Rome's first citizen. Marcellus's succession gave Livia the doubtful position of stepmother of the *princeps*'s wife. It was hardly the access to power the sources would argue she craved. Against this argument must be weighed the conceptual defeat Agrippa's inheritance represented. In appearing to favour Agrippa as his successor, Augustus implicitly denied genetic and dynastic principles. Although neither Tiberius nor Drusus shared direct blood links with Augustus, their claims of legitimacy as potential heirs rested on kinship with their stepfather – not, as Agrippa could boast, the recommendations of experience, merit and proven ability.

Shrewd as she was, Livia probably recognized that Augustus had acted, even *in extremis*, with sound political common sense. In the company of members of his family, officers of state and Rome's leading senators, he had behaved in a manner that appeared to take account not of the former but the latter. It was an appropriate course for the man who had claimed only four years previously to have restored the Republic. Ruffling family feathers, the failing Augustus remembered constitutional propriety. He entrusted public affairs to his fellow consul, his private concerns to his leading general, discounting nepotism.

Perhaps he understood that Marcellus was still too young and green, and his hand was forced. Perhaps Marcellus already showed the first signs of succumbing to the same illness as Augustus. Perhaps Cassius Dio's assessment is correct and Augustus was swayed by the claims of old affection, Agrippa 'a man whom Augustus loved for his virtue and not through any necessity'.[8] Possibly his behaviour was simply cynical, dictated by that instinct for self-preservation Edward Gibbon later attributed to Rome's rulers. 'The masters of the Roman world surrounded their throne with darkness, concealed their irresistible strength, and humbly professed themselves the accountable ministers of the senate, whose supreme decrees they dictated and obeyed.'[9] Whatever Augustus's motives, it seems to be the case that he felt himself close to death. In that eventuality, the reasons for his decision would be of little consequence.

For Augustus, succession to the principate became so significant an issue on account of his failure to produce a male heir. For Livia, as much as her maternal ambition, it was Augustus's repeated serious illnesses which kept the issue at the forefront of her mind. While Marcellus lived, Livia cannot have entertained Tiberius as a serious contender for the principate. Marcellus had married Julia: his children would be Augustus's grandchildren, great-grandchildren by adoption of Julius Caesar. Even in the event that Marcellus and Julia themselves failed to produce a male heir, Marcellus could look sideways to the progeny of his two sisters, the Claudia Marcellas, to supply a candidate. Through their grandmother Octavia, any such children would share Augustus and Marcellus's link with Caesar, as great-great-great-nephews and nieces of the deified dictator. In 23 BC Livia found herself in a dilemma. Augustus's death threatened her own hold on power, but in the event of Agrippa's succession and Tiberius's marriage to Vipsania, probably advanced Tiberius's cause; Augustus's recovery, and Marcellus's restoration to centre stage, guaranteed Livia's position for the remainder of Augustus's life but marginalized Tiberius. If, as Velleius afterwards suggested, Livia already at this point clung to dreams of being both wife and mother to the *princeps*, her position was impossible. Unless, of course, Augustus recovered and Marcellus died. As we know, this is precisely the course fate directed for Rome. But no one in attendance at Augustus's death bed, awaiting Musa's miracle, could have known that.

Recovery when it came kept Augustus busy but did little to grant Livia equanimity. Augustus offered to read his will aloud in the Senate House. He meant to demonstrate conclusively that he had not named in it any successor, an undertaking contrary to the Republican principles he so recently professed to have restored. In the event, probably for superstitious reasons, the Senate declined Augustus's offer. At the same time, the convalescent *princeps* struggled to defuse the rivalry of the brothers-in-law Agrippa and Marcellus. Recent family ties notwithstanding, there was evidently no love lost between the two men whose claims to Augustus's legacy were so divergent. Marcella, unlike her mother Octavia in the previous generation, does not appear to have acted with any success as intermediary between husband and brother. Suetonius states that Agrippa resented Augustus's preferment of Marcellus; Cassius Dio reverses the offence, attributing to Marcellus resentment at Augustus's public acknowledgement of the older man's claims in handing him his signet ring.[10] Augustus's chosen resolution despatched Agrippa to Syria – one of the territories within that unwieldy province he himself had received from the Senate in 27 BC – leaving Marcellus free to bask in the *princeps*'s adulation in Rome. By this means, Agrippa, as Augustus's legate, received the singular distinction of proconsular imperium, while Marcellus enjoyed the temporary solace of his rival's absence and, as Dio explains, 'no occasion for friction or quarrelling might arise through their being in one another's company'.[11] Neither Livia's position nor that of Tiberius was materially affected either by the two men's squabbles or Augustus's solution.

It is impossible to conjecture Livia's thoughts at this juncture. She cannot fail to have been relieved by Augustus's recovery, while her hopes for Tiberius stood neither challenged nor changed. Undoubtedly, she must have derived limited pleasure from Marcellus's prominence in Rome, balanced though this was by Tiberius's burgeoning senatorial career. For every advantage granted to Marcellus, Tiberius received a corresponding lesser grant. The year of Marcellus's aedileship saw Tiberius elected to the quaestorship. The meticulous even-handedness of Augustus's behaviour towards his son-in-law and stepson served merely to reinforce the discrepancy in their relative positions. Tiberius's pride may have revolted at the indignity as greatly as his mother's. In the short term, there could be no way out.

The short term, as it happened, proved to be of short duration indeed. Before autumn turned to winter, Marcellus had died at Baiae. Irresponsive to Musa's cold comforts, he probably fell victim to the same nameless fever by which Augustus was laid low. A devastated Octavia put on the mourning weeds she would wear until her death, incapacitated by sorrow and disappointment and, as Seneca tells us, envenomed against Livia above all other mothers. At sixteen, Julia became a widow for the first time. Augustus found himself without a son-in-law or the immediate prospect of heirs of his blood, and temporarily lacking any nominated successor from within his family. Of the young men who remained in that large household on the Palatine, only two shared Marcellus's political neutrality, related neither to Mark Antony nor Cleopatra: Tiberius and Drusus.

Augustus probably ordered public mourning for Marcellus. It served as a preliminary to the first of the really grand 'imperial' funerals the *princeps* exploited for propaganda purposes, a model for the sepulchral spectaculars by which he later commemorated Agrippa, Octavia and Drusus. Despite the undistinguished status of the Octavii, the funeral included a parade of ancestor masks, bolstered no doubt by the young man's distant connection with Julius Caesar. Augustus himself delivered an emotional oration. Servius recorded that a phrase from that oration was afterwards used by Virgil, laureate of Augustan Rome, to describe Dido falling in love with Aeneas in the *Aeneid*.[12] The publication of Augustus's family eulogies would afterwards become a feature of Rome's public life, and many enjoyed extensive circulation. Marcellus became the first member of Augustus's family to be buried in the *princeps's* new mausoleum, erected in 28 BC to the north of the Campus Martius between the Via Flaminia and the Tiber.

Wretched though she may have been, there is a suggestion that Octavia was not reduced by grief to utter helplessness. From the depths of her sorrow, she mustered the energy to smother at birth the incipient hopes Marcellus's death may have inspired in Livia. Her thoughts turned to her stepson Iullus Antonius, that son of Mark Antony and the much vilified Fulvia who would afterwards serve as consul and proconsul of Asia. As both Livia and Octavia were quick to realize, for Augustus the most pressing consequence of Marcellus's death was the need for a new husband for Julia. Augustus was forty, by Roman standards no longer young. Twice in the last three years ill health had brought him to the brink of death. Realistically he could not hope now to live to witness the majority of any grandson Julia bore him. But there was still time for him to put in place a son-in-law who would serve as a loyal and trustworthy regent during that grandchild's minority. The question was, who?

Were Livia's thoughts of Tiberius? It would be surprising if, at this point, the answer to that question were negative. In 25 BC common sense must have guided Livia's concession of Marcellus's prior claim to Julia's hand. Now death had voided that claim. Since Marcellus was Octavia's only son and Augustus himself had given birth only to Julia, Augustus's family could supply no alternative to Tiberius. For his part, Tiberius had already embarked on that senatorial career which would eventually equip him for supreme office, while his attendance on Augustus in Spain in 26 BC, alongside Marcellus, had provided him with an introduction to Rome's legions. Tiberius possessed distinguished Republican ancestry shared by none of Augustus's family. He was also Julia's near contemporary.

But Livia appears not to have counted on her sister-in-law. If Plutarch is to be believed, Octavia's intervention ran directly and deliberately counter to Livia's plans. To thwart Livia, Octavia was prepared to sacrifice the happiness of one of her four daughters. That she succeeded is in part testament to her continuing influence over Augustus and the esteem and affection with which the *princeps* regarded his sister – 'quite a wonder of a woman', as Plutarch described her. It is also undoubtedly the case that Octavia's scheme, whatever its motivation, had the recommendation of political expedience.

Julia's second husband was neither a member of Augustus's family nor of Julia's own generation. He was Marcus Agrippa. 'Since Marcellus died very soon after his marriage and it was not easy for Caesar to select from among his other friends a son-in-law whom he could trust, Octavia proposed that Agrippa should take Caesar's daughter to wife, and put away her own,' Plutarch writes.[13] Agrippa returned from Syria in the mourning months after Marcellus's death and divorced his wife Marcella, Octavia's daughter. The following year, 21 BC, he married his dead brother-in-law's widow and became the son-in-law of his oldest friend. With hindsight it appears the obvious corollary to that symbolic surrender of his signet ring made by Augustus two years earlier at a moment of fear for his life. Marcella, the first of many women of the imperial family to find herself reduced to the status of pawn in Augustus's political matchmaking, was married to her stepbrother, the still unmarried Iullus Antonius.

Again, the sources do not comment on Livia's response, indicating that at this point her reaction was not considered noteworthy, itself grounds for refuting any claim of unseemly ambition, but she may have felt herself for once outnumbered in Augustus's household. A solution the sources attribute at least in part to Octavia was the means of further exalting Augustus's right-hand man at Tiberius's expense. Furthermore, it has been suggested that the plan found an eager second in that other friend of Augustus's childhood, Maecenas. Dio tells us that Maecenas offered Augustus hard-hitting advice concerning Agrippa: 'You have made him so powerful that he must either become your son-in-law, or be killed.'[14] The second option, as Maecenas surely realized, was neither desirable nor viable. Agrippa was recalled to Rome. Octavia, Maecenas and Agrippa presented a united front. Agrippa married Julia and, his authority enhanced by his august bride, applied himself to the task of quashing disaffection in the capital. Augustus took the opportunity of leaving Rome for a second tour of the provinces. This time his destination was the east. Livia almost certainly accompanied him. Behind them, Augustus left disturbances and discontent as a result of his earlier curtailment of the cult of Isis and his renunciation, in 23 BC, of the consulship which he had held consecutively for the last nine years. Livia abandoned for the moment hopes of any public statement of Tiberius's preferment on Augustus's part. She left behind her the knowledge of her outwitting and the perpetrators of that adroit manoeuvre, as well as accusations – if such there were – of her malign role in Marcellus's death. In truth, she would be able to put behind her neither ambition nor popular suspicion.

CHAPTER 20

Three cities of Judaea

In her late sixties, Livia received a bequest that included three cities of Judaea. The donor was a Judaean princess called Salome, not John the Baptist's vengeful nemesis, but the sister of Herod the Great. Salome died around AD 10, six years after her brother. From Herod himself, that notorious pro-Roman client king reputedly responsible for the Massacre of the Innocents of St Matthew's Gospel, Livia had already received five million silver drachmae; on her death, Salome added the cities of Iamneia, Phasaelis and Archelais.[1] The extent of the princess's generosity can be judged from the fact that, in AD 4, Salome was considered a major beneficiary of Herod's will on the strength of her inheritance of the income of Phasaelis, north of Jericho, an area rich in date palms.[2] Livia's bequest represented a tripling of that of the King to his sister, including as it did two further cities of the eastern Mediterranean kingdom on the site of modern-day Palestine, together with estates and a balsam plantation. It was a grand tribute to a friendship of long standing.

The most likely explanation for the origin of Livia's friendship with Salome of Judaea is a meeting that took place in the spring of 20 BC.[3] Augustus and Livia were in Syria, then a large province briefly under Agrippa's recent legateship. The journey was part of a three-year eastern tour that kept them absent from Rome until 19 BC. They had spent the winter on the island of Samos in the north Aegean before travelling to Asia Minor. Strabo lists the Judaeans as one of the seven tribes of Syria.[4] Apprised of Augustus's arrival, Herod and his sister travelled across country. In inspiration, their journey was an act of homage. Herod owed his throne

Livia, 'most eminent of Roman women in birth, in sincerity and in beauty'. Large numbers of portrait busts of Livia have survived, including this well-known image from the beginning of Augustus's principate, complete with nodus hairstyle.

Unique in its record of service to the Roman Republic, Livia's family included legendary female role models for the young Livia Drusilla. Among them was the virtuous matron Claudia Quinta, who in 204BC single-handedly pulled ashore a grounded ship containing a statue of the goddess Cybele, the 'Great Mother' an episode later depicted by artists Garofalo (above) and Mantegna (below).

As she was? Livia's iconography, stubborn in its resistance to any visible ageing process, depicted an idealized vision of Roman beauty which survived throughout Livia's long life and beyond. The long, straight nose, rosebud lips and rounded cheeks are characteristic.

Augustus's personal propaganda was as heroic as his achievements. As in Livia's official portraiture, depictions of Augustus – including the Prima Porta statue (above) – beguiled the viewer with an idealization of Roman good looks. A sardonyx cameo from the first century (below right) briefly reverses the pecking order of Livia's marriage, making her, not the smaller deified Augustus, the dominant figure.

Romans, make your choice. Octavian's eventual victory over Mark Antony was as much ideological as military. Octavian partly defeated his former colleague by demonizing the latter's mistress, Cleopatra, who became a byword for all that was licentious, extravagant and 'foreign' – as in this painting of 1866 by Alexis van Hamme. Livia, by contrast, embraced simplicity and restraint (below).

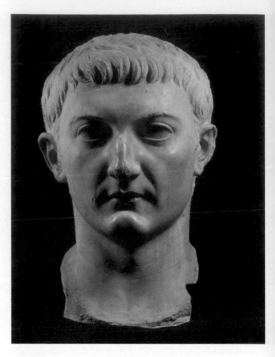

Portraits of Livia's sons by her first marriage, Tiberius (above left) and Drusus (above right), resemble those of their mother: eyes, nose, mouth and facial shape are all closely assimilated. By contrast, this bust of Tiberius's father-in-law and Augustus's righthand man Agrippa (left), betrays none of the patrician disdain of the Claudii.

The naturalistic wall painting of Livia's summer dining room in her villa at Prima Porta (above) is among the great achievements of early-imperial Roman art.

Early commentators on the first years of Tiberius's reign repeatedly indicated Livia's proximity to the centre of power – made manifest in a cameo triple portrait of Tiberius, Livia and a personification of Rome (below right), and the magnificent Great Cameo of France (below left), in which it is Livia who is seated alongside the central figure of Tiberius.

Long before Robert Graves's *I, Claudius* sealed Livia's vilification in the eyes of posterity, neoclassical artists chose to portray Rome's first empress as a heroic and virtuous figure. Here Ingres (above) and Jean-Baptiste Joseph Wicar (below) depict the same scene: Octavia fainting as Virgil reads aloud verses referring to her dead son Marcellus from Book 6 of the *Aeneid*. Livia looks on. Ingres's Livia is a concerned but dignified figure.

to assiduous long-term courting of Rome's leaders; he was neither Jewish nor a member of the Hasmonean dynasty who were Judaea's rightful rulers. An ally of Mark Antony, in 30 BC he successfully transferred his allegiance to Octavian. Evidently he secured the approbation of his new protector. On the occasion of Augustus and Herod's meeting in Syria in 20 BC, Cassius Dio reports that Augustus 'transferred to Herod the tetrarchy of one Zenodorus', whom Strabo clearly regarded as little better than a robber baron.[5] That 'tetrarchy' – literally, the fourth part of a country or province – included the territory of Ituraea, like Judaea Jewish in religion, which ran south from the Lebanon/Anti-Lebanon valley as far as Jordan. This handsome gift no doubt oiled the wheels of friendship. Herod remained loyal to Rome and Salome conceived a lasting affection for Livia. Thirty years later that affection bore splendid fruit.

Livia's whereabouts as spring turned to summer are not recorded. On 12 May 20 BC, we presume, she awaited – at first with anxiety, afterwards with pride – Augustus's return from the Parthian frontier. The *princeps* would not be alone: he was accompanied by Tiberius. Stepfather and stepson had taken joint action in the latest development in Rome's ongoing struggle against Parthia's eastern empire. Augustus demanded the return of Roman standards lost by Crassus and Mark Antony. Tiberius led troops against Armenia Major, where a Parthian protectorate had been established under the nominal rule of Artaxes. Even before Tiberius reached the Armenian border, pro-Roman forces within the country revolted against Artaxes and killed the puppet king While Augustus accepted the return of Roman standards, Tiberius crowned Rome's newest client king, Tigranes.[6] Cassius Dio adopts a sardonic tone in describing the double victory: 'Augustus received the standards and the prisoners as though he had defeated the Parthians in a campaign; he took great pride in the settlement, and declared that he had won without striking a blow what had earlier been lost in battle . . . Tiberius achieved nothing that was worthy of the scale of his preparations, since the Armenians killed Artaxes before the Roman expedition could arrive. Still, he put on a lordly air, especially after sacrifices had been offered up to commemorate the event, as though he had accomplished something by martial prowess.'[7]

Dio's disdain notwithstanding, Livia doubtless derived significant pleasure from the achievements of her husband and elder son acting in concord. It is reasonable to assume that Tiberius's part, but for the intervention of fate, would once have been played by Marcellus, as Livia must have known. Although Agrippa's marriage to Julia could no longer be denied, Tiberius, Livia may have surmised, had shown himself in Armenia Major a worthy successor to his stepfather. Happily, the Roman people inclined to the opinion of the *princeps* and his wife rather than that of Cassius Dio: Augustus was afterwards honoured with a triumphal arch. Characteristically, Velleius Paterculus laments the paucity of Tiberius's recompense: he received the insignia of a praetor, an office he was yet to attain, while sacrifices were offered to the gods.[8] 'For who can doubt that, when he had recovered Armenia, had placed over it a king upon whose head he had with his own hand set the mark of royalty, and had put in order the affairs of the east, he ought to have received an ovation?'[9] It was perhaps an assessment shared by Livia.

Livia and Augustus's eastern tour of the late 20s repeatedly overlapped with matters connected with Livia's family. The couple travelled to Sparta and twice over-wintered in Samos. Both city and island shared Claudian connections. The former was the site of Livia and Nero's final resting place on their eastward flight from Octavian in the dark years of the Civil War. It was from Sparta, driven there by the indifference of Mark Antony in Athens, that Livia had fled at night through a burning forest, charring her hair and dress, and endangering both her own life and that of the infant Tiberius. The reasons for her flight are lost. They probably had more to do with Nero than the Spartans. Twenty years later, Augustus rewarded the Peloponnesian city with a territorial grant, the Ionian island of Cythera. To commemorate Sparta's previous hospitality, he attended a formal banquet.[10] If Livia ever doubted the scale of the reversal of her fortunes effected by her marriage to Octavian in 38 BC, this return to Sparta under wholly altered conditions must have proved to her its magnitude. Perhaps too it offered pause for thought at that 'whimsicality of fate' which brought her back as the wife of the very man from whom previously she had fled.

The impression of fortunes reversed was surely reinforced by Livia's visits to Samos. Twice on their eastern tour, Livia and Augustus enjoyed lengthy sojourns on the grape-growing island. During each visit, sources suggest, Livia asked Augustus to grant freedom to the islanders. On the first occasion, the *princeps* refused his wife's request; his refusal survives in the letter which, unusually, he wrote to the Samians, explaining his decision. In the same letter he outlines the vigour of Livia's efforts on their behalf.[11] Perhaps Livia redoubled those efforts the following winter. Augustus yielded to entreaty and granted Samos freedom in either 20 or 19 BC. It is reasonable to assume that Livia again provided the driving force. Its explanation must lie in a client–patron relationship between Samos and either Marcus's family or that of Marcus Livius Drusus. Inscriptions discovered on the island honour Livia's parents, while statues of Livia found in the island's large sanctuary of the goddess Hera, the Heraion, bear her family name 'Drusilla', seldom used by Livia following her marriage to Octavian-Augustus.[12] The incident is illuminating. It highlights Livia's influence and tenacity, and her willingness to request from Augustus favours for third parties, as well as her continuing loyalty to her immediate Claudian heritage. Although it demonstrates that Augustus's compliance was far from certain, it indicates an approach to real power on Livia's part. On Samos, as at Sparta, Livia must have been struck by the nature and potential of her position since Augustus's settlement of 27 BC. Thanks to her husband's respect for her good judgement, the once fugitive daughter of Marcus Livius Drusus Claudianus found it in her power to win freedom for the island clients of her proscribed father.

The 'freedom' of the assembly of twelve cities known as the Ionian League was of a different variety. The cities were granted by Rome the right to mint their own coinage. At some point during Livia and Augustus's eastern tour, the maritime city of Teos, near Izmir in modern-day Turkey, issued coins commemorating the imperial couple. One such, probably Livia's numismatic debut, minted between 21 and 19 BC, makes explicit reference to her divine status.[13]

It was a significant moment not only in Livia's life but in the history of Rome's imperial family. Deification was not an aspect of everyday political life in Rome. Although religion infiltrated the institutions of state, Republican constitutional mechanisms had sought to curtail the degree of power which could be vested in a single individual. By this means the Republic denied specific statesmen the ability to reach a position of excessive lionization. Rome's gods, though frequently 'human' in behaviour and appearance, were not the embodiment either of deceased or living leaders. That was an eastern tendency, mistrusted by Rome, a characteristic of Hellenistic monarchy, with its associations of despotism and excess. Cleopatra, as we have seen, enjoyed divine status in Egypt, associated particularly with the Nile goddess Isis. In Rome, Julius Caesar had become a god. But despite graffiti slogans hailing him as such in his lifetime, Caesar, whom Republican Romans feared precisely on account of his inclinations towards eastern-style monarchy, had had to die to achieve immortal status. Not yet forty, Livia was very much alive. She was also, unlike Caesar, an unelected member of Rome's ruling class, a woman, without official position or constitutional status.

Livia's official deification remained sixty years away, effected posthumously during the reign of her grandson Claudius. The process which may have begun on a coin minted in distant Teos, issued at the time of Livia and Augustus's visit to Rome's eastern provinces, gathered momentum throughout Livia's lifetime. As in every aspect of her life, however, Livia is unlikely to have been declared a goddess had Augustus not already become a god. The phenomenon of Augustus's deification – discounting the award to Julius Caesar, an essentially unRoman occurrence – began in provincial centres. It arose out of the native and Hellenistic customs of the eastern empire and provided a template for the relationship between ruler and subject as traditionally understood in those areas.[14] Deification was the ultimate trump card of eastern kings, the untouchable social apex of a hierarchical society. Typically, the ruler cults of the east embraced a king's female relatives, and so it would prove with Augustus and Livia.[15] Where Augustus led, Livia was able to follow. She lent strength to her cause through her association at home with carefully chosen Roman cults and, abroad, through such 'god-like' actions as bestowing freedom on an island or a gift of territory to a city.

The ten times married Herod did not have a talent for family harmony. Almost alone among his relatives, Salome remained constantly loyal to her difficult brother. Only once did she oppose Herod's will – in the matter of her marriage. Such was the strength of her feeling on that occasion that Salome appealed to Livia, requesting that her Roman counterpart intercede for her with her brother. Livia demurred. She exercised circumspection in cases where interference in the internal politics of a client kingdom would be inferred at Rome, aware of the imperatives of Roman politics even where the interests of her friends were concerned. Rightly, she surmised that Salome was not a simple victim of thwarted romance, even if the Judaean princess herself did not realize as much.

A man called Syllaeus professed love for Salome. He was the senior minister or vizier of Obodas, ruler of the neighbouring Arab kingdom of Nabatea. Herod suspected Syllaeus of plotting to murder Obodas in order to become king of Nabatea himself. Syllaeus understood that any such action on his part would give rise to unease on the part of the Romans. Marriage to Salome was not a contract of love: in uniting Syllaeus and Herod as brothers-in-law, it promised to bind Nabatea to Judaea, the former sharing by association the latter's high standing at Rome. Happy that the weak King Obodas continue to occupy the neighbouring throne, Herod quashed the romance without apparently issuing any veto to Salome. Instead he insisted that, in order to marry Salome, Syllaeus convert to Judaism. That this condition was impossible, he recognized: the Nabatean Arabs would not countenance a Jewish king. Syllaeus declined Herod's condition. Lacking an alternative recourse, Salome appealed to Livia.[16]

Livia's advice was to follow her brother's wishes. We do not know how closely she was acquainted with the circumstances of Salome's 'romance' or the extent to which Syllaeus's cunning was public knowledge. But we know that the policy Livia advocated for Salome was one she had followed herself, however unwillingly, in the matter of Tiberius's marriage. It is impossible that Livia drew pleasure from either of Julia's marriages. Perhaps, in the case of Julia's marriage to Agrippa, Livia went so far as to express her objections to Augustus. Her protests unavailing, she recognized the inadvisability of further complaint. Her role became one of waiting and trusting. It was the counsel she shared with Salome. That Salome accepted Livia's advice in the long term – despite what we read of the vigour of her initial objections to Alexas, Herod's alternative choice of spouse for his sister[17] – is proved by the munificence of her testamentary bequest: no fewer than three cities of the kingdom of Judaea.

We cannot be certain of Livia's motives in requesting from Augustus freedom for the islanders of Samos. Nor do we know if the *princeps*'s beneficence towards the city of Sparta arose at Livia's prompting or simply by way of tribute to her. Family connections provided Livia with powerful incentives for desiring both events. Claudian clients were scattered across the ancient world. Her changing fortunes facilitated Livia's vigilance and assistance towards those clients. Her role as Augustus's wife brought her material gains like Salome's bequest and presumably further clients of her own. As Augustus grew in power, Livia – freed from guardianship of her financial affairs as long ago as 35 BC – also won an empire.

CHAPTER 21

'The man set apart by such an alliance would be enormously elevated'

In northwest Libya, on the Mediterranean coast, survive the ruins of the ancient city of Leptis Magna. Once a Phoenician settlement, Leptis Magna became one of the principal cities of the Roman province of Africa. It grew rich through trade, fat with the profits of slavery, gold and ivory. Its buildings and their embellishments reflect that wealth. In the Old Forum, in the oldest part of the city, archaeologists have discovered portraits and inscriptions relating to Rome's imperial family in the early years of the first century. Among them is the only surviving portrait identified with certainty as Vipsania Agrippina.[1] Carved from pale marble, broken at the tip of the nose, it shows a pleasant-looking woman of sombre expression, her heavy-set features closely assimilated to those of her father's portrait corpus.

Since the sources are silent concerning Livia's regard for her first daughter-in-law, we may infer a relationship that was at best affectionate, at worst tolerant. As we have seen in Seneca's account of Octavia's hatred for Livia, such silence did not survive even covert antipathy. Yet however cordial the feelings between Tiberius's mother and his wife, Livia could not delude herself that Tiberius had made an important match. Vipsania's invisibility in the portraiture of Augustus's regime – surviving in a single isolated image in a city remote from Rome on the coast of North Africa – provides an accurate measure of her significance. The absence of portraits depicting Tiberius and his first wife – unless such images were destroyed following the couple's divorce –

demonstrates the finality of their exclusion from Augustus's dynastic schemes.

Tiberius's marriage to Vipsania, after an engagement of thirteen years, finally took place in 19 BC, the year Livia and Augustus returned from the eastern provinces. Augustus had regained his strength; he had reorganized the client kingdoms of Syria and Asia Minor; he had been received as a living god in territories where local ruler cults imbued kings with divinity. For her part, Livia had erased the ignominy of the past, her helter-skelter dash towards Greece in Nero's train, fleeing the forces of the Triumvirs; she too had enjoyed intimations of divinity; she had savoured Augustus's presence away from the crowded intimacy of the Palatine, where Octavia, Agrippa and Maecenas all exercised sway over the *princeps*. Augustus marked his homecoming, Cassius Dio tells us, by investing Tiberius with the rank of an ex-praetor and allowing Drusus, like Tiberius before him, 'to stand for various offices five years earlier than was the practice'.[2] Drusus was elected to the quaestorship for the following year and Tiberius married his child bride, the fourteen-year-old Vipsania. It was, in its way, a year of celebrations for Livia.

The extent to which we attribute to Livia at this point joyousness or otherwise – in the face of the blanket silence of the ancient commentators – depends on a broader conjecture about Livia's plans for her sons. If we assume that Livia interpreted Julia's marriage to Agrippa as representing an end to Tiberius's eligibility for the succession, we might postulate a chilly satisfaction in Tiberius allying himself with the man who, after Augustus, was Rome's leading citizen. It is also possible that by way of distraction Livia took pleasure in the promise of Drusus's senatorial career. She may have chosen to overlook the five-year dispensation Drusus shared with Tiberius, and its memories of a greater award once granted to Marcellus. More than either of these responses, it seems likely that Livia's thoughts focused on Julia.

Julia's marriage to Agrippa had proceeded without Augustus and his wife, the second time the *princeps* had been absent from the wedding of his only daughter. Within a year, in 20 BC, the nineteen-year-old bride gave birth to the couple's first child. In accordance with Augustus's hopes, it was a boy. The first of three sons, he was named Gaius Caesar, an unambiguous statement of his grandfather's aspirations for him. The year of Augustus's return to Rome, Gaius was joined in the nursery by a sister, Julia, known to history as Julia the Younger.

It was, at the very least, a shadow on the face of the sun for Livia. While Julia remained childless, Tiberius as Agrippa's son-in-law could hope to occupy the second stage of Augustus's succession plans. This was the hierarchy Livia had inferred during Marcellus's pre-eminence, Tiberius riding the symbolic left-hand trace-horse. With the birth of Gaius, Tiberius's best hope became that of regent for the son of his step-sister following Agrippa's death. In the eventuality of long life on the parts of Agrippa or Augustus, Tiberius would forfeit even that role. The sources tell us nothing of Livia's response to the news.

Had she given up hope? A sour-tasting vignette suggests not. In the aftermath of victory at Actium, Octavian despatched two men to visit Cleopatra 'and instructed them carefully what they should say and do'.[3] Cassius Dio identifies the men as 'Gaius Proculeius, a knight, and Epaphroditus, a freedman'.[4] Granted an audience with the vanquished Egyptian queen, the men seized Cleopatra and 'removed from her any means of ending her life', before transferring her, a prisoner, to the monument in which she set about the task of embalming Mark Antony's body. Although, as we know, Cleopatra subsequently outwitted her gaolers to achieve romantic immortality at the fangs of an asp, Octavian was pleased by their diligence. Clearly knight and Triumvir had a relationship of some trust. In his account of 'the misfortunes of Augustus', Pliny records momentary 'desperation' on Augustus's part, 'which caused him even to beg Proculeius to put him to death, when he was hard-pressed by the enemy in a naval engagement'.[5] Proculeius's non-cooperation in this instance contrasts with his service towards Cleopatra. Dio reports that Augustus afterwards held him 'in the highest honour'.[6]

In 21 BC that honour did not suffice to persuade Augustus to marry his only daughter to Proculeius – as Tacitus's Tiberius would later remind the ambitious equestrian Sejanus, when the latter aspired to the hand of his niece Livilla. 'Augustus, you say, considered marrying his daughter to a knight. But he foresaw that the man set apart by such an alliance would be enormously elevated; and is it surprising, therefore, that those he had in mind were men like Gaius Proculeius, noted for their retiring abstention from public affairs?'[7]

Proculeius's champion, it has been suggested, was Livia.[8] The reasons ascribed to her are cynical in the extreme. Proculeius did not enjoy good health. In pursuit of relief from his sufferings, he unwittingly brought about his own demise. The gruesome circumstances are recounted in Pliny's discussion of the properties of gypsum. 'There is one remarkable fact connected with this substance: Gaius Proculeius, an intimate friend of the Emperor Augustus, suffering from violent pains in the stomach, swallowed gypsum, and so put an end to his existence.'[9] If she knew of Proculeius's affliction, Livia can have had only one motive: by involving Julia in a marriage certain to be of short duration, to win time for Tiberius, at that point still unmarried. Livia may have been encouraged in her bid by the relationship of trust and friendship obtaining between Augustus and Proculeius and the latter's 'safe' reputation for lack of political ambition. But it is surprising that she should propose for Julia a husband of equestrian rank when she herself drew little comfort from Vipsania's token connection with the *equites*.

It was not, of course, a solution Augustus favoured – whether for reasons of his own or through the admonishments of Octavia or Maecenas, we shall never know. Livia's efforts, if such they were, did not succeed. Perhaps Tiberius's explanation to Sejanus is the likeliest answer. It is an unsettling anecdote, its origins probably with Livia's detractors. Instead, despite a considerable age gap, Augustus chose Agrippa for Julia, his motives overtly political. The decision made, Livia wisely concurred. When, subsequently, Augustus decided to adopt two of the sons born of the marriage, making them legally his sons as well as his grandsons, Livia seconded his wish.[10] Hers was a pragmatic response. It was also perhaps a case of *force majeure*.

We see in Livia's failure to marry Tiberius to Julia – if such a failure existed – a reminder of the proscribed nature of her influence. Throughout their marriage, Livia exercised power with Augustus's complicity. At this point, it would appear, Augustus extended the same tolerance to his sister Octavia. He was in the habit of actively seeking advice from Maecenas and Agrippa, the latter by his marriage enfolded in the very bosom of power. He also trusted his own counsel. The demonized Livia of Tacitus's account, whom modern readers inherit via Robert Graves, is a figure who has stepped outside the bounds of female passivity to indulge, like Sallust's Sempronia, 'many crimes of masculine daring' and grasp the reins of fate. In truth, Livia's abilities were heavily circumscribed. Her daring may have been, in Roman terms, 'masculine'; her opportunities mostly were not. If, as seems likely, her wishes concerning Julia's second marriage differed from those of Augustus, it was Augustus's wishes which prevailed. It is impossible that Livia should not have understood this or that she sought to protest against it. She would not – as we have seen Agrippina later try – urge the claims of her case on the strength of her own status. The precepts of a Republican education rooted power firmly in Roman manhood. In 21 BC, under Augustus's essentially conservative principate, that truism continued to hold good for the most 'powerful' woman in Rome.

There is no reason to suspect that Tiberius's future role occupied Livia's thoughts at this stage to the exclusion of other matters. If she indulged in ambitious fantasies as we assume – acknowledging that such assumptions are highly speculative – she did so at least in part in order to perpetuate beyond Augustus's death the position she currently enjoyed. The experience of touring the eastern provinces had revealed to Livia the full implications of her place as wife of the *princeps*, following Augustus's settlement of 27 BC. That settlement continued to be refined, each fresh revision and award concentrating greater power in Augustus's hands. Traditionally patrician matrons had channelled their ambition through their sons. They did so in pursuit of an access to power otherwise denied them by Rome's constitution and practices. But Livia already enjoyed that privileged access. Despite her frustration at the marriages of Julia and Tiberius, she may have experienced a sense on returning to Rome that she could afford to enjoy the moment, as well as planning for the future in the form of Tiberius's career. If Livia chose this point to devise the engagement of her younger son Drusus, she acted astutely and with an apparent determination not to be wrongfooted for a second time as she had been over Tiberius's marriage.

Three years after Livia and Augustus's return to Rome, Drusus married Antonia Minor. The younger of Octavia's daughters by Mark Antony, Antonia was Drusus's near contemporary. The stepcousins already knew one another well, brought up in the same large, child-filled household. Their union smartly side-stepped the possibility of discord between Livia and Octavia. It offered the further recommendation to Livia that any children of the marriage would combine her own blood with that of Augustus, centring Drusus and his children on the *princeps*'s dynastic radar.

It was probably, as Livia may have acknowledged to herself, too little too late. In 17 BC Julia gave birth to a second son, Lucius Caesar, and, as Dio tells us, 'Augustus immediately adopted him together with his brother Gaius.' On this occasion – in contrast to his public evasiveness concerning Marcellus a decade earlier – Augustus made his intentions clear. 'He did not wait for them to attain manhood, but straightaway appointed them as his successors in authority to discourage plotters from conspiring against him.'[11] Adept at preserving appearances, Livia played the role of willing partner in Augustus's plans. At the very least, the boys' adoption, and their residence in that Palatine house so recently thronged with a previous generation of children, granted her the opportunity to influence and direct Rome's designated heirs. There is an element of the tawdry novelette in any suggestion that Livia may have been mindful of the fragility of infant life in Rome. The fecundity of Julia and Agrippa contrasted with her own barren marriage; Lucius would not be their last son.

Augustus's cult of moderation outlived his defeat of Cleopatra. Rome's first *princeps* was measured in his habits. He ate and drank sparingly. 'Habitually abstemious', as Suetonius describes him, he was frugal in his tastes. He 'preferred the food of the common people, especially the coarser sort of bread, whitebait, fresh hand-pressed cheese, and green figs of the second crop'.[12] By choice he drank only Raetian wine from vineyards in the Athesis valley, the only wine of the Graeco-Roman world matured in wooden barrels rather than earthenware vats.[13] Following Roman custom, Augustus diluted it with water; he also drank it in strictly controlled quantities. On all but special occasions he dressed simply, the purple stripe of his togas 'neither narrow nor broad'. He lived without ostentation in houses eclipsed by those of Rome's upper classes, retiring to the unaccustomed luxury of Maecenas's Roman mansion when ill and in need of a fillip. Although 'Palatine' provides the derivation of today's 'palace', there was little that was palatial about the House of Augustus on Rome's most sacred hill. While satisfactory for the purpose of accommodating Augustus, Livia and the changing cast of children they reared, it proved an inadequate hub of empire, too cramped for the expansive business of administration. After 28 BC official events and large meetings took place in the complex of the Temple of Apollo Augustus built adjoining the house, with its Greek and Latin libraries, and storage space for documents and records.[14] Augustus himself accomplished many of the tasks of empire in a small upstairs study, which Suetonius tells us 'he called "Syracuse" – perhaps because Archimedes of Syracuse had a similar one – or "my little workshop".[15]

In this overcrowded house, its facade decorated as we have seen with bay-leaf wreaths and a civic crown, Livia spent her days in a manner considered insufficiently interesting to merit the attention of Rome's chroniclers. Undoubtedly much of her time was hijacked by the unwieldy business of household management. Despite not rivalling the palaces of later emperors or the more splendid townhouses of the Roman aristocracy, Livia and Augustus's house was thronged with slaves. It fulfilled in addition a busy public role, notably in the morning *salutatio*, which Augustus continued to honour as any private senator.

At the end of the Republic, Cicero's wealthy wife Terentia had supervised the couple's houses as she oversaw her extensive property – with as little interference from her husband or guardian as possible. Although Cicero was interested in domestic affairs to the extent of translating into Latin Xenophon's *Oeconomicus*, Terentia apparently tolerated no meddling on her husband's part. She relied on the assistance of her steward, the freedman Philotimus, and a subsidiary staff of slaves each entrusted with more or less specialized roles.[16]

The evidence of the mausoleum dedicated to Livia's slaves suggests a pattern of household management affiliated to that of Terentia a generation earlier.[17] As in aristocratic houses of the late Republic – Marcus and Alfidia's included – a *dispensator* or steward oversaw the cumbersome arrangements. The *dispensator* was accountable to Livia. Beneath him were the household footsoldiers: cooking and cleaning slaves, including a catering officer, who may also have overseen the cellars, with their Pucine wine for Livia and Raetian vintages for Augustus, a store-room clerk and specialist bakers. Slaves attended to the day-to-day running of that woolworking in which both Livia and Augustus took pride. Livia's own involvement was almost certainly symbolic, spinners, weavers, fullers, patchers, menders and makers accomplishing the much-vaunted 'home' manufacture of the *princeps*'s clothes. There were secretarial staff, doorkeepers and footmen, waiting staff and specialist positions like that of *nomenclator*, the slave who reminded Livia and Augustus of the names of clients and petitioners at the morning *salutatio*. A number of Livia's slaves took care of that extensive toilette for which Ovid claimed she scarcely had time: dressers, hairdressers, masseuses, perfume-makers, shoe-makers, launderers and wardobe slaves. All save the masseuses and the dressers were men. Three of Livia's dressers – Dorcas, Nice and Gemina – became freedwomen, a detail suggestive of a degree of intimacy between mistress and maid.[18] Surprisingly, given Livia's adherence to Augustus's code of restraint and the absence of jewellery from her surviving portraits, her permanent staff included a pearl-setter, *margaritarius*.

This was the busy Roman world of Livia's childhood writ large. The populous household of slaves ministered to every aspect of patrician life, from menial tasks to artisans' trades. Such was the ubiquity of slaves in late-Republican and imperial Rome that wall paintings survive in which amorous couples cavort in rooms where slaves are busy, subordinates apparently invisible to their masters. In at least one respect Livia was a generous mistress: she appears – at a higher than average rate – to have rewarded her slaves with their freedom. Augustus's benignity towards his slaves survives in a well-known anecdote in which he intervened to restrain the cruelty of a fellow slave-owner. A wine-slave belonging to the immensely rich Publius Vedius Pollio broke a valuable fluorspar goblet. In Augustus's presence, Vedius ordered the man to be thrown to the lampreys in his fish pond. The sentence was one of instant death. Lampreys are blood-sucking, eel-like creatures considered in Rome, as in medieval Europe, a culinary delicacy. 'The boy,' Dio records, 'fell on his knees before Augustus and implored his protection, and the emperor at first tried to persuade Pollio not to commit so appalling an action.'[19] When Pollio paid no heed, Augustus ordered instead that all his fluorspar goblets be collected and broken one by one. Pollio 'restrained himself and said nothing'. The slave escaped his sentence.

The location of the houses to which, following their marriages, Tiberius took Vipsania and Drusus Antonia has not survived. Although both Livia's sons would spend much of the next decade absent from Rome, since their wives did not accompany them for the whole of their campaigning, they must have maintained establishments in the capital. Like Nero's house and that of Livia and Augustus, these may have been on the Palatine; at the time of his second marriage, Tiberius is recorded as living in a conspicuous house on the Carinae, on the southwest side of the neighbouring Esquiline Hill, also a fashionable residential district.[20] Livia's sons remained close to her in the early years of their marriage, geographically close to Augustus and the centre of Roman administration, which imperceptibly shifted uphill from the Senate House and the Forum. For the moment, unlike their mother, Tiberius and Drusus existed on the margins of Augustus's power. The marriage of the former is attested by a single sculpted portrait. It was found in a ruined city of North Africa and postdates not only the death of Vipsania in AD 20, but that of Augustus, would-be architect of the fate of both husband and wife.

CHAPTER 22

'Outstandingly virtuous'

'The wife of Caesar is so outstandingly virtuous that antiquity cannot outstrip our era in praising chastity,' wrote the poet Ovid to his wife. 'By having the beauty of Venus and the character of Juno [she] has alone been found worthy of a god's bed.'[1]

Livia was approaching her seventies. Banished to the Black Sea in modern-day Romania for transgressions which remain a riddle, Ovid fastened his hopes of recall on the ageing wife of the *princeps*. The fulsome praise of a desperate man – and a poet to boot – need not be interpreted literally. But Ovid's blandishments fasten on characteristics Livia had taken pains to annexe for herself: virtue, chastity, the attributes of goddesses. His encomium is testament to the efficacy of a policy of public rectitude which Livia had cultivated through four decades. More than a blameless private life or the carefully considered benefactions of temple restorations, it was a policy she embraced physically – from the Republican understatement of the *nodus* coiffure, copied from Octavia, to her discreet and simple jewellery and an item of dress she wore until her death: the *stola* or long tunic, woven mantle of virtuous Roman womanhood.

There was no mistaking the potency of glamorous dress for the elegist Propertius. Tormented by love for his mistress Cynthia, he wrote;

> 'You want to know why I keep on writing these poems of love . . .
> All she has to do is enter a room, a dazzle
> of flowing silk from Cos, and a book is born.[2]

That flowing silk was more than a fabric. 'What good is it, prom-
enading that way, your coiffure amazing, your couture an impressive
shimmer of Coan silk, as your skirts swing this way and that?'[3] Coan
silk was a luxury import, spun on the island from caterpillar filaments
in the manner of its Chinese counterpart, iridescent and nearly trans-
parent: a statement of exoticism, allure and availability.[4] It was the
antithesis of the effect Livia cultivated in dress, cloaking the female sexuality Rome feared in the formlessness of the *stola*. In the service of those
denied an active role in politics, signs and symbols become politicized.
Augustus had policies and power; Livia exploited the symbolism of
costume, her appearance her manifesto.

The streets of Rome were bright with women's fashion. In more care-
free mood prior to his banishment, Ovid had advised in the *Ars Ama
toria* on the colours women ought to affect in dress – not the costly
purple of the Tyrian murex, tortured from the secretions of a sea snail,
but shades inspired by nature: the blue of the sky, the green of the sea,
saffron, amethyst, Paphian myrtle, pale rose, Thracian crane, acorn and
almond.[5] Ovid's advice aimed at helping women to win and hold on to
a man. It was the opposite of Livia's aim. Livia's choice of dress had
nothing to do with flattering her appearance or commanding the attention of the opposite sex. It was not concerned with colour or fabric. Her
preferred dress was as much a uniform as that ceremonial garb adopted
by Julius Caesar at the zenith of his power. Like Caesar's wreath of golden
laurel leaves and scarlet leather boots inherited from the kings of Alba
Longa, the *stola* was an example of visual language. Livia employed it
in Augustus's service. Inevitably she too benefited from its virtuous connotations.

In the *Res Gestae*, the account of his life's work which Augustus requested
at his death be engraved on bronze tablets outside his mausoleum, the
princeps made much of a programme of legislation which on balance
had been neither successful nor popular. 'By new laws passed on my
proposal I brought back into use many exemplary practices of our ancestors which were disappearing in our time, and in many ways I myself
transmitted exemplary practices to posterity for their imitation.'[6] These

laws and practices were concerned with nothing less than a moral revolution in Rome. As with Augustus's claim to have 'restored' the Republic, they appeared to nod towards a past golden age of greater virtue, in this case specifically in the domestic sphere.[7] The laws themselves were enacted in 18 BC the year of Livia's fortieth birthday, when she could be said to have attained by Roman standards the rank of 'matron'. Aside from Augustus's own 'exemplary practices', which he does not elaborate, the weight of embodying this keystone policy fell on the women of the *princeps*'s family. Foremost among them was Livia.

The legislative programme in question came to focus chiefly on women's fidelity and the birthrate. It took the form of two principal acts, the Lex Iulia de Adulteriis Coercendis and the Lex Iulia de Maritandis Ordinibus. The former addressed the sexual constancy of married women, criminalizing adultery for the first time in Roman history; the latter outlined a system of penalties and incentives aimed at encouraging larger families. Both were chiefly concerned with the upper classes, providers of Rome's administrators and leading soldiers, although they appeared to cast their nets more widely. The former prescribed harsh sentences for errant wives, who faced compulsory divorce, possible banishment and a ban on future remarriage; in practice their correspondents were less severely treated, their punishment secondary to that of their mistresses. The latter act was more evenhanded in its treatment of the sexes, recognizing that the declining birthrate arose in part from the reluctance of patrician bachelors to marry. Unsurprisingly, the legislation won Augustus few plaudits among those fellow members of the senatorial class who were its chief target. Livy had predicted as much. 'For now we have reached a point where our degeneracy is intolerable – and so are the measures by which alone it can be reformed.'[8] Augustus made few efforts to sugar the pill.

He faced an uphill task. He lived in an age of moral cynicism. The last years of the Republic and the early principate witnessed a literary flowering among a new young generation of poets. Their subject matter was adulterous love – that of Catullus for Lesbia, Tibullus for Delia, Propertius for Cynthia. They cared neither for marriage nor Augustus's heavyweight morality. 'Call no man happy,' Martial quipped, 'until his wife is dead – particularly if she is rich.'[9] Ovid observed that the man concerned with his wife's adultery was lacking in savoir faire, a bore without knowledge of the social conventions.[10] Augustus – his deathbed claim of transmitting 'exemplary practices' aside – did little to lead by example. In a society which, despite its louche posturing, offers few instances of serial philandery, Augustus established a reputation for affairs more roving than any poet, those liaisons with Tertullia, Terentilla, Rufilla and Salvia Titisenia to which Mark Antony once scornfully referred. 'Here's a copper coin for the criticism of elderly men with exalted morals,' Catullus tells Lesbia. It was not a jibe which could be made against Augustus without irony. Two years after proposing his legislation, Augustus left Rome for Gaul. Gossip attended his departure, as Cassius Dio reports. 'There were some who even suspected that he left on account of Terentia, the wife of Maecenas, and that since Rome was full of rumours concerning their relationship, he had planned to join her abroad beyond the reach of such gossip. It was said that his desire for her was so great that he had once made her take part in a contest of beauty against Livia.'[11] The senators present at the debate on the *princeps*'s new laws did not spare their leading citizen.

'The senators . . . hinted mockingly at [Augustus's] own relations with a large number of women,' Dio tells us; they demanded a response from him. 'When he was forced to reply, he retorted, "You yourselves should guide and command your wives as you see fit; that is what I do with mine."'[12] With Augustus himself unable to fight his corner, Livia was called into the ring. Even by this relatively early stage in the principate, however, she had clearly acquired a reputation for independence and strength of character. Augustus's listeners balked at this image of the *princeps* overruling his strongminded patrician wife. 'They pressed Augustus still more eagerly, for they desired to learn what guidance he professed to give to Livia. Augustus uttered a few words very unwillingly about women's dress, their other ornaments, their going out and their modesty.'[13] In a single sentence, Livia's clothes became a matter of high politics, as powerfully charged as Cynthia's filmy skirts of swinging Coan silk, as central to her public persona as the beauty of Venus or the character of Juno.

The garment Livia chose as the visible means of broadcasting her obedience and fidelity to Augustus was as we have seen, the *stola*, recorded in literature as early as the second century BC but hitherto rare in daily life. A long sleeveless shift of heavy fabric, it hung vertically from the shoulders, perhaps fastened with ribbons, and reached as far as the ground, even hiding the feet. It covered a woman's undergarments and effectively shrouded her figure. Over it was worn a large mantle or *palla*, which further cloaked the figure in folds of impenetrable fabric. The *stola* was an exercise in concealment, a barrier between the wearer and the viewer, a halt to lasciviousness. That Livia's beauty outstripped that of Terentia despite the carapace of the *stola* is a powerful testament. Its one attraction appears to have been its colour – deep red or occasionally purple.[14] It was probably made of fine, dense wool. The suggestion that it might have been woven at home enhanced its virtuous connotations, binding a woman's public appearance to that private domestic task of weaving by which we have seen Romans – and Augustus in particular – set such store.

The colour of the *stola* recalled the official costume of Rome's magistrates, the *toga purpurea*. Championed by Livia in her role of exemplary Roman matron in response to Augustus's moral legislation, the *stola* would acquire similarly distinguished associations. As Livia's *nodus* hairstyle came to represent a patriotic choice – renouncing eastern elaboration of the sort previously worn by Cleopatra – so too the unlovely, shapeless tunic hung heavy with symbolism. It became a uniform – as Ovid called it, 'the badge of chastity'.[15] As if to emphasize the point, wearing the *stola* was forbidden to prostitutes – who, like men, were obliged to wear the toga – or to adulteresses, who were forced to adopt the prostitute's toga following conviction. This is the explanation for Cicero's taunt of Mark Antony in the *Second Philippic*: 'He took you out of the prostitute's trade, gave you a *stola* as it were, and settled you down in steady wedlock.'[16] Mothers of three or more children were rewarded by the Lex Iulia de Maritandis Ordinibus with the right to wear a special form of *stola*.[17]

For a critical period at the beginning of Rome's principate, dress acquired more than ordinary significance. A cumbersome woollen tunic became a reward for state-ordained good behaviour. The policy required the cooperation of Livia and the women of Augustus's family, whose high public profile – further heightened by these means – invested something essentially unglamorous with an aura of desirability. A symbiotic relationship developed quickly. The more the *stola* came to be associated with public reward of feminine virtue, the greater by association the appearance of virtue of its most prominent wearers. As it happened, Livia's private life was beyond reproach – even Tacitus, in his obituary notice of Livia, was forced to concede that 'her private life was of traditional strictness'.[18] Its lustre shone more brightly thanks to the positive implications of her clothes, held up to scrutiny in the Senate House by Augustus.

In that section of his *Natural History* devoted to pearls, Pliny cites two famous contemporary pearl-wearers. Although we know that Livia employed a pearl-setter in her household, Pliny's examples leave us in no doubt that the author disapproved of women's fondness for the jewels. He refers to Cleopatra and Lollia Paulina. Lollia Paulina was the granddaughter of an immensely rich provincial governor, who was afterwards threatened with prosecution for extortion; she was briefly married to Caligula.

> I once saw Lollia Paulina, the wife of the Emperor [Caligula]. It was not at any public festival or solemn ceremonial, but only an ordinary wedding entertainment. She was covered with emeralds and pearls, which shone in alternate layers upon her head, in her hair, in her ears, at her neck, in her bracelets and on her fingers. Their value amounted in all to forty million sesterces ... treasures which had descended to her from her grandfather, obtained by the spoliation of the provinces. Such are the fruits of plunder and extortion![19]

Velleius Paterculus describes Lollia Paulina's grandfather as 'a man who was ever more eager for money than for honest action'. In her excessive ostentation, it was clear, the granddaughter had inherited the sins of the grandfather.[20] Emeralds and pearls provided a symbol of that dishonesty and sinfulness.

Disapproval of luxury had a long history in Rome. It was among those factors which had enabled Octavian to demonize Mark Antony and Cleopatra, as we have seen. At moments of crisis in the Republic's history, virtuous women surrendered their jewellery to the State to be liquidated for funds. By extension, a delight in jewellery was unpatriotic, opposed to the collectivism at the heart of Republican mythology, even dangerous. 'There is nothing that a woman willl not permit herself to do, nothing that she deems shameful, when she encircles her neck with green emeralds, and fastens huge pearls to her elongated ears,' Juvenal spat.[21] Pliny's misgivings about pearls extended to all precious stones, a mistrust of an impulse that combined vanity with extravagance. Augustus took up the theme on that day in 18 BC when the Senate queried the extent of his authority over Livia. Reluctantly, he uttered 'a few words . . . about women's dress, their other ornaments', consigning Livia not only to the *stola* but to a habit of abstemiousness in terms of jewellery, a harsh proscription for one of the richest women in the world.

Imported precious stones flooded the Roman market, a trade that Pliny estimated as worth a hundred million sesterces a year.[22] Wealthy Roman matrons indulged in competitive displays of their jewellery. But Livia, loyal to Augustus's dictat, remained hors de combat. There is no evidence of jewellery in the portraiture that survives from Livia's lifetime. Even this apparently insignificant aspect of personal adornment, exploited by Augustus for political ends, had acquired a symbolic dimension. Simply dressed in a *stola* and *palla*, without precious stones or the gold jewellery which had earlier been limited by the Oppian Law, Livia continued to distance herself from the golden image of Cleopatra placed by Caesar in the Temple of Venus Genetrix. Once items of clothing had served as the virtuous woman's gifts to the gods, as Hecuba chooses a robe to present to Athene in the *Iliad*.[23] Livia's splendid robes were sacrificed to Augustus and an impetus for moral renewal which she, but not he, strove to embody.

Suetonius records that the Emperor Caligula referred to Livia as '*Ulixes stolatus*', 'Ulysses in a *stola*'.[24] The modern translation of 'Ulysses in a petticoat' captures the scornful disaffection Suetonius tells us that Caligula felt towards members of his family: it fails to convey either the force or the significance of his mordant tag. That Livia's great-grandson, who had partly been brought up in her Palatine household, couples her name with that garment she adopted to serve legislation passed before his birth indicates how thoroughly Augustus's wife came to be associated with Ovid's 'badge of chastity'. It also partners Livia with a clever and ingenious epic hero, whose adventures testify as much to the faculties of the mind as the more commonplace heroic qualities of bravery, strength or physical stamina. Caligula's disdainful epithet includes a graceless compliment – perhaps, as has recently been suggested, a recognition of Livia's skill in concealing within the clothes of virtuous femininity a less passive, more incisive mind.[25] In 18 BC Livia had no choice but to embrace an outward manifestation of policy-making which Augustus placed at the centre of his domestic agenda. Its implied bondage, if Caligula is correct, may have provided her with unexpected freedoms.

CHAPTER 23

'Tiberius closer to Caesar'

Death came in triplicate as the century pursued its course. The years 12, 11 and 9 BC all witnessed significant losses in Augustus's family. Each affected Livia's own position or that of Tiberius. Only one caused Livia lasting sadness. In 9 BC, aged twenty-nine and at the height of his powers, her younger son Drusus died. His death had been preceded by that of Agrippa, in 12 BC, and his aunt Octavia the year after. In quick succession, Augustus lost his principal helpmate, an adored sister and an affable and popular stepson who gave every indication of corresponding closely to the Roman ideal. Livia found herself, nearly twenty years after marrying Augustus, at last uncontested in the role of senior matron or *materfamilias* of his household. For the second time, despite her youth, Julia confronted widowhood. In all but name, Tiberius became the second male of Augustus's once sprawling Palatine family. Three splendid funerals set the dead on their final journey. In Drusus's case, the parade of ancestor masks, including both Claudians and Julians, was particularly extensive; Seneca describes the formalities as more redolent of a triumph than a funeral. Augustus buried all three in his mausoleum on the Campus Martius, Octavia rejoining her beloved Marcellus after more than a decade.

Drusus's death following a riding accident in September 9 BC abruptly foreclosed a period of considerable happiness in Livia's life. In 16 BC Tiberius had attained the praetorship. He was prevented from fulfilling the duties of office by Augustus, who took him with him to Gaul to stamp out German raids in the province. There was credit not disgrace in Tiberius's enforced dereliction of duty – and satisfaction for Livia in his replacement in Rome by Drusus. At twenty-two Drusus was only months older than Marcellus had been at the time of his first magistracy.

The coupling of Livia's sons in office set the pattern for succeeding years. In 15 and 14 BC the brothers fought alongside each other, their task the subjugation of the bellicose strategic German provinces of Raetia and Vindelicia, north of Cisalpine Gaul. Their partnership, according to Velleius Paterculus, was Augustus's idea. 'In this work he gave Tiberius as a collaborator his own brother Drusus,' we read.

> The two brothers attacked the Raeti and Vindelici from different directions, and after storming many towns and strongholds, as well as engaging successfully in pitched battles, with more danger than real loss to the Roman army, though with much bloodshed on the part of the enemy, they thoroughly subdued these races, protected as they were by the nature of the country, difficult of access, strong in numbers, and fiercely warlike.[1]

It was a heroic undertaking, which secured the Alps for Rome; and one certain to have given pleasure to Livia. To the record of Claudian achievements listed by Suetonius, and the triumphant iconography of Marcus's *armaria*-lined atrium, both her sons would add military victories rewarded by ovations and the insignia of the triumph. On 1 January 13 BC, alongside his brother-in-law Publius Quinctilius Varus, husband of Vipsania's half-sister Vipsania Marcella, Tiberius became consul, Rome's highest constitutional office. Not yet thirty, he had achieved more than any Neronian Claudian for two centuries.[2] There was little reason to doubt that Drusus would match his brother's record. Velleius describes him unambiguously as 'a young man endowed with as many great qualities as men's nature is capable of receiving or application developing';[3] Valerius Maximus consigned him to history as 'the exceptional glory of the Claudius family and a rare paragon of his country'.[4]

Livia's happiness was more than maternal pride. In either 14 or 13 BC Vipsania gave birth to a son, another Drusus, known as Drusus the

Younger. In Livia's affections he joined Germanicus, the son of Drusus and Antonia born in 15 BC. Between them, Livia's grandsons combined blood of the Claudii with that of the Octavii, in a heritage that embraced Agrippa and, more doubtfully, Mark Antony, Antonia's father. Despite Augustus's adoption of Gaius and Lucius Caesar, it is impossible that Livia abstained from thoughts of the future. In the absence of any child arising from her own marriage, she must have exulted in this mingling of bloodlines in the third generation. Both Germanicus and Drusus possessed a genetic blueprint capable of recommendation to Augustus. The prominence of Julia's elder sons notwithstanding – Julia gave birth to a third son, whom Augustus did not at this stage adopt, after Agrippa's death in 12 BC – Livia's grandchildren were well placed for the future, especially in a regime which, as Livia must have been aware, had yet to win sanctions for the endorsement of any direct hereditary principle.

But the place of Germanicus and Drusus in their grandmother's hopes would shortly be eclipsed. In the spring of 12 BC, Cassius Dio tells us, 'portents were noticed in such numbers . . . as normally only occur when the greatest calamities threaten the state.'[5] Owls flew through the streets of Rome, a comet hovered in the night sky, and Romulus's sacred hut burnt down as the result of a distinctively Roman accident: crows dropped on to its roof 'flaming fragments' of meat snatched from a sacrificial altar. The calamity worthy of such dramatic heralds was the death of Marcus Agrippa. It occurred in Campania in southern Italy, brought about by unknown causes. Agrippa was en route for Rome from Pannonia, a journey cut short.

Augustus did not allow personal sadness to occlude the demands of politics. Pregnant with her fifth child, Julia was a widow again. There were no dynastic reasons for her to marry for a third time, but in his legislation of 18 BC Augustus had established a timescale for the prompt remarriage of widows. He did not choose to make an exception of Julia. After the birth of her baby – whom Augustus named Agrippa Postumus in honour of his father – he married his only daughter to his elder stepson Tiberius. Velleius, whose account is the most nearly contemporary of the surviving sources, offers no explanation for Augustus's action. His focus – presumably with an eye on future developments – is the benefit Tiberius obtained from Agrippa's misfortune. 'His death brought Tiberius closer to Caesar, since his daughter Julia, who had been the wife of Agrippa, now married Tiberius.'[6] Velleius mentions no part played by Livia in Tiberius's preferment nor any discussion between Augustus and his wife concerning the decision. Livia is notably absent from all the sources' accounts of Julia and Tiberius's marriage.

A tradition has grown up which ascribes Tiberius's success, third time lucky, to the absence of alternative suitors for the hand of the *princeps*'s daughter. The same tradition invariably implies a vigorous behind-the-scenes role for Livia, which we have seen is not supported by textual evidence. Dio describes Augustus's decision as being made 'with some reluctance'. He explains this reluctance not in terms of personal objections to Tiberius but on the grounds that 'his own grandsons were still boys' – a suggestion that Augustus had rather have chosen no one at all, regretting instead the infancy of Gaius and Lucius Caesar which demanded this intermediary stage in the succession.[7] At this point proof of disharmony between stepson and stepfather is lacking. In addition, as we have seen, Tiberius had established over the previous decade an exemplary record of service to Augustus and the state. This in itself constituted public eminence equal to that likely to be conveyed by marriage to Julia, as well as a powerful recommendation for his suit. If there are grounds for any theory of 'victory by default' on Tiberius's part, it is possible that, in the absence of any definite antipathy, Augustus did not find Tiberius's an easy nature – he lacked the amiable manner and apparently untroubled disposition of his brother Drusus. The only conclusion we can reach with complete certainty is that Livia's elder son was an obvious candidate for the vacancy even without the championing of his mother – the sources express surprise at the speed of the marriage and the strength of Augustus's determination, not the fact of its happening. They are less clear about the immediate implications of Tiberius's second marriage. This did not necessarily at this stage imply his elevation to the status of Augustus's heir, particularly given the earlier adoption of Gaius and Lucius Caesar, as both Tiberius and Livia would have been aware.

In the *Annals*, Sejanus tells Tiberius, 'I have heard that Augustus, when marrying his daughter, had not regarded even knights as beneath his consideration.'[8] Tiberius's response, as we have seen, is neither concurrence nor disagreement. His argument that marriage to the *princeps*'s daughter would unnaturally elevate the man chosen and throw him in the way of temptation probably reflects Augustus's thinking. In the interests of self-preservation and maintaining the claims of Gaius and Lucius Caesar, Augustus was safer selecting a son-in-law from within his own family who would not incline to usurping the principate for himself. Inevitably this circumscribed the pool of contenders.

Tiberius was the frontrunner. Octavia's stepson and son-in-law Iullus Antonius – the husband of Octavia's daughter Marcella Major– was stigmatized by his paternity and indeed would later die in unresolved circumstances that appear to confirm Augustus's wisdom in discounting him. In Velleius's account the victim of suicide, executed for treason in Dio's version and adultery in that of Tacitus, in all three narratives, ironically, Antonius is brought to his death by an adulterous involvement with Julia, which may have overlapped with the murky world of political conspiracy. That left Drusus, like Tiberius already married in 12 BC. Unlike Vipsania, however, Drusus's wife Antonia was not dynastically negligible. Any children of the couple were Octavii through Antonia's mother, their sons Augustus's great-nephews as well as his step-grandsons.

If Augustus acted unwillingly, his reluctance was nothing compared with that of Tiberius. Tiberius's marriage to Vipsania, after an engagement that spanned most of his formative years, proved notably happy. Already the parents of a son, another Drusus, in 11 BC the couple were expecting a second child. Without the intervention of Julia and Augustus, it is possible they would have enjoyed a long and happy marriage like Augustus's own. We do not hear of inconstancy on the part of either spouse. Certainly, Tiberius cherished neither affection nor illusions in relation to the woman who was at the same time uniquely his stepsister, mother-in-law and proposed second wife. Refusal, however, was clearly not an option. Augustus did not confuse affection with political exigency. In pursuit of his purposes he had persuaded Nero to divorce the pregnant Livia and Agrippa the pregnant Caecilia Attica; now he insisted Tiberius act in like manner. Suetonius describes Julia's third marriage as 'hurried'. Tiberius, he tells us, 'took this very ill. He loved Vipsania and strongly disapproved of Julia, realizing, like everyone else, that she had felt an adulterous passion for him while still married to his father-in-law Agrippa.'[9]

Julia's wayward nature, lacking in allure for Tiberius who had known her since childhood, was perhaps among Augustus's reasons for hastening her remarriage. Eyebrows do not appear to have been raised at this conjunction of step-siblings. Augustus had acted with customary ruthlessness, his focus – traditional in the Roman marriage sphere – political rather than personal, apparently heedless of the likely outcome of a marriage inspired by policy without emotional warmth. Suetonius's brief account closes with a chilling intimation of the *princeps*'s thoroughness. 'Tiberius continued to regret the divorce so heartily that when, one day, he accidentally caught sight of Vipsania and followed her with tears in his eyes and intense unhappiness written on his face, precautions were taken against his ever seeing her again.'[10]

What then of Livia? Those rumour-mongers whom Cassius Dio reports as attributing Marcellus's death to Livia's malign intervention had expressed as early as 23 BC the cupidity of Augustus's wife for her sons' advancement. On that occasion, the removal of Julia's husband had brought no obvious benefits either to Livia or to her sons. The consequence of Agrippa's death was different. If, as Dio would have us believe, Livia had coveted the prospect of a Claudian principate in 23 BC, how much more zealous must her desire have grown in the intervening decade, as the rich possibilities of princely office revealed themselves more fully.

But this is a one-sided argument. Did Livia let herself dare to hope in 23 BC, only to see those hopes summarily crushed? Did she then set aside such aspirations, confronting apparently insuperable odds, content instead that first Tiberius and afterwards Drusus ascend the ladder of Rome's magistracies, the *cursus honorum*? Both men had done so with undoubted success, Tiberius becoming consul at the precocious age of twenty-eight. The question is whether Livia's make-up inclined more to the Roman habit of pragmatism or to Ulysses-like planning and plotting. If we take into account Caligula's verdict, the evidence is stacked equally.

It would be surprising, whatever her previous thoughts, if Livia did not conceive definite ambitions for Tiberius in 11 BC. First Marcellus, then Agrippa had married Augustus's only daughter. In each case, to his intimates if not to Romans at large, Augustus had made it clear that the marriage involved a symbolic aspect, signifying the new role of Julia's husband as *princeps*-elect. Circumstances had changed by the time of Tiberius's marriage, notably with the adoption of Gaius and Lucius Caesar, whom Augustus had openly declared his successors. But the boys were still children, Gaius the elder only eight at the time of his father's death. Given Augustus's precarious health, a strong likelihood of regency existed. That regency would fall to Tiberius. In the latter's case, marriage with Julia may not have held out for him the certainty of succession: but it promised to make Livia's son, if not *princeps*, at the least '*princeps*-tutor'.

Livia presumably exerted considerable force on Tiberius to accept Augustus's plans. At his accession to the principate in AD 14, Tiberius would refuse the appellation 'son of Julia' (as Livia was then known), offered by the Senate.[11] The tag was an acknowledgement of Livia's role in making Tiberius emperor. If, as the sources through their silence suggest, Augustus's decision to marry Tiberius to Julia did not arise at Livia's prompting, part of her contribution – recognized by the Senate – was perhaps compelling Tiberius's agreement to the plans of 12 BC. Against this argument is the question of the viability of Tiberius's refusal.

There are possible grounds for apologists to exonerate Livia from the charge of excessive ambition. The Claudii, we know, enjoyed an unrivalled history of service to the State. Part of Augustus's Roman revolution was his implicit transference of the concept of the State, Louis XIV-like, to his own person. For Livia, post 27 BC, the service of the State meant attentiveness to Augustus's wishes. She was, as Tacitus described her without intent to flatter, 'a compliant wife'.[12]

We can only speculate on Livia's response to Tiberius's resistance. It is doubtful that she was swayed by the sentimental argument of his love for Vipsania or the fact of Vipsania's pregnancy – she herself had divorced Nero while pregnant and even forsaken her sons in pursuit of her marriage. The foremost concern of aristocratic Roman mothers, of whom Livia can be seen as an archetype, was not the happiness of their sons but, as we have witnessed in the extreme example of Volumnia and Coriolanus, a son's adherence to his duty to Rome and his success in the magistracies of the state. In the consulship of 13 BC Tiberius had attained the pinnacle of senatorial achievement; he had also won both triumph and ovation. The principate offered one higher prize. It is certain that at this stage Augustus had little intention of extending the promise of that prize to Tiberius; equally certain seems the likelihood of Livia at last allowing herself the indulgence of hope.

There was one further argument Livia may have kept to herself. At best, Tiberius's engagement to Vipsania arose from the circumstances of the moment, the need of Augustus to flatter Agrippa or of Livia to win Agrippa's support for Tiberius in the face of Octavia's pre-eminence. With Agrippa's death that need no longer existed. The circumstances which bred Tiberius's first marriage had altered irretrievably. It is possible that Livia considered the marriage forefeit as a result. In this she would appear as much a statesman as Augustus.

In the autumn of 9 BC Livia accompanied Augustus to the ancient riverside city of Ticinum to receive Drusus's body. There she met Tiberius, who had travelled 'in wild haste, almost in a single breath', according to Valerius Maximus, across the Rhine and the Alps from Pannonia.[13] Slowly the sorrowful cortege returned to Rome, past burning pyres and crowds of onlookers. It was a gratifying if upsetting spectacle for a grieving mother.

Only once in Livia's life do we read of her succumbing to overwhelming emotion – on this, the occasion of Drusus's death. An execrable poem once ascribed to Ovid clumsily sought to offer her consolation. 'See how Fortune has raised you high, and commanded you to occupy a place of great honour; so, Livia, bear up that load. You draw our eyes and ears to you, we notice all your actions . . . Stay upright, rise above your woes, keep your spirit unbroken . . . Our search for models of virtue, certainly, will be better when you take on the role of first lady.'[14] The poem probably postdates Livia's lifetime. In 9 BC she sought consolation from a different source.

Livia consulted an Alexandrian philosopher, who Cassius Dio tells us was known to Augustus. In Seneca's account, he described himself as a confidant of both husband and wife. His name was Areius or Areus Diodymus and his advice has a decidedly modern ring to it. Areius,

Seneca records, explained to Livia her tendency to repress her feelings in public and the need to adopt a less guarded approach to Drusus's death within the safe confines of her inner circle of friends.[15] At the forefront of Livia's mind loomed the example of Octavia and her black-crêpe orgy of bereavement. At Areius's prompting she placed portraits of Drusus both in her private rooms and in public places; unlike Octavia, she encouraged her friends to talk about the dead man. Augustus shared her grief. Suetonius states that he 'felt so deep a love for Drusus that, as he admitted to the Senate on one occasion, he considered him no less his heir than were Julia's sons, whom he had adopted'.[16]

Impossible, then, that those writers should be correct who, as both Suetonius and Tacitus report, record Drusus's death as the result of poisoning ordered by Augustus . . .[17] Malign sources portray Drusus as a martyr to belated Republicanism, forcibly removed on suspicion of a retrograde wish to restore Rome's erstwhile status quo. Rumour takes no account of rank. Nor of probability or rationale. It is a lesson we must bear in mind in assessing Livia's life.

CHAPTER 24

'What more can I ask
of the immortal gods?'

Thirty-six crocodiles met their death in the Circus Flaminius in a public spectacle in 2 BC. The Circus, close to the Tiber, had been specially flooded for the occasion. Nearby in the same year a large artificial lake was dug. It too was flooded – to provide the setting for a re-enactment of a naval battle involving thirty ships and three thousand men; ships sank and men were killed. In the arena, Cassius Dio records, two hundred and sixty lions were slaughtered. Gladiatorial contests occupied the Saepta, also claiming their toll of fatalities. It was a year of celebration and festal Rome ran with blood.

The occasion was the long-awaited dedication of the Temple of Mars Ultor at the centre of the new Forum of Augustus. Augustus, however, was celebrating more than the completion of handsome building projects. On 5 February, the Senate conferred upon him the title 'Father of the Country'.[1] It was essentially a formality, but an important one nevertheless. 'Until then,' Dio reports, 'he had only been so addressed, without the title having been established by decree.'[2] Augustus delighted in his newest honour. 'With tears in his eyes,' according to Suetonius, he answered the assembly. 'Fathers of the Senate, I have at last achieved my highest ambition. What more can I ask of the immortal gods than that they may permit me to enjoy your approval until my dying day?'[3] As in the stories of gods and men which Augustus's life increasingly resembled, that slaking of highest ambition would be followed by a crash. Its fallout provided Rome with a spectacle more unexpected and involving than the slaughter of crocodiles or lions.

At its centre was a woman, Augustus's daughter Julia. Her behaviour shocked not only her father but popular opinion across Rome. Something of the magnitude of the scandal can be judged from Velleius's outraged account.

> In the city, in the very year in which Augustus ... had sated to repletion the minds and eyes of the Roman people with the magnificent spectacle of a gladiatorial show and a sham naval battle ... a calamity broke out in the emperor's own household which is shameful to narrate and dreadful to recall. For his daughter Julia, utterly regardless of her great father and her husband, left untried no disgraceful deed untainted with either extravagance or lust of which a woman could be guilty, either as the doer or as the object, and was in the habit of measuring the magnitude of her fortune only in the terms of licence to sin, setting up her own caprice as a law unto itself.[4]

Heedless of her father's moral legislation, Julia had begun her career of sexual liberation at an early age. In the year Augustus dedicated the temple he had vowed as long ago as Philippi, her misdemeanours caught up with her amid a whirlwind of publicity.

By the end of 2 BC Livia and Augustus, happy in their marriage, shared a sense of bereftness. The year that began so well found Augustus by its close 'father of the country' but alienated from his only child, whom he had banished to the volcanic island of Pandateria in the Tyrrhenian Sea. If the *princeps*'s latest honour encouraged Livia to consider herself by association 'mother of the country', she too would have acknowledged a bittersweet irony. Her marriage to Augustus, despite the promise of her two sons born to Nero, had proved barren. She had failed to win over to her own course of uncompromising moral rectitude that stepdaughter she had looked after from birth. Her younger son Drusus had died following a commonplace-seeming riding accident at the age of twenty-nine. Unexpected as those thunderbolts the Romans read as omens, four years before Julia's disgrace, in 6 BC, Livia's elder son Tiberius had abandoned Rome for voluntary exile on Rhodes. His course shocked and confused not only his mother and stepfather but the ordinary Roman in the street. Newly invested with tribunician power and proconsular authority, the highest honours in Augustus's gift previously shared only by Agrippa, Tiberius had left behind him his wife, his mother and his stepfather, after a petulant hunger strike and an inadequate explanation. Julia's adultery and Tiberius's 'insulting retreat' both joined Pliny's list of Augustus's 'misfortunes'.[5] Livia shared in those misfortunes. Neither the father of the country nor his wife ended the year able to take pleasure in their children or even to think of them with equanimity.

Julia's fall from grace came as a surprise to readers of poetry. Sometime after 16 BC Propertius had published his final elegies, including a poem in which a deceased woman, Cornelia, consoles her husband and children. Cornelia was the daughter of the same Scribonia whose brief, unhappy marriage to Octavian ended at Julia's birth. Propertius's Cornelia acknowledges her kinship with the *princeps*'s daughter. She also reveals Julia's status as a paragon of Roman virtues. 'My mother's tears and the city's grief exalt me, and my bones are protected by Caesar's moans. He laments that living I was worthy sister to his daughter, and we have seen a god's tears fall.'[6]

Julia was popular and admired in Rome. As disbelieving as Cornelia would have been had she lived, the people protested vigorously against her banishment, vocal in their demands for her return.[7] Augustus refused to relent. The daughter who had been acclaimed as the living Aphrodite on coins minted in the eastern empire had offended her father too gravely. Julia traduced that moral legislation which Livia made it her life's study to uphold. Her transgression stimulated prurience and condemnation in equal measure from Rome's (male) historians. We must decide for ourselves the likelihood of Augustus's daughter – a woman so proud of her birth, according to Macrobius, that she disdained Tiberius's Claudian descent[8] – offering herself nightly for sale on the rostra of the Forum in view of every passing Roman partygoer or insomniac. 'Turning from adultery to prostitution,' Seneca relates, 'she had stationed herself at the statue of Marsyas, seeking gratification of every kind in the arms of casual lovers.'[9] Augustus was initially as incredulous as the Roman crowd; learning more, Cassius Dio tells us, 'he was overcome by a passion so violent that he could not keep the matter to himself, but actually spoke of it to the Senate.'[10] It was Augustus's response which destroyed the reputation of the Julia of Propertius's elegy, not Julia's indiscretions. Historians have debated Livia's role in informing him of his daughter's caprices.

As with every incursion of Augustus's family into Rome's political arena, there were implications for Livia in Julia's inglorious downfall. We cannot know the nature or even the probability of Augustus's discussions of his political agenda with the women of his family, although we know from Suetonius that the *princeps* was in the habit of 'first [committing] to notebooks' statements to Livia which he considered 'important'.[11] Livia in turn, as we have seen, raised with Augustus subjects that particularly concerned her, like the freedom of Samos, and dedicated herself to upholding Augustan policy through the only means available to her – involvement with Rome's religious life and the promulgation of a carefully calibrated visual imagery. During her lifetime Octavia had behaved similarly, sharing Livia's reputation for honour and virtue. The best-known of her daughters, Drusus's widow Antonia, would act in like fashion.

A clear presumption existed that where the women of Augustus's generation led, their juniors would follow. As the *princeps*'s only daughter, Julia was the most prominent of that second generation of Augustan women. She had been strictly brought up in her father's household by Augustus and Livia as the inheritor of their moral outlook, and afterwards serially married to those exemplary Romans whom her father designated in turn his preferred successors. In Augustus's denunciation of his only daughter to the Senate was a powerful exposure of the fraudulence of public appearances and an admission of a very personal failure.

More worrying for Augustus, Julia's contempt for the laws by which he had sought to reform Rome's character mirrored the feelings of many upper-class men and women. In 2 BC Julia revealed herself as the worm in the bud, symptom of the degree to which Augustus's most cherished policies had failed to win either hearts or minds in a loose-living city. It was an act of unforgivable disloyalty. Augustus could not be unaware that it contrasted starkly with Livia's behaviour: Macrobius preserves instances of the *princeps* berating his daughter with her failure to meet the standards set by her stepmother, and her cheerful dismissal of Livia's chilly example. In the tussle between the two women – for Augustus's heart and for ideological dominance – Livia would emerge victorious. Two decades later, when Augustus's will was read, it was revealed that 'he had given orders that "should anything happen" to his daughter Julia', her body must be barred from his mausoleum.[12] To the surprise of modern readers, the same document adopted Livia as his daughter. The relative rewards of 'good' and 'bad' behaviour could not be more starkly expressed.

Julia's errant behaviour consisted at the very least of repeated adulterous liaisons over a lengthy period. Among her partners was that son of Mark Antony, Iullus Antonius, brought up in Octavia's household and known to Julia from childhood. He would later die as a consequence of his involvement with Julia, executed perhaps, perhaps committing suicide. Irrespective of her lovers' identities, Julia's misdemeanours posed a double challenge to Augustus. More than overruling her father on a political level, by declining to conform to the spirit of his legislation she challenged him symbolically. The 'father of the country' had failed to moderate the behaviour of his only daughter. This was a significant weakness in a society which, at least theoretically, ascribed control of women to men. That Augustus survived this onslaught is in part attributable to Livia, whose consistently exemplary personification of the traditional virtues of Roman wives and mothers, coupled with a blanket official silence concerning Julia in the aftermath of her banishment, granted Augustus the appearance of the upright father unfairly crossed by a wayward child. In time Augustus even made light of his tribulations. 'Among friends, he said that he had two darling daughters that gave him trouble, the Republic and Julia,' Macrobius relates.[13] Such sophisticated insouciance scarcely told the whole story. Suetonius records a bleaker outlook: 'he would sigh deeply and sometimes quote a line from the *Iliad*, "Ah, never to have married and childless to have died."'[14] Where Julia was concerned he spoke in earnest; he did not regret his marriage to Livia. But Livia could not undo Julia's transgressions or erase the stain of her exposure. Her only means of benefiting Augustus was adherence to the unspotted private life she had espoused in 38 BC, remaining the same 'model of virtue' she was hailed as in the 'Consolation to Livia'.

Such an explanation ignores the possibility – conjectural but plausible – that it was Livia who brought about Julia's downfall.

Although Tiberius's behaviour differed from that of his wife, Livia and Augustus must have shared a sense of exasperation through these troubled years. Each confronted the apparently senseless folly of an adult child and their own powerlessness in the face of wilful nihilism. In adopting Gaius and Lucius Caesar in 17 BC, Augustus had implicitly elevated Julia's status. He even offered her proof of her centrality to his plans in a coin issue of 13 BC, on which her portrait appears between those of Gaius and Lucius.[15] It was a unique example of official numismatic commemoration of a female member of his family by Augustus, a compliment he never extended to Livia. Daughter of one *princeps* and mother of his chosen successor, Julia had good reason for satisfaction with her lot. Yet she deliberately jeopardized her marriage and acted in a manner certain to offend her father's sensibilities.

Tiberius had twice held the consulship: in 7 BC, the year of his second term of office, he celebrated Rome's first triumph for twelve years; the following year Augustus granted him extraordinary powers. But he preferred to live as a private citizen in retirement on Rhodes, fruitlessly absorbed by passions for astrology and Greek philosophy, remote from the politicking of the Senate, distant from the provincial battlefields on which he had repeatedly demonstrated his worth to Augustus and Rome's legions. Pre-empting Julia's disgrace, Tiberius's behaviour arose perhaps from the unhappiness of his marriage, perhaps from his disaffection at the prominence accorded by Augustus to Julia's sons and the adulation lavished upon the two young boys by the Roman crowd. To Livia, the action of turning his back on the centre of power at a moment of preferment must have seemed an inexplicable perversity. It also imposed on his mother the unenviable task of brokering a reconciliation with her stubborn and unforgiving husband.

Augustus's policies, as we have seen, merged distinctions between Rome's public and private spheres, in particular in relation to his own family. On behalf of the Senate, Valerius Messalla addressed Augustus on 5 February: 'May good and auspicious fortune attend you and your [house], Caesar Augustus, for in praying for that we are praying for lasting good fortune for the state; the Senate and People of Rome hail you as Father of your Country.'[16] Livia, Octavia, Julia, Tiberius, Drusus and Marcellus all served at different moments as torchbearers of the Roman virtues extolled by Augustus's regime. As early as 17 BC, reviving the Saecular Games as the symbol of the dawn of a new age, Augustus had publicly offered prayers which included his family: 'For the sake of these things, as this ewe is sacrificially offered, may you be and become willingly propitious to the Roman people, the citizens, the College of the XV Viri, me, my house and family.' [17] In gestures large and small Augustus's family had consolidated that emergent public profile – from the installation of portraits of Livia and Octavia in the Temple of Venus Genetrix to the permanent monuments of the Forum of Augustus and the porticoes of the *princeps*'s wife and sister. Augustus dedicated the Theatre of Marcellus following his nephew's untimely death; on his death in 12 BC Agrippa bequeathed to the people of Rome the city's first public baths. In 7 BC Livia dedicated her shrine to Concordia. By celebrating in a single structure Augustus's triumph over civil discord and the harmony of her own marriage, Livia had declared in the centre of Rome her place in public life. Even if the truth were less anodyne, she did so in the very manner Augustus's politics outlined for his family, by emphasizing her non-political role of wife. The day she chose for the formal dedication was 11 June, the Matralia, Rome's nearest equivalent to Mother's Day, when married women and widows who had been married only once offered to the dawn goddess Mater Matuta cakes baked in earthenware pots.

These actions provided the context for Julia's promiscuity and Tiberius's abandonment of his marriage. Husband and wife each undermined Augustus's legislative programme, with its pink-tinted 'Republican' ideal of happy, faithful, fertile marriage. Both had behaved in a manner antithetical to Livia, whose public life was a blameless endorsement of her husband's official morality. In truth, Julia's behaviour – considered by Romans shocking in a woman – was not so far removed from Augustus's own, those repeated dalliances which Livia had learned to ignore. The scandal of her fall from grace exposed the hypocrisy at the heart of Augustan policy-making.

Pliny records the agonies suffered by Agrippa on account of Julia's infidelity during the course of their marriage. Suetonius, we know, attributed Tiberius's reluctance to marry Julia in part to her attempt to seduce him while married to his father-in-law. Julia's downfall in 2 BC represented the culmination of more than a decade's lawlessness. Inevitably questions arise about the timing of her disgrace and the part played by Livia in her expulsion from an increasingly depleted Palatine household.

Unusually, however, given the opportunity for historiographical mischief, the sources attribute no role to Livia in Julia's downfall, an omission which is almost certainly significant. This is not to deny the occasionally uncomfortable nature of the women's relationship. Rather, it suggests that any malevolent intent on Livia's part was sufficiently skilfully disguised to elude even Rome's busy gossips. Certainly it would appear that the women had little in common. In Macrobius's testament, recorded four centuries later, despite Livia having brought Julia up from earliest infancy, their relationship appeared to lack both warmth and mutual understanding. Yet, this scarcely amounts to malice or the motive for such drastic and potentially self-defeating action. Only a powerful wound to her own family pride and a mother's love for Tiberius could have forced Livia's hand, surely? Did she blame Julia for Tiberius's departure for Rhodes? If so, it was Julia who had jeopardized Tiberius's hopes of the principate at the very point when Augustus had endowed him with greatest power. In 11 BC Livia may have felt gratitude towards Julia as the means, through marriage, of Tiberius's preferment. Ten years on, she may have considered her stepdaughter dispensable.

Tacitus tells us that Julia 'looked down on [Tiberius] as an inferior'.[18] Is this how she drove him away? It has been suggested that Julia's point was not her own eminence as Augustus's daughter, but contempt for Tiberius's descent from the undistinguished Claudii Nerones, Nero's family.[19] She had recently taken a lover. He was also a Claudian, like Livia one of the Claudii Pulchri. His name was Appius Claudius and he was a great-nephew of that infamous Clodius who figured so prominently in the Rome of Livia's birth, a man unlikely to have featured among the ancestor masks of Marcus's atrium or the proud legends of Livia's childhood.

Livia eschewed acts of political rashness. If she facilitated Julia's removal from Augustus's household, her motives were Augustus's best interests, Tiberius's best interests ... or her own best interests. Throughout her marriage she had striven to uphold the strictures of Augustus's moral legislation. Her efforts had won her public plaudits and an unrivalled reputation. But they did not win her the respect of her ebullient stepdaughter, who scorned Augustus's attempts to encourage her to emulate Livia's behaviour, her dress, her friends. In the year in which Augustus, hailed as 'Father of the Country', at last became Rome's absolute ruler, his wife may have grown weary of this unbeliever in their midst.

From distant Rhodes Tiberius wrote what Suetonius describes as 'a stream of letters' to Augustus, requesting that the *princeps* forgive his daughter and reconsider her exile, 'though well aware that Julia deserved all she got'.[20] Over time he changed this position. Shortly after Tiberius's accession, Julia died. The cause of her death was malnutrition or starvation, sanctioned by Tiberius. This does not amount to the forgiveness he had once begged of Augustus. In the interval, Tiberius's heart hardened towards Julia. There is no justification in the sources to attribute that hardening to Livia's influence.

CHAPTER 25

'Try not to guess what lies in the future'

Virgil's reading of extracts from the *Aeneid* in front of Augustus and his family was noteworthy not on account of the poet's skill in recitation, described nevertheless as 'sweet and strangely seductive',[1] but for the effect of his work in progress on one of his listeners. In response to Marcellus's death, Virgil incorporated Augustus's nephew into his epic account of Rome's foundation. Discovered in the underworld, Marcellus is saluted in tones of heroic lamentation. 'Alas, poor youth! If only you could escape your harsh fate! Marcellus you shall be.' As the words were uttered, his mother Octavia fainted.

This anecdote – afterwards painted by the French neoclassicist Jean-Baptiste Joseph Wicar, with Livia catching her milk-white sister-in-law as she falls – demonstrates the place of poetry in Augustan court life. Augustus's dinner parties were frequently accompanied by a form of entertainment: storytellers, musicians, actors, even circus performers diverted the *princeps*'s guests.[2] As with Virgil, it is probable that Maecenas, artistic maestro of the regime, organized readings of the work of his other protégé, Horace. Livia, we know, left behind her no trace of bookishness. Given the likelihood of in-house readings of Horace's work, she did not need to read poetry to be familiar with the poet's thoughts. In the decade following Tiberius's retirement to Rhodes, Livia would have done well to abide by an injunction from the first book of Horace's *Odes*, published in 23 BC. 'Try not to guess what lies in the future, but as fortune deals days enter them into your life's book as windfalls, credit items, gratefully.'[3] The ten years of Tiberius's absence, commencing at the low point of 6 BC, would transform Livia's life. The reversal of her fortunes came about only in part through her own doing.

In 13 BC Augustus had returned to Rome cloaked for the last time in the garb of conquest. He had spent the previous three years, as Cassius Dio reports, 'dealing with the multitude of problems which faced him in the various provinces of Gaul, Germany and Spain'.[4] Aided by Tiberius and Drusus, he oversaw Roman gains across the central and eastern Alps. Today, a ruined monument survives above Monaco commemorating Augustus's defeat of no fewer than forty-eight Gaulish tribes.[5]

At home, on 4 July, the Senate voted Augustus an altogether more splendid monument. The Altar of Augustan Peace, 'Ara Pacis Augustae', remains one of the great sites of Rome. Excavated in 1937 as part of Mussolini's government's fascination with a lost imperial heyday, it stands today, reassembled and pristine, at the centre of a purpose-built museum designed by the American architect Richard Meier.

Originally conceived, Dio tells us, as an altar for the Senate House, it ultimately took the form of a freestanding monument erected in the northern part of the Campus Martius. It took three and a half years to complete, and was finished in time for dedication in 9 BC. It consists of a wide stone altar surrounded by high-walled precincts, lavishly decorated to the exterior with foliate panels, mythological vignettes and a processional portrait of the dramatis personae of the Augustan regime. It is approached by steps from the east and west sides. Its principal decorative features are the friezes on the long north and south sides, depicting members of Augustus's family in the company of priests, officials and senators at a formal religious ceremony, probably an idealization of the dedication of the altar itself.[6] The best-known of its panels shows the figure of Mother Earth, Tellus, surrounded by symbols of fertility. Recent scholarship has suggested an alternative identification of this female figure as the dynasty's adopted deity, Venus Genetrix.[7] This appealing explanation points to a deliberate attempt on the part of the altar's builders to assert in marble an association between Augustus's family – in their guise as descendants of the goddess, the Julians – with idealized, fertile Roman motherhood.[8] In addition, the recognizable presence of so many of Augustus's family on an altar of peace grants to each of the featured individuals an associative role as a protector of that peace which Augustus had brought to Rome. As if to underline the altar's family focus, the date of its dedication was set for Livia's forty-ninth or fiftieth birthday on 30 January. This subtle but significant compliment emphasizes Livia's association with peace above that of anyone other than Augustus. In years to come, Ovid indicates, sacrifices were also offered on Livia's birthday rather than the anniversary of the altar's foundation, a further example of her 'safe' infiltration of Roman public life through religion.[9]

As Tiberius's self-imposed exile gave way to the scandal of Julia's fall, did the Ara Pacis continue to delight Augustus and his wife? This grandiose gesture of family unity soon became as much a souvenir of a vanished moment as the stiffly posed groups of old wedding photographs. First Agrippa, then Drusus, died. Tiberius departed for Rhodes. Iullus Antonius died in uncertain circumstances that reflect little credit on either himself or his associates. Julia was banished to Pandateria, debarred from male company, even her intake of wine supervised. Of the inner circle of Augustus's family broadcast on the friezes of the Ara Pacis, only Augustus and Livia, Antonia Minor and Gaius and Lucius Caesar remained. The boys, of course, were legally Augustus's children, although Gaius is depicted between the figures of his parents Agrippa and Julia. Antonia had her own children with whom to busy herself, among them Germanicus – contender in adulthood for the most popular figure in the early empire, admired even by Tacitus – and the physically infirm Claudius, afterwards a surprisingly successful emperor.

Having lost one son, Livia was understandably vigilant in the service of the other. She appears to have made it her purpose to plead Tiberius's case to Augustus. She did so, however, less frequently than we might imagine and with a sense of fulfilling a duty she regretted. It was demanding work. Augustus was autocratic in his management of his family. The omens were dark for Tiberius the day Augustus explained his departure to the Senate as an act of desertion. Livia balanced knowledge of her husband with anxiety about her son's future. Suetonius describes her, not wholly appealingly, as being forced on one occasion to resort to 'wheedling' Augustus in Tiberius's name. Even in that instance she attained success of a strictly limited nature – persuading him to grant Tiberius 'the title of ambassador . . . as an official cloak for disfavour'.[10] She did so probably against her own better judgement: according to the sources, Tiberius could hardly persuade her to broach the subject with Augustus.

Suetonius's account of Livia's behaviour during Tiberius's absence confounds expectations. It forces us to pause in our assumption that, following Agrippa's death, Livia dedicated herself singlemindedly to securing the principate for her elder son. In Suetonius's account, Livia intervenes on Tiberius's behalf when the latter expressly requests her to and, finally, when she feels that Tiberius's life is at last in danger. Once a friend of Gaius Caesar's had offered to sail to Rhodes and 'fetch back the Exile's head' for Gaius – happily a souvenir the latter declined – both Tiberius and his mother were forced to recognize the very real precariousness of his position. No longer content with astrology and philosophy, 'Tiberius pleaded most urgently for a recall to Rome; Livia supported him with equal warmth.'[11] At that point, we read, 'Augustus at last gave way', although even then he left the final decision to Gaius. This cavalier dismissal shows the extent to which Augustus allowed his anger at Tiberius's 'desertion' to overwhelm any affection he felt towards Livia's son or gratitude for his previous sterling service to the State. Evidently Augustus did not at this stage share Velleius Paterculus's opinion of Tiberius: 'the most eminent of all Roman citizens save one . . . the greatest of generals, attended alike by fame and fortune; veritably the second luminary and the second head of the state.'[12] It was not an opinion to which, during the years of Tiberius's absence, Livia was able to win over her husband. As a result – worryingly for Livia? – those years witnessed Tiberius's certain eclipse as second luminary and second head of state; even fame and fortune temporarily bypassed 'the Exile'.

It is clear that in Suetonius's account the parameters of Livia's life are broader than simple maternal ambition for Tiberius. Suetonius is writing from Tiberius's point of view and does not concern himself with Livia's state of mind. Nevertheless, there is no indication that it is Tiberius who occupies Livia's every waking thought. Perhaps Livia was angry with her son, realizing that she had wasted in vain her 'express pleas' for him not to leave Rome in 6 BC. She may have considered that, in leaving Julia,

Tiberius had weakened his nearest tie to the principate, thereby undoing any progress either she or Tiberius himself had made towards that elusive goal. Perhaps she understood the extent to which Tiberius's recalcitrant nature demanded time and space to make its own decisions; she recognized the conditions necessary for Tiberius to relent. In the wake of Julia's downfall, it may be that Livia was concerned not with Tiberius at all, but with Augustus. The revelation of Julia's offences may temporarily have appeared to Livia sufficiently grave to unsettle the *princeps*'s regime. Was her concern with her own position? Did Augustus attribute Tiberius's stubborn determination to pursue his own course to that Claudian pride that came to him partly through his mother? Perhaps Augustus made clear to Livia at the point of Tiberius's departure that he considered the subject closed. A rumour reported by Dio that Tiberius travelled to Rhodes not of his own volition but because Augustus had exiled him on the grounds that he was plotting against the youthful Gaius and Lucius seems to indicate a degree of anger on Augustus's part which may have been slow to dissipate.[13]

Livia was temperate in her emotions. At her one recorded moment of emotional crisis – Drusus's death – she took advice on how best to address her unhappiness, followed that advice and, in doing so, won the admiration of onlookers and writers, among them Seneca. Tiberius's eccentric flit from Rome in the wake of Augustus's bestowal of tribunician power and proconsular authority did not rival the anguish of Drusus's death. Far from collapsing under the setback, Livia governed her response to the extent that the sources felt no need to record it. We do not know her private feelings or details of any communications with Tiberius. There are reasons to assume that Augustus was similarly excluded from her innermost thoughts.

Not for the first time, Livia embarked on a waiting game. Tiberius did not intend to remain on Rhodes indefinitely. Suetonius and Velleius agree that he had asked Augustus for leave of absence in order to rest. Although implausible, such an excuse on the part of a thirty-six-year-old man of proven stamina, crowned with every glory, appears to indicate an intention of returning at some future date. Livia could not predict the duration of Tiberius's absence, but she could be reasonably certain that, with Augustus's sanction, Tiberius would in time return to Rome.

In the meantime, sword-toting friends of Gaius notwithstanding, his position of retirement on an unassuming island in the eastern Mediterranean was possibly safer than Rome with its intrigues and power struggles. Four years after Tiberius's departure, his estranged wife Julia proved the severity of the penalties in store for those who offended Augustus's government. In the following year Augustus pointedly omitted to renew Tiberius's five-year grant of tribunician power on its expiry; instead, *imperium* passed to Tiberius's elder stepson Gaius. To those like Livia concerned with developments within Augustus's family, there was a clear inference that, despite his own precarious health, Augustus had decided to bypass the middle generation and entrust his power to those grandsons he had adopted as long ago as 17 BC. Wittingly or otherwise, Tiberius had scored an own goal.

How Livia responded to this knowledge, which Augustus may have discussed with her, is matter for conjecture. Her own uncertainty, based on daily familiarity with Rome's shifting temperature, contrasted with that of Tiberius. Tiberius, Dio tells us, shared his exile with an Alexandrian grammarian and expert astrologer called Thrasyllus. Together the two men consulted the stars in the hope of decoding the future. They drew comfort from what they saw. Thrasyllus may have been a charlatan; certainly he issued his predictions with confidence. Dio reports Tiberius as being 'very accurately informed as to what fate held in store both for himself and for Gaius and Lucius'.[14] If the vision afforded to Tiberius and Thrasyllus was indeed accurate, the knowledge promised greater succour to the former than to those children of his exiled wife. Within two years of Augustus relenting and Tiberius's return to Rome, both Gaius and Lucius were dead.

The wife of the Father of the Country needed to prove herself. Her elder son had discarded a career of notable distinction in order to stargaze and study on an island more Greek than Roman. He left Rome accompanied not by the trappings of glory but by a single senator, Lucilius Longus, a handful of equestrians and those lictors and *viators* appointed to attend him in his capacity as tribune of the plebs invested with *imperium*.[15] Livia did not see him off at Ostia. Her other son lay dead. The stepdaughter to whom she had been a mother throughout her life had offended not only specific moral legislation but sensibilities rooted deep in the Roman psyche, flaunting her depravity in Rome's public places, desecrating the rostra of the Forum in her pursuit of casual sex. So complete was Julia's rejection of Livia's example that she behaved in a manner which turned her stepmother's policy on its head. Where Livia avoided the appearance of any intrusion into Rome's male arena, Julia embraced it, selling sexual favours at the heart of the men-only zone of the Forum. As she embarked on a lifetime's exile, Julia took with her to joyless Pandateria Scribonia, her blood mother divorced by Augustus on the day of her birth. For Livia it was the final rebuff. She had failed to make Julia the daughter Augustus wanted; she had also failed to create any relationship of love and affection with her. In adversity, Julia chose the company of the mother she had never had. Only Drusus's widow Antonia upheld the standards Augustus had made central to his government; Antonia was not Livia's but Octavia's daughter. The Senate had acclaimed Augustus Father of the Country. Although Valerius Maximus compared the brotherly love between Tiberius and Drusus to that of Castor and Pollux[16] – a tribute either to Nero or to Livia – Livia's record as mother within her own house did not bear scrutiny or, on this count, invite a corresponding honour.

Happily, for all her avoidance of public display of the sort responsible for Julia's downfall, Livia had not, as we know, confined her activities to the domestic life of her own family. She had adopted a policy which, in one sense, placed her in the position of mother and father to all those she benefited. It was a policy earlier practised by wives of the pharaohs and, less contentiously, by wealthy upper-class women throughout Roman history.[17] Livia gave allowances to parents to enable them to bring up children who would otherwise have been exposed at birth; she also formed a habit of contributing to young girls' dowries. Both gifts created bonds between Livia and Romans outside Augustus's household, extending the bounds of her 'family' and the nature and degree of her influence. Dio explains that the parents and daughters in question were drawn from senatorial ranks, adding that, at her death, the Senate voted Livia the unusual honour of an arch, 'because she had reared the children of many, and had helped many to pay their daughters' dowries, in consequence of all which some were calling her Mother of her Country'.[18] Although Tiberius did not ratify the title, in death Livia had achieved parity with her husband. She had also, through her choice of recipients, helped strengthen ties between Augustus's government and the ruling class.

'I believe that far more wrongs are put right by kindness than by harshness,' Livia tells Augustus in Dio's *Roman History*. The context for what is presumably an imaginary conversation between husband and wife is a lengthy debate about the appropriate punishment of conspirators.[19] A testamentary epitaph discovered in Rhegium, in the far southeast of Italy, the site to which Julia was transferred from Pandateria in AD 4, attests to a freedwoman of Livia's among Julia's slaves.[20] Mother and stepdaughter enjoyed a relationship of limited concord. But Livia, it appears, continued to assist Julia after her banishment: the gift of slaves was one of the few she might offer the disgraced prisoner with impunity. In AD 4 Livia had reason for generosity. Ten years after his departure for Rome in 6 BC, Tiberius had beeen adopted by Augustus as his heir.

CHAPTER 26

'Perpetual security'

Velleius Paterculus was a worthy spin doctor. Twenty-seven years after Augustus adopted Tiberius, a capitulation chiefly notable for its bad grace, Velleius recorded the events of what he describes as 'a day of good omen . . . for all' – 27 June AD 4. First Marcellus had died, then Agrippa. Their deaths separated by two years, Lucius and Gaius were the latest victims of Augustus's succession jinx.

> Caesar Augustus did not long hesitate, for he had no need to search for one to choose as his successor but merely to choose the one who towered above the others. Accordingly . . . in the consulship of Aelius Catus and Gaius Sentius . . . he adopted him, seven hundred and fifty-four years after the founding of the city . . . The rejoicing of that day, the concourse of the citizens, their vows as they stretched their hands almost to the very heavens, and the hopes which they entertained for the perpetual security and the eternal existence of the Roman empire, I shall hardly be able to describe to the full . . .[1]

Tiberius's return to Rome – foreshadowed, Suetonius tells us, by the omen of an eagle which, never previously seen on Rhodes, landed on the roof of his house – ended in a sort of victory. It was almost certainly not accompanied by the public rejoicing of Velleius's account. The authorship of that victory was attributed by her detractors to Livia, 'that feminine bully' condemned for this very reason by Tacitus.[2] It would become, in the writing of Rome's history, an unforgivable incursion of maternal ambition into the male arena of power. The truth, of course, was less simple.

Augustus had repeatedly sought to choose candidates for the succession from within his own family. Marcellus was his nephew, Gaius and Lucius his grandsons. Each shared with Augustus Octavian and, in small measure, Julian blood. Tiberius lacked kinship with either family, his only connection with Augustus the fact of his mother's remarriage. In AD 4, unlike the occasion of his marriage to Livia in 39 BC, Augustus took no pleasure in Claudian distinction or patrician descent. Uniquely he explained his adoption of Tiberius as arising 'for reasons of state'. Ten years later, he reiterated this graceless acceptance of defeat in the wording of his will: 'Since an unkind fate has robbed me of my grandsons, I make Tiberius my heir.'[3] It was a loveless asseveration. A letter written by Augustus to Gaius three years previously demonstrates the pathos of the former's changed fortunes: 'My darling little donkey, whom Heaven knows I miss when you are away ... I beg the gods that I may spend however much time is left to me, with you safe and well, the country in a flourishing condition – and you and Lucius playing your part like true men and taking over guard duty from me.'[4] Ties of affection bound Augustus to Julia's sons. Unusually, he had overseen their upbringing himself, teaching them literature, how to swim and even to master handwriting modelled on his own. Presumably in time he had introduced them to the finer points of statecraft as he understood it. Although the sources offer no record of a complementary role for Livia in relation to Augustus's boy heirs, Suetonius preserves an instance of the doting love both Augustus and Livia were capable of feeling towards young children, in this case a great-grandchild. 'An extremely likeable boy', a child of Julia's younger daughter Agrippina and Drusus's elder son Germanicus, died in early childhood. 'Livia dedicated a statue of him, dressed as a cupid, to Capitoline Venus; Augustus kept a replica in his bedroom and used to kiss it fondly whenever he entered.'[5] Such a combination of whimsy and devotion was not one either spouse chose to express towards Tiberius. In Livia's case we may assume maternal affection; Augustus's emotions at this point are less certain, compounded for the most part of regret at the premature loss of Gaius and Lucius.

*

Augustus made it plain that his agreement to Tiberius's return was con-
ditional. Chief among the *princeps*'s conditions was his son-in-law's retirement from public life. On Rhodes, Tiberius had forfeited the special
powers which elevated him above other members of Augustus's family.
Now those powers belonged to Gaius Caesar, an arrangement entirely
satisfactory to Augustus. In the interval since Tiberius's departure, Gaius,
now twenty-two, and Lucius, nineteen, had attained the majority they
required to embark on a serious role in Roman power. Their maturity,
albeit unproven by experience and lacking Tiberius's distinction, rendered their erstwhile stepfather obsolete. Consolidating this obsoles-
cence was the fact that Augustus had dissolved Tiberius's marriage to
Julia. In the process, as Livia would have appreciated keenly, he had sev-
ered a link between himself and his remaining stepson.

Tiberius had acted judiciously in ascribing his wish to return to Rome
to a desire to see his family. After initial refusals, Augustus's agreement
condoned a continuing family role for the younger man. Shortly after
his arrival in the capital, Tiberius celebrated his son Drusus's formal
introduction to public life – swapping the *toga praetexta* for the *toga
virilis* and inscribing his name on the lists of citizens and those eligible
for military service in the Forum. Afterwards, he moved house. He left
behind the large house which had previously belonged first to Pompey
the Great, then to Mark Antony. In its stead he chose a more modest
dwelling place in a less conspicuous district – the Gardens of Maecenas,
also on the Esquiline Hill. The move represented a calculated step away
from Rome's administrative centre and political hub, which lay to the
northeast.[6] Suetonius states that, obedient to Augustus's proscriptions,
he lived there 'in strict retirement' for nearly three years.[7]

After her fears that his life had been in danger, Livia must have been
relieved to have Tiberius back in Rome. She was too shrewd to ignore
the pronounced changes in his position following the folly of his retirement. Acquainted with Augustus's implacability, she may have struggled
to reconcile herself to the certain diminution of his prospects – only
she can have known the vigour of her efforts on Tiberius's part over the
past seven years and the strength of Augustus's resistance. If she retained
any spark of hope, it lay in the increase in Tiberius's chances of renewed
good fortune which residence in Rome brought. Although it is unlikely

that any of those who had ranged themselves behind Gaius and Lucius, as the sources intimate, spared a thought for Livia and her shattered hopes, her position embraced a degree of pathos.

Possibly at this juncture Livia drew comfort from a sense of regrouping in the wake of recent disasters. Julia was banished, breaking Tiberius's strongest connection with the principate, but Livia remained married to Julia's sons' adoptive father and female head of the household in which the boys had been brought up, a role of some influence. She continued to enjoy an exemplary reputation. Since Julia's departure, she occupied uncontested the position of first lady of Augustus's court, which only the marriage of Gaius – engaged in time to Livia's granddaughter Livilla – or Lucius could now challenge. In addition, after Drusus's death, in opposition to Augustus's Lex Iulia de Maritandis Ordinibus, his widow Antonia had chosen not to remarry but to live instead with her mother-in-law Livia. Mourning the loss of one child and what she may have regarded as the lost prospects of another, Livia at least enjoyed the company of a sympathetic and attentive daughter-in-law, a woman whose character and reputation for virtue in some ways mirrored her own. Valerius Maximus expressed this manifestation of Antonia's fidelity to Drusus's memory strikingly. 'After his death, although she was beautiful and in the prime of her life, she lived with her mother-in-law rather than remarrying. Together in one bed, Antonia let her youthful vigour waste away while the other woman grew old as she went through widowhood.'[8] Part of the importance of Valerius's account is its emphasis on Livia's age. With hindsight we know that, at sixty, Livia had almost a third of her life ahead of her. But to her contemporaries, even perhaps to herself, time was running out for a woman who still had one great purpose to achieve.

Antonia took with her to the Palatine house her children Germanicus, Livilla and Claudius. Claudius, whom Cassius Dio describes as 'sickly in body, so that his head and hands shook slightly',[9] was already familiar with Livia's house. He had probably spent time there during his mother's absence on campaign with Drusus, considered too infirm to accompany his parents.[10] Antonia clearly bore Livia no ill will as a result of the honours showered on her at Drusus's death, which had not been shared with her daughter-in-law. Arguably, in 9 BC Antonia as much as Livia merited the Senate's grant of *ius trium liberorum*, 'the right of three children', with its freedom from formal guardianship and increased legal rights of inheritance – a formality in Livia's case, since she already enjoyed these privileges. Although Livia had been pregnant three times, she had borne only two children – in contrast to Antonia, who gave Drusus two sons and a daughter. Livia's bereavement, but not that of Antonia, was also noted by the Senate with a vote of statues. Antonia's strength did not derive from public tokens. The interweaving of the two women's households after this date is attested by the presence of Antonia's slaves and freedwomen among those of Livia and Tiberius in Livia's *columbarium*; it can reasonably be interpreted as pointing to a degree of domestic harmony between them

Did Livia importune Augustus on Tiberius's behalf following the latter's return to Rome in AD 2? The sources are silent, but the answer is surely not. With Tiberius at home, and happy in her arrangement with Antonia, Livia may have been inclined to count her blessings. Although we cannot prove her actions, it is probable that she had devoted at least part of the last quarter-century to promoting Tiberius's cause – all, apparently, in vain. It was a moment to enjoy the security and gains of her own position. First Octavia, then Julia had asserted their closer consanguinity with Augustus in the preferment of their sons. Two of Julia's sons remained Augustus's nominated successors, while the third, Agrippa Postumus, might be expected to share their good fortune in some measure, but Julia, like Octavia, no longer held sway over the *princeps*.

If, however, Tiberius's return to Rome did indeed once again inspire Livia to lofty aspirations, she would not have long to wait before receiving a glimmer of hope. On 20 August, en route for manoeuvres in Spain, Lucius Caesar died suddenly at the Gaulish port of Massilia. He was nineteen. So swift, unforeseen and inexplicable was his demise that the sources concur in their silence on the circumstances surrounding the death. Dio's 'the spark of Lucius's life had . . . been extinguished at Massilia' is typical.[11] It would not be long before this unexpected blow to the succession plans inspired a familiar refrain, that of Livia's involvement – what Tacitus describes, exploiting literary stereotypes with greater dramatic effect than accuracy, as the 'secret hand' of his 'stepmother Livia'.[12]

Livia's weapon was either long-distance poison, the same rumour that attached to Marcellus's death, or the services of a paid assassin. While the former was in all likelihood physically impossible, the latter points to a degree of reckless risk-taking wholly out of character for Livia, particularly given the minimal gain Lucius's death represented so long as Gaius remained alive. None of the ancient authors who report the accusation provides either evidence or even comment; nor do they trouble to specify the particulars of Livia's feat of cross-border malevolence. Excluded from the public formalities of Lucius's funeral, Tiberius, Suetonius records, instead composed a commemorative lyric poem entitled 'A Lament for the Death of Lucius Caesar'.[13] Had he suspected any involvement of his mother on his own behalf in Lucius's death, it would have been a remarkably cynical gesture.

Less than two years later, again confronted by family tragedy, Tiberius refrained from writing poetry. On 9 September AD 3 Gaius Caesar was wounded during a ceasefire in the siege of Artagira in Armenia. Velleius describes the outcome in unrevealing shorthand: 'his body became less active and his mind of less service to the state.'[14] Weakened and suffering, possibly unsettled as a result of recent revelations of duplicity among his advisors, Gaius decided to forswear his position and, like Tiberius before him, retire from Roman life – in his case to Syria. Augustus persuaded his 'son' to postpone any decision-making until his return to Rome – advice of the sort he may have discussed with Livia. Unlike Tiberius, Gaius did not live to make good his return. He set sail for Lycia in modern-day Turkey in a cargo vessel and died in the town of Limyra at the beginning of AD 4. His death caused widespread dismay – in the town of Pisa, commercial and religious activity was suspended while the townsfolk devoted their days to mourning.[15]

The coincidence of the deaths of Lucius and Gaius – together clearly advantageous to Livia's ambitions – proved more than Roman gossips could swallow, at least in those accounts which postdate Livia's lifetime. 'And so suspicion fell upon Livia of having been involved in the deaths of both men,' Dio tells us from the safe remove of several centuries, 'particularly because it was just at this time that Tiberius returned to Rome from Rhodes.'[16] That Lucius and Gaius, both so young, should die so close together – Velleius elides the interval to 'about a year'[17] – gave rise to suspicions of foul play irresistible to ancient authors bent on mischief-making.

A decade had passed since Tiberius's ill-advised departure for Rhodes. Then rumour had attributed his disappearance to jealousy of Augustus's unreasoning fondness for his stepsons, and he in turn had confessed his anxiety to avoid any suspicion of rivalry. In justifying his return to Augustus, he had invoked Gaius and Lucius again. 'Now that both were fully grown and the acknowledged heirs to the throne,' he explains in Suetonius's account, 'his reasons for keeping away from Rome were no longer valid.'[18] By AD 4, two years after Augustus finally relented and sanctioned Tiberius's homecoming, those acknowledged heirs to the throne were both dead.

This was not Livia's doing and it need not have benefited either mother or son. Augustus had indicated clearly as early as the marriage of Julia and Marcellus in 25 BC that his preference was for an heir of his own blood. In AD 4, Julia's third son, Agrippa Postumus, survived his brothers as Augustus's last grandson. Augustus's sister Octavia bequeathed her brother two grandsons, Germanicus and Claudius, who shared blood links with their great-uncle. Claudius's physical disabilities did not recommend him as a successor – even his mother, Antonia, referred to him as 'a monster: a man whom Mother Nature had begun to work upon but then flung aside'.[19] Germanicus, by contrast, like his father Drusus, was an attractive boy of ability and winning ways. The year after Gaius's death he married Julia's younger daughter Vipsania Agrippina, known as Agrippina. In a fourteen-year marriage, they produced nine children. All shared not only Augustus's but Octavia's blood and even that of Livia, repeated intermarriage within Augustus's extended family making husband and wife at last joint great-grandparents in the fourth generation. With Gaius and Lucius dead, both Livia and Tiberius, accustomed by now to being overlooked in the succession stakes, ought realistically to have expected Augustus's choice to fall on Agrippa Postumus or Germanicus.

Augustus's track record of fortitude in the face of family misfortunes perhaps failed him at Gaius's death. Although Suetonius is at pains to indicate that 'the deaths of Lucius and Gaius did not break his spirit'[20] – presumably to reassure the reader that his subsequent actions were not taken in a state of derangement – Augustus was approaching his sixty-seventh birthday. This was a greater age in AD 4 than today, particularly for a man with a long history of indifferent health, who had begun work on his mausoleum more than thirty years previously. He could not know how much longer he had left to resolve the issue of the succession which, on balance, appeared to have consumed as much time and energy as any of his policies of Roman rule. Genetic egotism promoted Agrippa and Germanicus; common sense dictated a resurrection of Tiberius's once illustrious career. As always, Augustus behaved sensibly and for the good of the State. He said as much in the act of Tiberius's adoption on June 26, trumpeting the sinking heart with which he invested Livia's son with his ultimate prize. He attached two qualifications to Tiberius's triumph: Tiberius shared his adoption with Agrippa Postumus and was required, before that adoption was formalized, himself to adopt Germanicus as his heir in preference to his own son Drusus. As Tacitus expressed it with customary waspishness, 'although Tiberius had a grown son of his own, he ordered him to adopt Germanicus. For Augustus wanted to have another iron in the fire.'[21] In due course a son of Germanicus did indeed become ruler of Rome, though the Emperor Caligula was a credit to neither of his great-grandparents nor to the principle of hereditary succession to which Augustus clung so tenaciously. In AD 4 Tiberius received anew those powers he had forfeited on Rhodes. Augustus despatched him promptly to campaign in Germany. It may have been proof of the extent of his ambivalence on a personal level towards his heir and stepson; it demonstrated clearly the keenness of Augustus's need for Tiberius.

How much was this Livia's doing? Tacitus's account lays responsibility squarely at her feet. Once, he claims, Livia had plotted by 'secret machinations' to manoeuvre her son into a position of power. He does not elaborate those 'secret machinations', allowing the reader to assume the worst about a woman he consistently demonizes. Failing, and seizing the advantage of Augustus's age – which, we conclude, brought with it a decline in either his acuity or his resolve – she now changed her approach. 'This time she requested it openly.' That she succeeded after decades of failure, and at a moment when Tiberius's currency had plummeted to an all-time low, indicates the shifting balance of power in the couple's relationship. Naturally that shift wears a sinister aspect. 'Livia had the aged Augustus firmly under control . . .'[22] All the faults of Tiberius's future government can be attributed to that control. Controlling wife, aged husband – both wear the taint of Tacitus's contempt. Tiberius, too, is corrupted by the 'ingrained arrogance of the Claudian family'. 'So we have got to be slaves to a woman,' Tacitus records people as saying. That no other source reports such expressions of popular disaffection is not matter for surprise. There is a gulf between masterly storytelling and reliable history.

Two other allusions are persuasive. Suetonius refers to Livia as 'begging' Augustus to adopt her son,[23] while Dio describes him at this point as a man who 'had reached a state of exhaustion through old age'.[24] Both confirm Augustus's own implicit statement that Tiberius's adoption was not a matter of choice but something forced upon him. Livia would not have been the woman to inspire such hostility in Roman writers had she not understood when to seize an opportunity. With Augustus tired by the repeated frustration of his plans and the Herculean effort of three decades of supreme power, Livia, it seems, made a final push. The result – Velleius's 'day of good omen . . . to all' – was the fulfilment of the ultimate ambition a Roman mother could conceive. As we have seen, it did not represent Livia's life's work and could not have come about without Augustus's concurrence. Nor is Livia likely to have regarded it as reason to relax her vigilance. At the forefront of her mind were the examples of Octavia and Julia. She was most likely unaware of those rumours of plotting and poison which have since besmirched her reputation – if indeed they existed at all.

CHAPTER 27

Purer than Parian marble?

The statue of Augustus discovered by archaeologists at Livia's villa of Prima Porta in 1863 is carved from Parian lychnites marble, the purest of all white Greek marbles.[1] Given the degree of official control exercised over Augustan visual propaganda, the choice of stone cannot have been accidental. 'The beauty of sparkling Glycera, purer than Parian marble, sets me on fire,' Horace wrote, establishing in poetry a symbolic correspondence between the stone's luminescent whiteness and a sense of moral purity.[2] Perhaps Glycera merited the associations of Parian marble. Did Augustus? Archaeologists have generally assumed that the Prima Porta statue replicates in stone a bronze original erected in the centre of the city. Augustus may have displayed moral purity, in the sense of fidelity, towards Rome; his track record where Livia was concerned is less sparklingly white.

'As an elderly man,' Suetonius records, 'Augustus is said to have still harboured a passion for deflowering girls – who were collected for him from every quarter, even by his wife!'[3] Famously Livia attributed the success of her long marriage to being 'scrupulously chaste herself, doing gladly whatever pleased Augustus, not meddling with any of his affairs, and, in particular, by pretending neither to hear nor to notice the favourites of his passion'.[4] There is no reason to discount Suetonius's statement of Augustus's enduring libido, however convincingly Livia chose not to notice it. We have seen that the *princeps* was probably repeatedly unfaithful to his second wife. Evidently Augustus was untroubled by the gulf between his own behaviour and that outlined in his programme of social legislation of 18 BC, embraced by Livia in the symbol of the *stola* and a private life impervious even to Tacitus's septic scrutiny. We may approach with greater scepticism the suggestion that Livia supplied her husband with nubile virgins. Such an undertaking was not only at odds with her stance of public rectitude but one she may accurately have considered too fraught with risk of discovery. There were limits to Livia's fondness.

And yet husband and wife loved each other. Augustus's last words, in one version of the tradition, were spoken to Livia: a commendation that she remember their marriage. The very length of that marriage, coupled with its childlessness, offers proof of affection, at least on the part of Augustus, who so easily might have divorced his barren bride. The statue of Augustus discovered at Livia's villa more than a century ago may indicate how fully that love was reciprocated.

In 20 BC, assisted as we have seen by Tiberius, Augustus had returned to Rome military standards lost in Parthia by Crassus. In thanksgiving for that victory – reversing a notable disgrace in Roman eyes – a public monument was erected. It incorporated a statue of Augustus. Some thirty-five years later, with Augustus dead, Tiberius commissioned a copy of that statue, which he presented to his mother. Associated with Tiberius and Augustus's collaboration in the eastern empire, it was, at one level, a statement of the men's closeness, reiterating even in private Tiberius's right to succeed his stepfather. But Tiberius may have had less egocentric motives in offering his mother such a gift in the first year of her widowhood. Faithful to the idealizing impulse of Augustus's public imagery, the statue is one of great beauty. It was perhaps as Livia chose to remember Augustus, a desire she may have confided in Tiberius.

'When the most famous sculptors or painters wished to carve or paint the most beautiful bodies possible,' Quintilian tells us, 'they rightly judged [as proper models] the well-known Doryphoros, suitable as it is for either military and athletic figures, and other physically beautiful bodies of youthful warriors or athletes.'[5] The Doryphoros, or 'spear-bearer', was the best-known work of a fifth-century BC Greek sculptor from Argos called Polyclitus. The sculpture Quintilian almost certainly had in mind is the Prima Porta Augustus or its bronze original. It is an example of Rome revisiting and reinterpreting Greece, Polyclitus's naked athlete translated to the martial world of an imperial triumph. It presents Augustus as a military leader, in the guise of a breast-plated *imperator* or 'supreme commander'. In depicting Augustus barefoot, traditionally a signifier of divinity, it hints at his more-than-human status. The figure of Cupid riding a dolphin beside his right foot consolidates this impression: in the Roman pantheon, dolphins were associated with Venus, claimed by Julius Caesar as an ancestress of Augustus's adoptive Julian clan. Although Augustus was more than forty when the original statue was produced, his appearance is that of a young man at the height of his physical prowess, perhaps as Octavian appeared to Livia, newly shaved, in the first years of their marriage. One arm extended in a gesture usually associated with public speaking, Augustus becomes the archetype of Quintilian's 'military and athletic figures, and other physically beautiful bodies of youthful warriors or athletes'. As such, his position of supreme power in Rome is ordained both by nature and the gods. The Prima Porta Augustus, cherished by a grieving widow in the privacy of her country estate, offers proof in pristine white marble of Velleius Paterculus's assertion that 'flattery always goes hand in hand with high position'. [6] At another level, thanks to its findspot, it is a statement of enduring affection – love capable of idealization even in the face of repeated betrayal. The statue may also have served Livia as a totem. Following Augustus's death, and with the deterioration of her relationship with Tiberius, its quasi-divine, militarily all-powerful Augustus was the surest safeguard of her own position of eminence, and a continuing justification for the respect and privileges she enjoyed throughout old age. Heroic, it stood within a stone's throw of that grove of laurels Livia cultivated for imperial triumphs, progeny of a distant portent of her own high destiny.

Cruelly the passage of time exposed the emptiness of public gestures of family solidarity like the Ara Pacis Augustae. Livia and Augustus's indifferent record in bequeathing to their family a model of that marital concord Livia had proclaimed at the shrine within her portico portended serious consequences. These operated not only in the long term, to shape Roman imperial history, but within their own lifetimes, in Augustus's protracted search for an heir.

It was an instance of sowing and reaping. In the case of their children's marital careers, both spouses would find that they had led by example. Augustus's well-known philandering found an echo in Julia's serial adultery. What the *princeps* discounted in his own behaviour, he accorded shorter shrift when the culprit was both a woman and his daughter, particularly when her sexual exploits entered the public arena in a context which may or may not have encompassed a political aspect and suspicion of conspiracy. Both Livia's sons made happy marriages, characterized, like their mother's marriage to Augustus, by personal loyalty and sexual fidelity. We have witnessed Tiberius's reluctance to divorce Vipsania Agrippina in 12 BC and his sadness at accidentally encountering her again. His love proved of long duration. In AD 30, ten years after Vipsania's death, her second husband, Asinius Gallus, perished – in Cassius Dio's account murdered to satisfy Tiberius. 'For Gallus had married the former wife of Tiberius and claimed Drusus as his son, and he was consequently hated by the other even before this incident.' [7] Livia's younger son Drusus earned the praises of Valerius Maximus for his sexual continence and the devotion he inspired in his wife Antonia the Younger. 'It is well known that he restricted his sexual pleasures to those he enjoyed with his beloved wife. By her famous deeds, Antonia . . . repaid her husband's love with her exceptional loyalty to him.' [8]

In the next generation, the record grew increasingly patchy. Drusus's elder son Germanicus enjoyed a fruitful and happy marriage to Julia's youngest daughter Agrippina. Germanicus's sister Livilla, however, became one of several villainesses of imperial Rome. Acting in partnership with her lover Sejanus, she murdered her husband, Tiberius's son Drusus the Younger, by slow poisoning. In doing so, she unwittingly exacerbated Livia's posthumous vilification by a host of later historians, by forging a proven connection between imperial women and poison. Livilla died for her sins, although the sources are unclear whether she was executed at Tiberius's behest or, startlingly, that of her appalled mother Antonia. [9]

Drusus and Antonia's third child, Claudius, was married four times. Since two of his wives were those she-wolves of imperial Rome, Messalina and Agrippina the Younger, he cannot be held entirely culpable for his busy record. Of his remaining cousins, both Agrippa Postumus, adopted by Augustus at the same time as Tiberius, and Julia's first daughter, Julia the Younger, met unfortunate ends. Both died in exile after banishment by their grandfather. The result was a family tree which, like that of the celluloid D'Ascoynes, came close to being chopped down, and family circumstances which conspicuously failed to mirror the reproductive programme outlined in Augustus's social legislation. From the happy marriage of Livia and Augustus, and the model of virtuous, family-minded Roman matronhood Livia had successfully projected over three decades, emerged a family chiefly remarkable for its pronounced dysfunctionalism.

At its simplest, the fault lay in Augustus's failure to produce a male heir. Post-27 BC, this created a lacuna of instability at the heart of the principate. Suetonius described the period of Tiberius's adoption: 'by this time it had become pretty clear who the next Emperor must be.'[10] Members of the *princeps*'s family could be excused a sense of déjà vu. On every previous occasion, the gods had willed otherwise. In the face of such long-drawn-out uncertainty, opportunism was inevitable. Augustus's own declared preference for a successor of his blood made every near male relative a potential candidate. His emphasis on the claims of kinship created an environment in which his family members inevitably regarded themselves as distinct from the body of ordinary Romans. Like Julia, they considered themselves governed by different rules, subject to a different authority. Livia's personification of old-fashioned virtues lacked persuasion confronted by such a licence to lawlessness. Given Augustus's less than blameless behaviour and the widespread unpopularity among the upper classes of those reforms Livia made her benchmark, it is not surprising that she succeeded in winning only a handful of devotees among the women of Augustus's family. The presumption of maternal ambition perhaps weakened Livia's case among her nearest relations: while she espoused the virtuous associations of the *stola*, all suspected her desire for Tiberius's advancement. They in turn trained their sights on personal goals. Augustus's Roman revolution was complete: as a single family squabbled for power, the public good enshrined in Rome's once cherished respublica slipped from view. The brutality of Augustus's behaviour towards relations he regarded as political pawns – those divorces he forced on Agrippa and Tiberius, his refusal to allow Julia a period of mourning her husbands – generated predictable responses.

On a tiny, empty island off the coast of Apulia in southeast Italy, called by Tacitus Trimerum, a baby briefly cried. It had been separated from its mother, a prisoner. Trimerum and the other rocky outcrops which make up the archipelago today known as the Tremiti Islands have a chequered history of harbouring prisoners. At the end of the eighteenth century, Ferdinand IV, King of Naples, built a penal colony on San Nicolo; later, these islands were among several used by Mussolini for the internment of political prisoners. The baby of course had not committed a crime. Through exposure it must atone for the sins of its mother – adultery, with a suspicion of conspiracy – and that of its father, almost certainly conspiracy. In AD 8 Augustus sentenced to death his newest great-grandchild, a son or daughter of Julia the Younger and either her husband Lucius Aemilius Paullus or her lover Decius Junius Silanus. The younger Julia, it seemed, was cut from the same cloth as her mother. That year, like her mother before her, she had been despatched to end her days in banishment. Like her mother, she would be debarred from burial in Augustus's mausoleum.

The year Julia's baby died in agony on that barren outcrop, its only surviving uncle continued his pointless existence equally remote from Rome. Insolent, brutish, even mentally deficient, Agrippa Postumus – all too briefly co-heir with Tiberius of Rome's Empire – frittered away futile days on the island of Planasia. Distant from the coast of Tuscany, suspended from Elba like an afterthought, Planasia is currently uninhabited following the closure a decade ago of its maximum-security prison specializing in Mafiosi. Two thousand years ago, the island was the site of a villa belonging to Augustus, a tiny open-air theatre and some baths.[11] But it is not to be expected that Agrippa Postumus, fond as he was of fishing, found the life there either agreeable or diverting.

The circumstances of the downfall of brother and sister are unclear. Agrippa Postumus's banishment came hot on the heels of a formal *abdicatio*. The process by which a father threatened a son with disinheritance, this was an early warning sign which Postumus surely ignored since Dio attributes his subsequent exile to a failure to mend his ways.

Unconvincingly his bad behaviour, as recorded, consisted of unfitness for military command, violent fits of anger, railing against Augustus for withholding his inheritance from his father and '[reviling] Livia as a stepmother'.[12] In Tacitus's version, of course, it is all the fault of the 'stepmother' and her firm control over her ageing husband. 'Through stepmotherly malevolence [she] loathed and distrusted the young Agrippa Postumus.' Later she gets rid of him 'at the first opportunity'.[13] Tacitus even finds a negative construction for the financial assistance we learn that Livia gave to Julia throughout the twenty years of her exile. It is a form of hypocrisy, scheming for the downfall of her enemies, then affecting the appearance of virtue by rallying to their aid once their fortunes falter. At an interval of two thousand years the truth cannot be recovered, obscured rather than elucidated by the cloak-and-danger insinuations of ancient writers. It is impossible to overlook the likelihood of a political aspect to both banishments. This being the case, Livia's obvious role is one of revelation, the harbinger of bad news to Augustus.

For the ancient authors it all came back to Livia. Tiberius had been adopted as Augustus's son and Augustus, as must have been increasingly obvious, had entered his final years, but still this was not enough for the villainous Livia of the sources. At all costs she must eradicate any child of Julia's who might yet threaten Tiberius's claim. For this reason, in AD 6 Agrippa was disinherited; the following year he was banished. One year later, his sister joined him in oblivion. Of the five children of Julia and Agrippa, two were dead and two in exile. Only one remained in Rome, and she was married to Livia's grandson Germanicus. It was surely a cause of sadness for Augustus. For the monstrous Livia of the sources, it was reason to rejoice. To the modern reader, it offers proof of the vulnerability to slander to which Augustus's need for a male heir exposed Livia. Only the absence of an heir of Augustus's blood, and what retrospectively appeared a lengthy search for a suitable successor, allowed the ancient authors to demonize Livia so conclusively as a scheming, ambitious mother hellbent on power. This is the central facet of Livia's posthumous reputation. But it is wholly unproven.

Livia commemorated her love for Augustus in a statue. Copied from a public monument, it was a private object, displayed in a house visible only to invited friends and family. It bore witness to her own eminence, of course, but showed the human face of that public position. The Prima Porta Augustus survives today, powerful and impressive, a reflection of the *princeps*'s careful self-presentation as much as an image of the handsome, successful man Livia married in 38 BC. In its suggestion of love given and returned, it is a more attractive testament than the sources grant to Livia. As with Livia's own portraiture, its heroic iconography conceals as much as it displays.

CHAPTER 28

'Blood-red comets'

It is not to be expected that Augustus would be allowed to die without a full complement of portents. Cassius Dio recalls one particular instance of such heavy-handed ominousness that it is hard to believe it was not the work either of a practical joker or, less amiably, parties grown weary of the ageing *princeps*. 'During a horse race which took place at the festival of the Augustalia, held in honour of Augustus's birthday, a madman seated himself in the chair dedicated to Julius Caesar and, taking his crown, put it on his own head.'[1] Combining gravitas with disingenuousness, Dio offers the inevitable interpretation: 'This episode caused universal alarm, since it seemed to have some significance for the destiny of Augustus, as indeed proved to be the case.'

When the end came, it merited more than madmen in fancy dress. Nothing less than a total eclipse of the sun would serve for Augustus's demise. Even nature obligingly added her pyrotechnics to underline the importance of this unprecedented event. 'Most of the sky seemed to be on fire; glowing embers appeared to be falling from it and blood-red comets were seen.'[2]

If Dio was right, there was solace for Livia in these meteorological effusions. Her common sense and instinct for political survival did not desert her at Augustus's death. As in life, she must define her position in relation to that of her husband. No one benefited more than Livia from the possibility of Augustus's deification, foretold in falling embers. She embraced those quirks of nature which seemed to point towards Augustus's death as something outside the common run, indisputable proof of his divinity. Aware of potential challenges ahead, the *princeps*'s widow welcomed the safety net of associative godliness. It was a sort of comfort in the face of a sorrow whose extent we cannot gauge. On this occasion, unlike at Drusus's death, Livia does not appear to have consulted Areus or to have betrayed in public unguarded expressions of grief. Her widowhood inspired remarkable honours on the part of the Senate, as we shall see. It did not generate a poem like the 'Consolation of Livia', intended to salve a suffering heart. Augustus's death lacked the suddenness of Drusus's or the pathos of youth slain in its prime. It was an event for which Livia had prepared herself on a number of levels.

Augustus's final decade is overshadowed in several sources by Livia's assumption of a central role in imperial politicking. At best, this is an interpretative approach. Since it is frequently the work of hostile authors writing after the event – Tacitus above all we must measure its value with care. Evidence of Livia's involvement, whether it took the form, as Tacitus claims, of 'secret machinations' or open requests, is scant. We are on firmer ground in viewing the ten-year period following Tiberius's adoption as one of physical decline on Augustus's part, matched by a partial loss of control in both domestic and foreign policy, and a gradual move towards a complete powershare by *princeps* and designated successor. Again there is no evidence of any role for Livia in this last process, although it is extremely likely that Augustus consulted his wife in matters relating directly to Tiberius. Letters written by Augustus to Tiberius, quoted by Suetonius as proof of the warmth of the men's relationship, refer to Livia in a manner that suggests husband and wife were indeed mother and father, as in law they were, acting and thinking in concord: 'I beg you to take things easy,' the older man wrote during one of Tiberius's later campaigns abroad, 'if you were to fall ill, the news would kill your mother and me.'[3] This is not, of course, the same as attributing to Livia any role as intermediary between the two men. Such a suggestion would have been as unwelcome to both as unnecessary. Tacitus's insinuations aside, it is hard to envisage any increased role for Livia at this point save in the case of Augustus's failing faculties. Although Tacitus hints at this, repeatedly referring to Augustus as an 'old man' in language suggestive of senility, other sources, as we shall see, are at pains to refute such an inference.

What had changed in AD 4 was not Livia's area of responsibility but her position. No longer was she simply the *princeps*'s wife, she was now also the mother of the future *princeps*. At a moment when Augustus's household had been purged of several members, this accorded Livia unprecedented prominence, unrivalled in Rome's past even by Republican paragons like Cornelia, whose public profile was largely symbolic. Livia found herself one of a reduced handful of imperial women, alongside Antonia the Younger and Augustus's granddaughter Agrippina, and indisputably their senior. Held in the highest esteem by the Roman people, she already possessed divine attributes in the provinces, alongside extensive clients and valuable estates. This alone was more than sufficient grounds for Tacitus's hatred.

Not until the moment the Senate formally acclaimed him, and the army demonstrated its loyalty, could Livia consider Tiberius's succession safe. Undoubtedly, however, the years after Tiberius's adoption saw a lessening of her anxiety about Augustus's ill health. Once, as we have seen, Livia had expressed her entire dependence upon Augustus's position, her survival bound up with his. With Tiberius acknowledged as *princeps*-in-waiting, unmarried and apparently disinterested in female society, she could relax, confident that her position would survive the regime's change of leadership. This confidence gave Livia buoyancy during Augustus's recurrent health scares, notably in AD 9. In AD 12, partly blind in one eye and no longer capable of public speaking, Augustus took a step away from the formalities of government, forswearing his visits to the Senate House and discontinuing the *salutatio* he had maintained even as *princeps*. Furthermore, as Dio tells us, 'the emperor requested the senators . . . not to pay their respects at his home, nor to feel offended if he ceased his practice of attending their public banquets'.[4] Augustus remained of sound mind – 'Despite these disabilities,' Dio hastens to reassure us, 'he fulfilled his duties no less meticulously than before' – but the end had begun. Livia must surely have made her plans. In the event, Augustus's semi-retirement from public affairs did not diminish either his own profile or that of his wife.

Augustus's fulfilment of duties had included a return to the fray in the form of further moral legislation. Undaunted by the spectacular falls from grace of the two Julias, or perhaps encouraged by their waywardness to further zeal, in AD 9 Augustus revisited the laws of 18 BC dealing with marriage and adultery. The Lex Papia Poppaea is named after the consuls responsible for its authorship; its contents are Augustus's own. The law is chiefly a qualification of its earlier counterparts, but extended the period within which widows and divorcees were required to remarry and distinguished between married and unmarried men without children, imposing differing scales of penalties. It also increased the inheritance rights of certain women. Again the law enforced the Augustan belief that weaknesses within the family engendered similar flaws in the state, and focused attention on Augustus's own family. The achievements of the *princeps*'s remaining female relatives provided only a partial endorsement of his programme. Livia was the mother of two children, while Antonia had refused to remarry after her widowhood. At this stage, Livia, Antonia and Agrippina – the last-named later revealed as a termagant in the Fulvia mould – could all convincingly pose as virtuous Roman matrons dedicated to the good of the state. At the end, as at the beginning, Livia's principal political service to her husband was her parade of virtue, a boldly Republican statement that confined women's place to the home and family.

That confinement was, of course, a case of mummery as Augustus's principate drew slowly to its close. Almost half a century had passed since a radical grant of sacrosanctitas awarded Livia public representation in the form of statues and portraiture. On the friezes of the Ara Pacis Augustae, dedicated on Livia's birthday and annually commemorating that anniversary with sacrifices, two figures were distinguished from the remainder by their dress. Each wore a wreath and veil – Augustus and Livia. In crisp-carved marble they appeared in the semblance of ruling couple, Livia the *materfamilias* of a politicized family which existed in a public parade of private life.[5] In the absence of equality between the *princeps* and his wife, Livia enjoyed nevertheless a highly unusual prominence far removed from that traditional domestic confinement she advertised in the *stola* and a life of careful religious observance. Appropriately, it would be in the religious sphere that the couple came closest to parity.

*

'A Caesar arrived with a Caesar, for me . . . those that you've sent me . . . the gods: and Livia is there, joined with her Caesars, so that your gift could be complete, as it ought to be . . . It's something to gaze at gods, and consider them present,' wrote the exiled poet Ovid to the orator Cotta Maximus.[6] It was late in Augustus's reign and Ovid longed to escape his banishment to the Black Sea coast. With questionable tact, given the authorship of Ovid's downfall, Cotta, who later held the consulship under Tiberius, sent him silver figures for his private altar. Those figures depicted Augustus, Tiberius and Livia. Increasingly, even in life, Augustus acquired the trappings of divinity. 'Wooed with prayers and bowls of unmixed wine,' Horace had written, 'your godhead shares his worship with the Lar that guards familial peace.'[7] The inclusion of Livia and Tiberius within this partial metamorphosis was a tribute to lives of prominent service and an association sufficiently powerful to survive Augustus's death. The existence of such small statues or busts cannot have displeased the *princeps*'s wife. By an unforeseeable irony, the woman excluded from her family's gallery of *imagines* on account of her sex had made her way into Roman atria in a form that would outlive those perishable wax likenesses. No funeral mask for an actor, she did so in the guise of a silver goddess.

From a distance we can recognize such instances as stages on the route to Livia's eventual deification. Livia herself could not have been so certain. Instead, such signs composed the building blocks of a future without Augustus. Livia, like her husband, understood the extent to which the principate, with its impulse towards hereditary monarchy, contravened deeply held Roman beliefs. The period of transition from Augustus's rule to that of Tiberius posed potential problems. Any intimation of divinity on the parts of Livia and Tiberius promised to oil troubled waters. Divinity provided both Livia and her son, each unrelated to Augustus or Julius Caesar, with a form of legitimacy.

In AD 10 Tiberius celebrated a triumph for earlier victories in Pannonia. Suetonius describes the scene. 'He broke his progress through the city at the Triumphal Gate, where Augustus, who was presiding over the ceremonies, waited for him at the head of the Senate. He then dismounted and knelt at the feet of his adoptive father before proceeding up the Capitoline Hill to the Temple of Jupiter.'[8] This touching piece of theatre united father and son in full view of the Senate and the Roman crowd. It is likely that Augustus, accepting Tiberius's homage, raised him to his feet. That symbolic gesture conveyed graphically to his onlookers Augustus's plans for the future. He had earlier outlined those plans in an explicitly monarchical statement, which in itself indicates Augustus's confidence of Rome's acceptance of his successor. Vetoing an award to Tiberius of a title to commemorate his military victories – 'Pannonicus' ('Pannonian'), 'Invictus' ('the Unconquered') and 'Pius' ('the Devoted) were all proposed – Augustus 'promised on each occasion that Tiberius would be satisfied with that of "Augustus", which he intended to bequeath him.'[9]

The plans Augustus formulated for Tiberius's rule became reality for the most part before Augustus's death. Although Augustus and Tiberius divided the empire between them, the former continuing to administer Rome, the latter to mastermind military campaigns in the provinces, their communication included extensive movement between the two spheres. Tiberius regularly returned to Rome; Augustus met Livia's son at points near the front.[10] In AD 13 Tiberius received from the Senate a renewed grant of tribunician power alongside a new grant, that of consular *imperium*. At the same time, Dio records, Augustus, with a show of reluctance, accepted a fifth ten-year term as head of state. Save in name, the two men's powers were equal. As if to confirm this development, gold coins issued in the same year by the provincial mint at Lugdunum in Gaul coupled Augustus's head on the obverse with that of Tiberius on the reverse, a compliment previously only shared by Marcus Agrippa.[11]

These were the powers on which Tiberius's claim to succeed Augustus rested. They owed nothing to Livia. In the Senate's gift, they could not have been bestowed arbitrarily by any individual, most of all a woman. Nor were they such as might be won by poison or murder of a perceived opponent. Half a century after Octavian's defeat of Mark Antony at Actium, the formal powers of Roman government remained the nominal preserve of the Senate, an exclusively male assembly. Augustus had not presumed to rule without them and nor would Tiberius. In the first instance, Augustus required senatorial endorsement to uphold his claim of having restored the Republic. In Tiberius's case, inherited Republican sympathies probably made an adherence to age-old formalities a prerequisite of taking up office. Tiberius was Livia's son and owed to Livia his proximity to the *princeps*. He did not owe his mother those formal awards by which he became, ahead of AD 14, second *princeps* of Rome, as Livia herself understood. Did she seek to counter this claim? Only, it seems, in unguarded private moments in sources which cannot be verified. A daughter of the Republic, she understood the mechanics of power. Undoubtedly she facilitated Tiberius's progress; but she was not the architect of his principate.

Murder formed the substance of the sources' accusations against Livia when at length Tiberius succeeded his adoptive father on 19 August AD 14. Not one murder but two. The seventy-two-year-old's victims were Agrippa Postumus, that difficult last son of Julia and Marcus Agrippa, and Augustus himself. In the latter case, as with Marcellus forty years previously, Livia's alleged means of disposal was poison.

Every circumstance of the death of Agrippa Postumus remains subject to debate, the only certainty being that Augustus's grandson did not die of natural causes. He was killed, unarmed in his island exile, by a staff officer probably acting on written instructions. Those instructions originated with Augustus or Livia or Tiberius, depending on the source consulted. Their despatch to Planasia arose alternatively as a result of a trip made to the island by Augustus in the spring of AD 14; on account of Augustus's fear that supporters of Julia would rally behind the exile to unsettle Tiberius's succession; or from Livia's 'stepmotherly malevolence', loathing and mistrust. Whether Augustus was sufficiently strong early in AD 14 to travel to Planasia, two years after excusing himself from the effort of visits from senators, and how disposed either to order the murder of his last-remaining grandson or to reinstate that grandson – described by Suetonius as 'becoming more mad day by day' – are unclear. The sources do not record Livia's reaction to the young man's death, although Dio offers her fears over the possibility of Agrippa's reinstatement as the motive for her murdering her husband. Tiberius for his part explicitly denied issuing the death warrant. Afterwards he pointedly abstained from any public discussion of the matter in the

Senate. Ovid supplies information on how Livia found out about what we assume was a secret visit by Augustus to Planasia. The poet's eleventh-hour appearance in the ring fails to clarify a murky incident that reflects well on none of its players, actual or conjectural. Given Tiberius's formal powers, granted by the Senate in advance of Augustus's death, as we have seen, and his unrivalled record of service to the state, Agrippa's death is probably a sideshow. If the Roman people sought an alternative to Tiberius in AD 14, their choice was more likely to fall on Livia's grandson Germanicus than Julia's wholly inexperienced youngest son, with his ungovernable anger and propensity for brutality. At twenty-nine, however, Germanicus could not rival Tiberius's qualifications for power.

The murderous Livia was apparently untroubled by any perceived threat from Germanicus at this stage. Leaving her grandson unharmed, she trained her sights on Augustus instead. Why Livia should wish at this moment to kill her husband of fifty-two years, a man already in failing health, is not known, unless Augustus had indeed decided to restore Agrippa Postumus to favour at Tiberius's expense. We cannot conclusively rule out this possibility, although it exists only as an inference in that source most virulently opposed to Livia, Tacitus's *Annals*. If Livia nurtured a long-term desire to rid herself of Augustus, she acted sensibly in waiting until Tiberius had received both tribunician and con-sular *imperium*. That she chose to take action in mid-August AD 14, a period when Tiberius had already departed for Illyricum on the eastern shore of the Adriatic and was not on hand to smooth the succession, appears less sensible.

Husband, wife and son ought to have known the time was ripe as spring turned to summer. Lightning melted the first letter of Augustus's name on the inscription of his statue on the Capitol. It was no ordinary storm damage, as Suetonius and Dio are at pains to explain. 'This was interpreted to mean that Augustus would live only another hundred days, since the remainder of the word, namely AESAR, is the Etruscan for "god" – C being the Roman numeral 100.'[12]

Despite the brevity of this life sentence, Augustus decided to accompany Tiberius on the first stage of his journey to Illyricum. With Livia, he set out for Beneventum, more than a hundred miles south of Rome on the Via Appia. At Astura, he modified his plans, choosing to travel instead by boat. Departing at night, he caught a chill combined with diarrhoea. The party headed for Capri, where it made an unscheduled but apparently successful convalescent stop, before resuming its course. After a detour to Naples to witness an athletics competion held every five years in Augustus's honour, Rome's first family continued as planned to Beneventum. Their destination reached, Livia and Augustus turned back towards Rome, while Tiberius maintained his course for Illyricum.

But Augustus never returned to Rome. Plagued by a recurrence of the same illness, he made a detour with Livia at his side to Nola, where he owned a house. It was, by chance, the same house in which his father had died. Comforted rather than otherwise by this coincidence, Augustus moved into the very room in which Gaius Octavius had breathed his last. More than thunderbolts or blood-red comets, this was the omen Livia could not ignore. Immediately she sent messengers entrusted with Tiberius's prompt recall.

The weakness of Roman emperors in the face of wives intent on murder has become proverbial. Agrippina the Younger, Augustus's great-grand-daughter, famously despatched Livia's grandson Claudius with a mush-room she had earlier entrusted to the ministrations of a convicted poisoner called Locusta. The exact manner of Claudius's death is not known. Perhaps it was the emperor's doctor, Xenophon, who gave the fatal dose; possibly Claudius's death was caused not by a mushroom but a deadly enema. What appears to be beyond dispute is Agrippina's intent to kill and her success, through whatever agency, in realizing that aim. She sacrificed her husband in order to ensure the succession of her son by a previous marriage, Nero, in place of Claudius's son Britannicus.

In Dio's account of the death of Augustus forty years previously, Livia takes drastic action. She is prompted by fear that Augustus plans to rein-state Agrippa Postumus as a candidate for the succession. 'So she smeared with poison some figs which were still ripening on trees from which Augustus was in the habit of picking the fruit with his own hands. She then ate those which had not been smeared, and offered the poisoned fruit to him.'[13] Obligingly Augustus died, and Livia's son, like Agrip-pina's son in years to come, succeeded his stepfather as *princeps*.

Thanks to the inclusion of this incident in the televised *I, Claudius*,

Tiberius's succession will for ever be attributed to a deadly fig and a scheming mother. It is surely significant that alone of the ancient writers, Dio records this version of Augustus's death. In the account written by Velleius Paterculus, the only version to survive from the lifetime of any of the protagonists, Livia is entirely absent from the deathbed scene, Augustus's death the result simply of old age. 'Since no care could withstand the fates, in his seventy-sixth year . . . he was resolved into the elements from which he sprang and yielded up to heaven his divine soul.'[14] Untrustworthy in many ways, Velleius is the only author to bequeath us an account of Augustus's death not coloured by knowledge of Agrippina's murder of Claudius as a preliminary to Nero's accession.

Livia acted with greater circumspection than to risk so late in the day a crime of such magnitude and easy detection. She summoned Tiberius at the earliest opportunity. Then, like Agrippina after her, she sealed off Augustus's house and the surrounding area with troops. Whichever source we choose to follow next – whether we prefer Augustus's last hours to be spent in earnest discussion with Tiberius, joking among friends or saving his final words for his wife – Livia controlled firmly the dissemination of facts about his condition. She allowed news of her widowhood to escape the barricades only once she was wholly certain of sufficient support for Tiberius to implement his immediate nomination as *princeps*. At that point, she surrendered control. As so often in the past, she had kept her head while those around her might have lost theirs.

CHAPTER 29

Augusta

In her eightieth year, Livia dedicated a statue of herself to her father. The recipient of this courtesy was not, however, Marcus Livius Drusus Claudianus but Augustus. In his will, dated 3 April AD 13, Augustus, as we have seen, had adopted his wife as his daughter. Like Augustus before her, adopted in the will of Julius Caesar, Livia found herself by testamentary adoption a member of the Julian clan. Accordingly, at the age of seventy-two, she changed her name to Julia. At a stroke, her husband of fifty-two years became, by law, her father.

The sources maintain a degree of sangfroid surprising to modern readers in relation to this procedure, which is probably unprecedented in Roman history. The ancient writers discount the emotional ramifications of such altered relationships, diverted instead by a twin development; its radicalism encompassed not emotional but political implications. Augustus's will bequeathed to Livia not only a new name but a title, 'Augusta'. As intimated before AD 10, the same document conferred on Tiberius the masculine equivalent, 'Augustus'. Livia's name henceforth – Julia Augusta – announced not only her membership of a new family but, for the first time, in a feminization of a title once awarded Octavian by the Senate in recognition of outstanding services to the state, a suggestion of a formalized position. Augustus's decrees of 3 April would have long-lasting consequences for Livia and especially for Tiberius.

From the outset, a number of the sources maintain, the new principate included at its heart a struggle between mother and son. A focus of their differences was their interpretation of Augustus's intention in creating Livia 'Augusta'. Octavian's receipt of the title 'Augustus' had underscored the ratification of his supremacy in Rome. Inheritance of the same title marked out Tiberius as the Empire's second *princeps*. What then were the implications for Livia? Disenfranchised by virtue of her sex, could she remain hors de combat as the bearer of this highly politicized moniker? Did she want to? For more than half a century she had moderated her behaviour in line with Augustus's wishes. Her future conduct would depend on her interpretation of the wishes of the dead man whom she now called father.

Livia applied herself at once to the letter of Augustus's will. Although Tiberius, Suetonius tells us, 'refrained from using the title "Augustus", though his by right of inheritance, in any letters except those addressed to foreign monarchs',[1] Livia embraced it: those slaves to whom she granted freedom – her freedmen and women – took the name Julius or Julia.[2] Perhaps the shared title suggested to her an ongoing relationship with Augustus to which she clung for emotional reasons as well as political expediency. Like adoption into the Julian clan, it expressed her proximity to the man the Senate was quick to declare a god. Perhaps Livia regarded it as a guarantee of inviolability.

If, however, she chose to consider the nomination as a green light to involvement in Roman public life, we discover a further piece of the jigsaw puzzle of Livia's posthumous vilification in the ancient sources. The ancient writers opposed on principle the emergence of a woman into the public arena. Augustus's opposition, as Octavian, to Cleopatra, his failure to produce a male heir, and his programme of moral legislation had all accorded Livia a degree of prominence unknown among women of the Republic. Now the testamentary award of a political title encouraged her to independent public activity. It was an affront to sexist sensibilities. Writers whose perception of Livia was shaped by her place in Tiberius's principate revisited her actions of the preceding half-century in the light of septuagenarian transgressions. In place of Livia's constructive role as Augustus's helpmate, they saw only ambition, an impulse to be feared among prominent women. It was a small step to accusations of poison and murder, the ultimate arsenal of aggressive ambition. As Octavian had demonstrated in his treatment of Cleopatra, the demonized enemy is a defeated enemy.

*

Cassius Dio describes the aftermath of Augustus's funeral. 'When these ceremonies had been completed, all the others departed, but Livia remained on the spot for five days, attended by the most distinguished of the knights; then she had his bones gathered up and placed in his tomb.'[3] We cannot state confidently that Livia's lonely vigil arose from devotion, nor on the contrary that it represents an exercise in keeping up appearances, behaving as Roman precedent demanded. At some point during those five days in which Augustus's pyre smouldered and Livia kept watch, an obliging senator, the ex-praetor Numerius Atticus, witnessed the deceased *princeps*'s ascent to heaven in the same way, as tradition maintained, as occurred in the case of Romulus. Livia rewarded him with a payment of a million sesterces. She could afford to be generous. Augustus's will divided his estate between his wife and his adopted son, one third to Livia, the remainder to Tiberius. The financial element of Livia's share amounted to fifty million sesterces. Such was the unprecedented magnitude of the bequest that the Senate was required to waive in Livia's favour the Voconian Law restricting female inheritance.

This represented a resounding victory for the Claudian element of Augustus's family. The death of Agrippa Postumus at the beginning of Tiberius's rule eliminated the late *princeps*'s final grandson. Any successor in the next generation could be at best Augustus's great-grandchild through Agrippina the Elder. Not only would such an heir share minimal quantities of Octavian and Julian blood, but through his father, Agrippina's husband Germanicus, he too would be a Claudian. In the meantime, Augustus's accumulated wealth, including his slaves and freedmen, passed in its entirety into the hands of a family to which he was unconnected save by marriage. How the leading players of that family chose to share their inheritance became an important dynamic of the early years of Tiberius's principate. Inevitably, the sources portray Livia and Tiberius as a family at war. Their picture is one of personal animosity between mother and son. In truth those differences, such as they were, were ideological as much as personal.

Augustus, we know, had behaved assiduously in restricting the scope of Livia's influence. Favours were not hers for the asking, as Livia discovered when Augustus refused her first appeal for freedom for the people of Samos or, on another occasion, her request that a Gaul be granted Roman citizenship. In their unprecedented position, negotiating a compromise between Augustus's declared republicanism and the realities of sovereign power, husband and wife maintained a cautious balancing act. Both, we assume, were aware of the rules of engagement. That Augustus valued Livia's advice appears to be proven by his discussion of political matters with her. That he prepared for such conversations by making notes in advance, careful to clarify his opinion in his own mind, may equally suggest he feared her ability to persuade him to her point of view against his will. Livia may have regarded Octavian's position as *princeps* and 'Augustus' with a degree of reverence; there is no evidence that her feelings for the man himself encompassed elements of awe. Propriety demanded discernible clear blue water between Augustus's public life and his domestic relationships. Both husband and wife maintained the semblance of that distinction. In practice it had frequently been an artificial divide.

Suetonius preserves letters from Augustus to Livia concerning the latter's grandson, the future Emperor Claudius. 'As regards the immediate question in your last letter, I have no objection to his taking charge of the priests' banquet at the Festival,' Augustus writes on one occasion.[4] We do not know if Augustus and Livia were separated at the time of this discussion, Augustus absent on business or Livia at her villa at Prima Porta. If not, we see clearly the shared habit of committing to paper requests that touched on the public arena, even if, as in this case, the issue concerned the couple's family as much as the official life of Rome. In this instance, having set out his opinion, Augustus entrusts the matter to Livia's judgement: 'In short, my dear Livia, I am anxious that a decision should be reached on this matter once and for all, to save us from further alternations of hope and despair.'[5] Although Augustus denied Livia official recognition in his lifetime in the form of any public position, these are letters written between equals, opinions canvassed, considered and, on occasion we must assume, accepted and acted upon. It is possible that Augustus discussed with Livia her continuing exclusion from Roman politics. Given her background and upbringing, this may not have been necessary.

A question then arises about Augustus's intention in creating Livia

'Augusta' in his will. Did he deliberately impose on Tiberius a problem he himself had been unwilling to address? Did he intend Tiberius to rule jointly with Livia? Did he imagine that the son would benefit from his mother's long experience and her close association with himself, his success and his popularity with the Senate and people of Rome? Or did Augustus simply mean to grant his widow a position of public respect and of continuing behind-the-scenes influence in private? Such an intention surely could not be realized through the grant of a title with such explicit political resonance. There are few indications of Augustus's political acumen failing him late in life. It would be surprising if he had chosen to act naively in a matter as significant as the future leadership of Rome.

If Augustus failed to discuss his testamentary intentions with Livia, the business of interpretation fell simultaneously to her and Tiberius. As events would prove, their thoughts in this matter were not alike. The Republican son of a Republican father, Tiberius opposed on principle a role for women in Roman public life. 'He repeatedly asserted that only reasonable honours must be paid to women,' Tacitus records.[6] He also opposed a culture of excessive formal recognition of any single individual, himself included. 'Of the many high honours voted him, he accepted none but a few unimportant ones,' Suetonius tells us. 'He declined also to set the title "Emperor" before his name, or "Father of the Country" after; or to let the Civic Crown . . . be fixed above his own palace door; and even refrained from using the title "Augustus".'[7] The reputation he desired was the same as that to which the office-holders of Marcus's atrium had once aspired. 'They will do more than justice to my memory if they judge me worthy of my ancestors, careful of your interests, steadfast in danger and fearless of animosities incurred in the public service,' he tells the Senate in Tacitus's account.[8]

Moderate in her habits, her public profile a model of restraint, eschewing any approach to extravagance that might suggest the Cleopatra-like excesses of eastern monarchy, Livia nevertheless does not appear to have shared Tiberius's regret at Augustus's overthrow of the Republic. Augustus's assumption of supreme authority contravened that oligarchic power-sharing which once was central to Roman government. What he maintained in its stead was the Republic's focus on the civic-mindedness of its servants. In this way husband and wife reconciled the apparent contradiction of the restoration of the Republic by a quasi-monarch. In 13 BC Augustus had not balked at presenting himself in a ruler's guise on the friezes of the Altar of Peace that bore his name. Wreathed and garlanded, he was distinguished from every other figure – *princeps*, father of his family and the State, godlike in his attributes. Only Livia shared the symbolism of Augustus's costume. Following his death and his grant to her of the title 'Augusta', she showed reluctance in discarding that wreath and garland.

Livia it was who masterminded Tiberius's accession, suppressing news of Augustus's death and surrounding the house at Nola with loyal troops. In this way at least Tiberius owed the principate to his mother. Astute and practical, Livia created an environment in which he could safely take control. This done, the sources momentarily lose interest in Augustus's widow, their focus Tiberius, his actions and outlook. Along-side the two handwritten notebooks of his will, Augustus had entrusted to the Vestal Virgins three sealed rolls. One contained directions for his funeral. While Tiberius finalized with the Senate the implementation of those directions, Livia disappears from view. Perhaps she made plans of her own. Alongside the official ceremonies of Augustus's funeral, Livia instituted a personal act of commemoration, according to Dio. 'Livia held a private festival in his honour at the palace, which lasted for three days.' Significantly, Dio adds, 'This ceremony is still carried out by the reigning emperor down to the present day.'[9]

At the outset of Tiberius's reign, Livia's actions – unwitting or otherwise – were those of a reigning emperor. In matters concerning Augustus, mother and son presented a semblance of concord. Dio describes 'decrees passed in memory of Augustus, nominally by the Senate, but in fact by Tiberius and Livia ... I have ... mentioned Livia's name, because she took a share in the proceedings, as if she possessed full powers.'[10] Except in the inference of the Augusta title, Livia did not possess full powers, nor need we accept unchallenged Dio's opinion that her behaviour gave rise to such an assumption. It may have seemed natural to her to interest herself in Augustus's funeral arrangements and his posthumous honours. That she did so in a manner which, intentionally 'private', became public is indicative of the problems which lay ahead. Those problems were of neither Livia's nor Tiberius's making.

'Goodbye, Livia: never forget whose wife you have been!' Augustus tells his wife with a kiss minutes before dying, in Suetonius's version.[11] His words have been interpreted as a statement of love, imploring Livia to remain romantically constant. Is this likely? Livia was seventy-two and of stern moral outlook; the probability of her conceiving a new emotional attachment at this point was slight. But to a woman whose heredity included the taint of excessive pride, newly invested with a title of unrivalled distinction, an alternative interpretation of Augustus's farewell may have suggested itself. Was it possible that Augustus admonished her to mindfulness of her status in Rome? In remembering whose wife she had been, Livia clung to the position she occupied by virtue of her marriage. Augustus's death changed that position. But his investment of Livia with a female version of his own title perhaps sought to prevent the march of time and preserve the earlier status quo. If so, it was an unfair burden to impose on Tiberius. Augustus had circumscribed Livia's prominence; Tiberius would find the task more difficult.

One of the three sealed rolls entrusted for safekeeping to the Vestal Virgins alongside Augustus's will contained, Suetonius tells us, 'a record of his reign, which he wished to have engraved on bronze and posted at the entrance to the Mausoleum'.[12] This was the document known as the *Res Gestae Divi Augusti*, the 'Acts of the Deified Augustus'. Briefer than the thirteen-volume autobiography written during his convalescence in Spain forty years earlier, the *Res Gestae* lists Augustus's version of his achievements in the service of Rome. It is a businesslike if vainglorious piece of work, with its tally of triumphs, ovations and salutations as *imperator,* its census figures and lists of laws passed and territories secured, but its portrait of Augustus's career is selective. It omits mention of the Proscriptions or the lengthy power struggle against Mark Antony. It omits evaluation of those measures whose success was at best qualified. It also omits any mention of Livia. 'Never forget whose wife you have been,' Augustus addressed his wife, confronting death. In Rome, it was impossible that Livia should have said the reverse to him. And so the official record of Augustus's principate, carved in bronze, despite references to that moral legislation for which Livia became an archetype and the temple restorations she seconded, excludes any contribution by Livia arising from her long marriage. In life, Augustus had exploited the women of his family as political pawns. In death, he overlooked their very existence.

In tone and outlook, the *Res Gestae* is a Republican document, a ledger-like account of service to the state. Its tenor may have been more agreeable to Tiberius than that of Augustus's will, fraught with problems as the latter would soon reveal itself. Tiberius, Tacitus tells us, determined at the very beginning of his principate to clip his mother's wings. 'He was jealous and nervous, and regarded this elevation of a woman as derogatory to his own person.'[13] In truth, Livia's elevation – apparently confirmed by the terms of Augustus's will, and almost certainly more 'derogatory' in Tacitus's mind than that of Tiberius – was not new. The silence of the *Res Gestae* aside, Livia had devoted fifty years to creating for herself a position of prominence unrivalled in five centuries of Claudian distinction. At the sound of the last trump, Augustus recognized those efforts by bestowing on his widow the blessing of his own divine blood.

30

'His mother Livia vexed him'

At a still unidentified point in the first half of the nineteenth century, a ring entered the collection of the British Royal Family.[1] Little is known about its origins or how it came to be included in the Royal Collection. It was neither particularly old nor new at the time of its acquisition, probably dating from the end of the eighteenth century. It takes the form of an onyx cameo framed in gold. On the cameo are carved three heads in profile, one male and two female. The male head has been tentatively identified as that of Tiberius, the female head closest to it as Livia, the third profile is unidentified but may represent a personification of Rome or an allegorical figure. 'Tiberius' wears the laurel wreath of office, 'Livia' a form of the *nodus* hairstyle. The features of the two portraits are closely assimilated, each strong-jawed, with long, straight nose and large, oval eyes. Most likely the jewel was a souvenir of the Grand Tour. It may have been modelled on a Roman original – a similar portrait in Florence's Museo Archaeologico has been suggested. The head of Tiberius dominates, carved from the darkest layer of stone. The shadowy profile of Livia beneath, tertiary-coloured and translucent, cannot be overlooked.

As in the eighteenth century, so in the first: Tiberius could not escape his association with Livia. Across the empire, couplings like that replicated in minature on a cameo set in a ring proliferated. At Cumae, near Naples, seat of the famous Sibyl, an ancient Greek colony rich in religious resonance, priests dedicated statues of the *princeps* and his mother.[2] At Tralles, in southwest Turkey, Tiberius and Livia shared a priest; their heads appeared together on the coins of eastern mints. [3] Often Augustus was included alongside his survivors, the source of their claim to honours – a triad of eminence and quasi-divinity. In the theatre at Volterra stood statues of Augustus, Livia and Tiberius.

The year after Tiberius's accession, the authorities of the city of Gytheum, a port in the Laconian Gulf, wrote to Rome's new ruler. Gytheum was in Roman Sparta, an area with close ties to the Claudii, where once, during their flight from Octavian and the forces of the Triumvirs, Nero, Livia and Tiberius had sought sanctuary. In altered circumstances, the city's authorities proposed a festival dedicated to the newly deified Augustus. They intended to honour not only the deceased emperor but leading members of his family, notably Tiberius and Livia, and set out their intention of commissioning statues or painted images of the imperial family. [4] Both the city's proposed honours and Tiberius's reply survive as inscriptions, our fullest record of ceremonies of the Roman imperial cult. [5] In this case, Tiberius declined images for himself: 'I myself am satisfied with the more modest honours suitable for mortal men.' He stated that Livia must make her own reply when she was fully acquainted with details of the honours proposed for her. We do not know the substance of that reply. Perhaps Livia's response to the Gytheans was less repudiatory than that of her son; perhaps the Gytheans chose simply to ignore the strictures of both *princeps* and exalted mother. Despite Tiberius's disclaimer, his own image joined that of Livia in Gytheum's festival of the Divine Augustus. At the beginning and again at the end of daily processions, offerings of incense were made to painted images set up in the city's theatre. Those images depicted Augustus the Father, Julia Augusta and *Imperator* Tiberius Caesar Augustus. [6] In the minds of provincial worshippers, the family was united not simply by their shared repute and eminence, but, since Augustus's will, by a common name.

In AD 18 the city government of Forum Clodii in Latium inscribed a decree outlining its official celebrations of birthdays within the imperial family. Noting the city's statues of Augustus, Tiberius and Livia, the decree stipulates, on Augustus's birthday, a public sacrifice and games held in his honour, a public banquet and sacrifice for Tiberius on his birthday and, on Livia's birthday, the distribution of wine and cakes to

female worshippers of Bona Dea.[7] In vain Tiberius resisted these trib-
utes to a divinity which, on his own part and that of Livia, had yet to
be attained. Torn between a genuine distaste for the culture of flattery,
of which deification was the ultimate manifestation, and a recognition
of the benefits inherent in his association with the divine Augustus, he
adopted a two-part policy. In mainland Italy he forswore all temples,
priests and altars to himself. As Dio reports, 'no sacred precinct was set
apart for him either by his own choice or in any other way ... nor was
anybody allowed to set up an image of him; for he promptly and expressly
forbade any city or private citizen to do so'.[8] By contrast he acquiesced
in the blandishments of provincial centres. The evidence of Gytheum
suggests that he did so with a degree of tactful kindliness which would
afterwards appear uncharacteristic. It must nevertheless have seemed a
killjoy instinct. From the outset of the principate and even earlier, the
empire's distant subjects made sense of their thraldom to Rome through
the cult of Rome's leader's divinity.

There is no reason to assume that Tiberius's policy of quashing cult
fervour arose from a desire to restrict honours paid to Livia. His focus
appears genuinely to have been himself. The corollary of his approach
would indeed be a curtailment of the worship of any member of the
imperial family save Augustus, an approach which inevitably affected
Livia but which, at that point, was technically correct. As the cases of
Forum Clodii and Gytheum prove, Tiberius's subtlety met with variable
success. Livia's association with Bona Dea, celebrated in Forum Clodii
on her birthday, was not necessarily akin to investing her with divine
attributes, nor was it an association within Tiberius's control. She had
enjoyed a long connection with the female-oriented cult, as we know;
her publicized restoration of the temple of Bona Dea Subsaxana dates
from the beginning of Augustus's principate.

Despite the insinuations of ancient sources bent on exaggerating tensions between Tiberius and his mother, the curmudgeonliness of
Tiberius's response to their joint worship was qualified. It was in fact
exactly that which he applied to the question of his own worship. The
extent and diversity of provincial honours paid to Livia during her son's
reign suggest unconcern on Tiberius's part at this aspect of his mother's
profile. He did not exploit the issue as a vehicle for point-scoring; his

sensitivity, even oversensitivity, was grounded in principle. In AD 23 cities of the Roman province of Asia competed to host a new temple dedicated jointly to Tiberius, Livia and the Senate. The gesture was one of thanksgiving, acknowledging Rome's punishment of the province's disgraced former governor, Gaius Junius Silanus, and the procurator Lucilius Capito. Tiberius assented to the proposal, and the temple was built in Smyrna on the Aegean coast, the site of modern-day Izmir. When, two years later, the province of Hispania Ulterior asked for permission to build a similar temple, the *princeps* reached a different decision. On this occasion, the Senate had been dropped by the Spanish envoys, who meant to dedicate their temple to Tiberius and Livia alone.[9] 'Disdainful of compliment,' Tacitus reports, 'Tiberius saw an opportunity to refute rumours of his increasing self-importance.'[10] He withheld permission, using the opportunity provided by what he recognized as an apparent inconsistency to explain his position on provincial honours. His speech on the subject was that in which he made claim to a place in the temples of his listeners' hearts. Whether, as Tacitus suggests, Tiberius regarded the encouragement of the imperial cult as a form of self-importance, we do not know. Nor need we assume he interpreted Livia's greater enthusiasm as an expression of that vice in her. As time passed, the differences between mother and son would increasingly focus on questions of role and status. With regard to Hispania Ulterior, Tiberius was overly mindful of the Senate's exclusion, the technicality that neither he nor Livia was yet, by senatorial decree, divine, and the absence, unlike in Asia, of any beneficial political purpose behind the scheme.

Tiberius, Suetonius tells us, 'complained that his mother Livia vexed him by wanting to be co-ruler of the Empire; which was why he avoided frequent meetings or long private talks with her . . . A senatorial decree adding "Son of Livia" as well as "Son of Augustus" to his honorifics so deeply offended him that he vetoed proposals to confer "Mother of the Country" or any similarly high-sounding title on her.'[11]

Among principal grounds for the worsening relations between Livia and Tiberius following the latter's accession was a dispute over the role of Livia in Tiberius's adoption as Augustus's heir. The evidence to suggest that this became contentious through the actions of either Livia or

Tiberius is inconclusive. Dio claims of Livia that, 'in the time of Augustus she had possessed the greatest influence and she always declared that it was she who had made Tiberius emperor'.[12] We need not accept Dio's word unsupported. Livia and Tiberius both knew enough of Roman politics to recognize that Livia alone could not have made Tiberius *princeps*. Dio's statement, if indeed Livia ever uttered its equivalent, is of a sort that she would surely have made only to Tiberius himself and then only under extreme duress. Throughout her marriage to Augustus, she had behaved with restraint and discretion. Are we to believe that at Augustus's death she discarded those virtues? Did she demand for herself public acknowledgement of the power which for so long she had taken pains to conceal, knowing that its concealment was its only safeguard? It is more likely that it was the Senate's misguided decree which sowed the seed of discord between mother and son.

We have seen that only Augustus, acting with the support of the Senate, could have elevated Tiberius to the position of *princeps*-in-waiting. It was Augustus who entrusted Tiberius with the military commands on which his reputation rested, and Augustus who possessed by senatorial grant the quiverful of powers which would eventually be formalized in the institution of the principate. In point of law Tiberius was 'son of Augustus', as he had been since AD 4. It was only by virtue of his kinship with Augustus, expressed in the relationship of father and son, that Tiberius was able to become his predecessor's principal inheritor.

Tiberius overlooked at this point the fact that Livia's marriage of 38 BC was the single condition which created the opportunity for her son also to become Augustus's son. He stamped on the Senate's suggestion that he be hailed 'son of Livia' – or 'son of Julia', as Tacitus and Cassius Dio more correctly report it. He understood the impossibility of such a concept in Rome, where legitimate filiation derived exclusively from the father.[13] Undoubtedly, he was also reluctant to elevate Livia to the status of 'king-maker'. Perhaps he misunderstood that, in creating Livia 'Julia Augusta', Augustus meant to enhance Tiberius's own legitimacy, eliminating at a stroke any suggestion that he owed his position to his mother's scandalous affair and remarriage.[14]

It was not a mistake Livia herself made, whatever the inference of Dio's account. She was surely behind the commission of a cameo produced

shortly after Augustus's death.[15] Reversing the hierarchy of that eigh-
teenth-century ring, she is the larger, dominant figure.[16] In her hands
Livia holds a bust – that of her son Tiberius. She is portrayed in the
guise of Venus Genetrix, kinswoman goddess of the Julians, her own
new family and, since AD 4, that of Tiberius too. By a quirk of fate, she
and her son share the same legal father. In the topsy-turvy flattery of
the cameo, presumably a private commission intended for limited circulation, Livia's status is the higher: daughter, wife and goddess. It was
a delusion which could be humoured only in private. Time would prove
that a mother's place did not outstrip that of the *princeps* and that deification did not arise from simple association. The cameo is an exercise
in make-believe. It is also the earliest surviving image of a living empress
masquerading as a goddess.[17] Had Tiberius known of it, it might have
provided him with cause for concern.

Livia was in her thirties, accompanying Augustus to the eastern empire,
when the provincial mint in the Ionian city of Teos issued coins asserting
her divine status. Since that point, her cult had gained significant
momentum. Overseas she was associated with a gaggle of goddesses,
from Ceres to Cybele, in addition to personifications embracing peace
and concord. That Cotta Maximus was able to buy a silver statuette of
Livia to send to his friend Ovid suggests that at home too her profile
had acquired aspects of divinity. None of these developments, however,
rivalled the radicalism of an appointment made in Livia's favour in the
immediate aftermath of Augustus's death.

'At the time,' Dio relates, 'the Senate declared Augustus to be immortal,
assigned to him sacred rites and priests to perform them, and appointed
Livia . . . to be his priestess. They also authorized her to be attended by
a lictor whenever she exercised her sacred office.'[18] Augustus had
bequeathed his widow a title, 'Augusta'. In the establishment of the
deceased Emperor's cult, the Senate outstripped that distinction. Having
appointed a college of priests to serve the new god and Germanicus to
the role of chief priest, it created a further vacancy – for Livia, who
became priestess of the Divine Augustus. The Senate not only conferred
on Livia an official position but, in the award of a lictor – a freedman
attendant employed on public occasions – visible acknowledgement of

that position. It was the first grant of its sort in Roman imperial history to a woman who was not a Vestal Virgin.

Unsurprisingly, Livia applied herself to Augustus's cult with the wholeheartedness she had earlier brought to her embodiment of his programme of moral and social reform. Together she and Tiberius agreed to build a temple to Augustus in Rome. It was a speaking gesture, indicative of Tiberius's endorsement of Livia's new role. 'Priestess and daughter', as Velleius Paterculus described her, Livia understood the benefits to herself of Augustus's divine honours: a reaffirmation of her right to respect and a continuing role in Tiberius's Rome.[19] She staged festivals in honour of Augustus and dedicated his image in her house on the Palatine. Indirectly her efforts also benefited Tiberius, son of Rome's newest god. But there is no evidence that Augustus's cult forged a lasting rapprochement between mother and son.

The year after his accession, Tacitus records, Tiberius 'had been annoyed by anonymous verses. These had criticized his cruelty, arrogance and bad relations with his mother.'[20] It was not the first time lampoons of this sort had circulated in Rome. In the decade before his death, an exasperated Augustus took decisive action in condemning such verses as treasonable.[21] But their taunts failed to disappear. 'You cruel monster!' ran one preserved by Suetonius, 'I'll be damned, I will, if even your own mother loves you still.'[22] In the years before Livia's death, Tiberius would abandon Rome for a second retirement, his destination on this occasion not Rhodes but Capri. Among explanations given for his withdrawal was his desire to escape from his mother.

As in the sources' portrayal of Livia's poisoning of Augustus, Tiberius and Livia suffer from a correspondence drawn, but not acknowledged, between their position and a later imperial parallel, in this case that of the Emperor Nero and his mother, *femme capable de tout*, Agrippina the Younger. In each case the ambitious wife of an emperor is attributed with positioning her son on Rome's throne by misdeeds. In the case of Nero and Agrippina, good relations between mother and all-powerful son 'of naturally cruel heart' proved of short duration.[23] The emperor made an unsuccessful attempt to kill his mother in a staged accident at sea. Equally unsuccessfully, he tried to poison her and to crush her in her bed by means of a collapsing ceiling made of lead. Thwarted but determined, he finally ordered her execution by hired assassins. His actions – extreme even by the standards of Julio-Claudian dysfunctionalism – did not echo those of his predecessor Tiberius.

But the topos of the ambitious mother and ungrateful son proved irresistible to Roman historians. There is no evidence to suspect Tiberius of harbouring murderous intentions towards Livia. Evidence of animosity between mother and son is mostly conjectural. Each understood their mutual dependence and the limits Rome set on their behaviour. The venom of Nero and Agrippina provided richer pickings for storytellers than the more moderate emotions of their wiser forebears. In the written record all are tarred with the same brush.

CHAPTER 31

Above the law?

The funeral of Livia's grandson Claudius in AD 54 was an event of some splendour, similar in scale to that of Augustus. Its solemn grandeur, Tacitus asserts, was attributable to Claudius's widow, the same Agrippina who would shortly meet a bloody end at Nero's hands. 'For Agrippina,' we read, 'strove to emulate the magnificence of her great-grandmother Livia.'[1]

At least in part, Tacitus's inference is misleading. The magnificence of Augustus's funeral, with its *imagines* of legendary Romans from Romulus onwards and parade of allegorical images of subject nations, was not Livia's but his own doing. Augustus enumerated its details in one of those three sealed rolls he entrusted to the Vestal Virgins alongside the notebooks containing his will. Livia's magnificence was of a different variety. She disdained extravagant gestures. Her own funeral would be a modest affair – if the sources are to be believed, a valedictory attempt on Tiberius's part to cut her down to size for one last time; perhaps in fact a ceremony in keeping with that sense of propriety which characterized all her appearances on Rome's public stage.

Yet at the end of her life, Livia found herself a woman of notable wealth, at the head of an impressive household of an estimated thousand retainers and a network of clients which spanned the Roman world. Her portfolio of land holdings included Salome's bequest of cities in Judaea, estates in Egypt boasting vineyards, papyrus marshes, vegetable farms and granaries,[2] an estate close to Thyateira on the Lydian border in Asia Minor and her villa at Prima Porta, where she cultivated a crop of symbolic richness in the laurels used for imperial wreaths. She also owned commercial property: brickworks in Campania, a copper mine in Gaul, apartment blocks in Rome. Her wealth extended to hard cash: in her will she would bequeath the future emperor Galba the significant sum of fifty million sesterces.

But these were private possessions, perhaps little-known to the ordinary Roman who, like us, might express surprise at Livia employing a pearl-setter when her appearance was so studiedly free of ostentation. As a member of Livia's family, Agrippina could have seen what was hidden from ordinary eyes. Agrippina's memoirs – now lost, but used at points by Tacitus – painted a negative picture of Livia. Did the younger woman, herself ambitious and acquisitive, consider that Livia's knowledge of her own regal riches, the eminence of her position as Augusta and the innate pride of the Claudii together engendered in her a sense of personal magnificence that did indeed shape her behaviour?

Livia's record under Tiberius appears to differ from her previous conduct. Repeatedly, if sporadically, she behaved in a manner which suggests consciousness of her unique position. She resumed the morning *salutatio*, which, we have seen, infirmity forced Augustus to abandon. She did so not as Tiberius's deputy – itself a highly unusual proposition – but apparently in her own right, perhaps in the so-called Casa di Livia which, while close to Augustus's Palatine house, is nevertheless discrete. Livia's *salutationes* were published in the *acta publica*, the public record, alongside the names of those attending.[3] This official sanction raises the undertaking above that of a private individual. It is presumably an example of Livia exploring the possibilities of the undefined role encompassed by the Augusta title, in this instance behaving in a manner later associated with widowed consorts who maintain the routine of their late husbands' courts. As if to emphasize her continuing public significance, Livia's birthday was celebrated by several of Rome's priestly colleges, not simply in the sacrifices made on the Ara Pacis Augustae. In addition, her name was included alongside that of Tiberius in annual vows made for the welfare of the *princeps*.[4]

It was a significant leap from that position Cassius Dio states she outlined for herself in relation to Augustus, almost a refutation of her claim that she avoided meddling in any of the *princeps*'s affairs. In Rome the *salutatio*, as Livia must have been well aware, was a masculine forum. It provided an opportunity for members of the public to make requests of senators, trusting in the power invested in senatorial office to satisfy those requests. But Livia possessed no such office, nor, we might assume, did she possess access to such power. Events would prove that, with Tiberius's blessing, not only she could achieve results equivalent to the personal intervention of senators, but her friends assumed as much of Livia.

Two years after Augustus's death, Livia and Tiberius together intervened in the legal process in aid of one of Livia's friends. Their joint intervention was sufficiently irregular to attract the attention of the ancient commentators. Livia's friend Plautia Urgulania owed a sum of money which she showed no inclination to pay. In Tacitus's account, but for the intervention of Lucius Calpurnius Piso, who adopts towards Plautia the role of avenging angel, she would have succeeded in reneging on its payment since 'her friendship with the Augusta had placed her above the law'.[5] Piso, however, had set his sights against the corruption of the capital and determined to make an example of the older woman. 'Defying the Augusta, he ... dared to hale her friend Urgulania into court from the palace itself'.[6] Plautia had ignored Piso's summons, instead setting off for Livia's house where she assumed, it seems, she would benefit from something akin to sanctuary. Her thoughts were apparently seconded by Livia. They differed from those of Piso, who followed her to Livia's house to repeat his demands. Since Livia supported Plautia's chosen course of resistance, it fell to Tiberius to mediate by upholding the formalities of the rule of law. Livia asserted that her dignity had been compromised. Resorting to language associated with the laws governing the preservation of the *princeps*'s majesty or '*maiestas*', she stated that Piso's persistence both humiliated and violated her.

Wisely, Tiberius dodged the issue of Livia's assumption of majesty. He decided that, 'without acting autocratically, he could back his mother up to the point of promising to appear before the praetor and support Urgulania' and set off from the palace to walk to court in the company of his military escort.[7] Deliberately hindering his own progress by stopping to greet members of the public along the way, Tiberius gave Livia sufficient time to relent. In the time that elapsed, honour intact, Livia, not Tiberius or Plautia, paid Plautia's debt.

It was an incident in which all involved successfully made the point they wished to make. Piso had demanded and achieved the removal of a legal irregularity. Plautia had flaunted friends in high places in order to resist an unwanted summons. Livia had asserted with grandiloquence the eminence and power of her position. Tiberius had defended the processes of law. On this occasion it was Tiberius, not Livia, who won popular plaudits. Unless mother and son had devised together their joint response to Piso's challenge, Tiberius cannot have derived from the incident any surety about Livia's future submissiveness. It would appear to be an unusual instance of Livia misjudging the behaviour required of her – resorting to the rank pulling to which she felt entitled in place of the carefully modulated behaviour by which she had attained that rank.

In AD 17 Livia and Tiberius acted together under happier circumstances. Travelling from Nicopolis in Achaia to Syria to quash unrest in the east, Tiberius's adopted son and Livia's grandson Germanicus broke his journey on the island of Lesbos. For the ninth and last time, his wife Agrippina the Elder was due to give birth. With the safe delivery of her baby, a daughter, Julia Livilla, mother and son supplied a wet nurse to the status-conscious woman who was respectively their step-granddaughter and step-daughter-in-law. The wet nurse chosen, Prima, apparently gave satisfaction: she may later have been rewarded for her services with her freedom.[8]

It was a gesture of family feeling which would subsequently be overlooked. Within two years of Livilla's birth, to widespread sadness in Rome, Germanicus was dead. He was the latest in a lengthening line of affable young men of Augustus's family to be struck down in their prime. 'The loves of the Romans seemed brief and ill-omened,' Tacitus commented, drawing parallels between Germanicus's unexpected death and those of his father Drusus and uncle Marcellus.[9] It was, inevitably, a short step to accusations of poisoning directed against Livia.

Livia was seventy-eight years old at the time. Germanicus was the elder son of that son whose death had caused her such paroxysms of grief that she had resorted to consulting the philosopher Areus to mitigate her pain. In time, in the event that Augustus's strictures were followed, Germanicus would have succeeded Tiberius as *princeps*, a second Emperor born not of Augustus's blood but of that of Livia and her favourite daughter-in-law Antonia. Livia's motive for this her final crime was her fear that Germanicus, like Drusus before him, intended instead to restore the Republic. Since Livia would almost certainly be dead at that point, it was a less than convincing argument. Nor was it one that was widely held in AD 19.

Germanicus himself believed he had been poisoned by the recently appointed Roman governor of Syria, Gnaeus Cornelius Piso, and his wife Munatia Plancina. Surviving trial documents indicate that he specifically testified against Piso.[10] 'Examination of the floor and walls of his bedroom revealed the remains of human bodies, spells, curses, lead tablets inscribed with the patient's name, charred and bloody ashes, and other malignant objects which are supposed to consign souls to the powers of the tomb,' Tacitus relates with a note of grim satisfaction. 'At the same time agents of Piso were accused of spying on the sickbed.'[11]

For the historian like Tacitus, bent on Livia's posthumous damnation, there were telling details. Plancina was a close friend of Livia's, her father the author of Octavian's 'Augustus' title in 27 BC.[12] By adoption, Germanicus and Agrippina stood in relation to Livia as step-grandson and step-granddaughter, a variant on that relationship of stepmother and stepchild which Tacitus consistently exploits to Livia's detriment. At the trials of Piso and Plancina in AD 20, Livia intervened on the latter's behalf, requiring Tiberius to address the Senate in her place in order to secure Plancina's pardon. Given the strength of feeling in Rome and the weight of evidence against Piso and his wife, it was an unwise, even ignoble act on Livia's part, which quickly gave rise to negative comment. The Senate's response suggests its sympathies lay elsewhere. Only the consul Cotta Messalinus in any way seconded Tiberius's appeal.[13] When, inevitably, the Senate acceded to the *princeps*'s request, it bestowed its pardon on Plancina without enthusiasm, as a favour to Livia 'for having served the state excellently'.[14] That service did not encompass the current instance. The Senate resisted the conclusion that Livia's partiality proved her own guilt and publicly continued to laud the woman it had for so long extolled as a model of female virtue. Inscriptions found in Spain, dating from the year of the Piso/Plancina trials, reiterate Livia's praiseworthiness for 'her many great favours to men of every rank'. In a remarkable break with Republican precedent, the inscriptions attest, 'She could rightly and deservedly have supreme influence in what she asked from the Senate, though she used that influence sparingly.'[15]

Great age does not always sharpen political sensibilities and seventy-eight was indeed a great age in AD 20. Undeniably, there is a sense as Livia's life drew to its slow close of her losing her sureness of touch and that legerdemain which once had characterized her exploitation of issues and events to her own benefit. Certainly the events surrounding Germanicus's death and the trials of Piso and Plancina served Livia ill. At Germanicus's funeral, from which Livia and Tiberius were both pointedly absent, all eyes focused on the grieving Aggripina. Tacitus describes the torch of Roman womanly virtue, once Livia's assured possession, passing ineluctably from Augusta to step-granddaughter. 'The glory of her country they called her – the only true descendant of Augustus, the unmatched model of traditional behaviour.'[16] That final tribute had formed the basis of Livia's reputation for more than half a century. To her credit – or perhaps because Tacitus's statement is without foundation – she exacted no revenge. Agrippina would afterwards suffer a dramatic fall from grace. Among her contemporaries, it was considered significant that her banishment to Pandateria, the vicious beating at the hands of a centurion in which she lost an eye, and her slow death from self-induced starvation, occurred only once Livia had died. Then, so the story ran, this ambitious, politically active granddaughter of Augustus lost the safety net of her step-grandmother's protection.

Despite tensions, the relationship of Livia and Tiberius remained amicable as late as AD 22, when, for the first time in her life, Livia succumbed to serious illness. 'Either mother and son were still good friends or, if they were not, they concealed it,' Tacitus comments of Tiberius's visit to his mother's sickbed.[17] That Rome shared Tiberius's opinion at this point is confirmed by the honours voted Livia on her recovery – a statue dedicated by the equestrians to the goddess Equestrian Fortuna and many of the privileges of Rome's highest-ranking women, the Vestal Virgins, including the right to sit with the Vestals at public games and in the theatre and to travel within Rome in a carriage, the '*carpentum*'. How much use Livia made of these privileges depends on the fullness of her recovery, information impossible to retrieve. Not for the first time she largely disappears from the sources following her illness. Although this may indicate a life of increasing retirement, it is also attributable to the ancient authors' preoccupation with current political developments, namely the rise and rise of the would-be *princeps* Sejanus.

Livia, however, continued to involve herself in small-scale petitions. It was just such an application for Tiberius's intervention in legal procedure which finally drove a lasting wedge between Livia and that son whose future had consumed so many of her energies. The matter was a request concerning the advancement of a man only recently granted citizenship. Tiberius – correct in his assessment of the legal issue at stake – declined Livia's petition and, as Suetonius records, 'quarrelled openly with his mother'. Livia reacted furiously. In her anger, she 'produced from a strongbox some of Augustus's old letters to her commenting on Tiberius's sour and stubborn character'.[18] It was a dramatic but self-defeating gesture. Tiberius's anger matched that of his mother, its source not the contents of Augustus's letters but the fact that Livia had kept them and used them to taunt him so long after the event. This incident, Suetonius cautiously claims, 'is said to have been [Tiberius's] main reason for retirement to Capri'. Tacitus offers the alternative explanations that Tiberius wanted to escape from Sejanus or to conceal the cruelty and immorality of his conduct. Unable to resist a chance to denigrate Livia, however, he ultimately attributes his departure in AD 26 to 'his mother's bullying'.[19]

Certainly Tiberius showed no signs of missing his mother in his self-imposed exile. During the remaining three years of Livia's life, Tiberius would visit his mother only once. In AD 29 he omitted even to attend her funeral, interesting himself in the business of her death only to the extent of capping those honours voted to her by the Senate. He annulled her will and vetoed her deification. A dozen years would pass before Livia's grandson Claudius formalized that metamorphosis. In the interval a troubled psychopath known to history as Caligula, the Emperor Gaius, decreed the divinity of his sister Julia Drusilla, the great incestuous passion of his short life. So unworthily did Livia escape becoming the first woman of the Roman Empire to be declared a goddess.

There were perhaps compensations of a form more familiar to us for the eighty-six-year-old widow. In 19 BC Livia and Augustus had visited the Greek city of Eleusis, west of Athens. Eleusis was the site of one of the ancient world's most sacred rituals, the Eleusinian Mysteries, shrouded in impenetrable secrecy but focused on the worship of Demeter and Persephone. We do not know if Livia became an Eleusinian initiate in 19 BC but the possibility certainly exists. Later, Eleusis would attract the scorn of the early Christians. An offshoot of an ancient pantheism characterized by the lofty vengefulness of its deities, it offered its initiates unusually the promise of rebirth – and the hope of a happy and joyful afterlife.

EPILOGUE

'You held your course without remorse'

Propertius opens Elegy 3.11 with a bang: 'Why are you astonished if a woman drives my life and drags, bound beneath her own laws, a man?'[1]

The question is deliberately provocative. The subject of Propertius's poem is contentious and highly charged – a lover's submission to his mistress. In Rome, no honourable template existed for such an impulse. Male submission was disgraceful, a source of contempt, the reason Romans tolerated active but not passive male homosexuality, the bar to a Roman soldier's surrender even in the face of certain defeat. The principal virtue of Rome's governing elite – its administrative, and military but also overwhelmingly its literary class – was '*virtus*' itself. Derived from the Latin word for man, '*vir*', *virtus* was not understood, as today, as an ethical concept of goodness but a definition of manliness in the form of a man's ideal behaviour.[2] *Virtus* became the Romans' defining quality, 'the badge of the Roman race and breed', as Cicero described it.[3] So close was the association of tribe and trait that the cult image of *Virtus* exactly matched that of the goddess Roma. Confusingly, women too could embrace *virtus*. In doing so, they accepted Rome's idealization of maleness and subscribed to their own subjection. They did not, like Propertius's mistress, drag a man 'bound beneath [their] own laws'.

Writing in the decade after Octavian's victory at Actium, Propertius defends his pose of submissiveness through comparison with Rome's recent fear of Cleopatra.[4] His point is simple. Although Romans seek to deny it, women *have* power. The poet's bondage to Cynthia reflects in miniature Rome's terror at Cleopatra's perceived expansionist threats.

265

In each case, mistress and monarch exploit the wiles of their sex, the Queen of Egypt as meretricious as any Roman femme fatale.

We do not know if Livia was familiar with Propertius's poetry. The elegist would become one of Maecenas's stable of poets invited to hymn Augustus's regime. Whether or not such sponsorship yielded a public reading of the third book of elegies, Livia understood too clearly the concept Propertius sought to stand on its head in 3.11. She devoted her public life to the Augustan status quo, that conservative romanticizing of a Republican golden age of political stability and domestic harmony. If Augustus exploited the rhetoric of *virtus* in pursuit of a better Rome, it was Livia who repeatedly acted as exemplum of its very specific requirements.

Her touch was sure. She took from Octavia the austere Roman *nodus* hairstyle and made it her own. She wore the *stola*, the shapeless '*noli me tangere*' of a garment made from woollen homespun which Augustus liked to maintain she wove herself in their Palatine atrium. She associated herself with recognizably female religious cults. Her charitable activities included contributions to the dowries of young girls and to parents of newborn babies. She assisted the victims of fire, the natural disaster most likely to rob Romans of their homes, implicitly strengthening her own associations with domesticity. 'In the domestic sphere,' as even Tacitus was forced to acknowledge, 'she cultivated virtue in the time-honoured fashion.' Mindful of the spirit of Augustus's much-vaunted legislation concerning marriage and the family, she donned a shining carapace of chastity, '*pudicitia*'. This ultimately earned her Horace's commendation as an '*univira*', Rome's cherished concept of the one-man woman, despite it being common knowledge that she had married Augustus in haste after embarking on an affair with him while still married to her first husband, Nero. 'Once, when some naked men met her and were to be put to death in consequence,' Dio relates, 'she saved their lives by saying that to chaste women such men are no whit different from statues.'[5]

Such statements were not spontaneous effusions. They arose as part of a larger policy of appearing to embrace the traditional parameters of Roman women's lives. Livia capitalized on the new possibilities generated by Augustus's politicization of private life to create a public exist-ence in which she seemed to confine herself to the private sphere of home and family. It was an accomplished balancing act, a puppetry of smoke and mirrors. It demonstrates the extent to which she recognized the restrictions of her position, even as the wife of Rome's leading citi-zen. In many ways her arena mirrored those two inches of ivory with which, eighteen hundred years later, Jane Austen concerned herself, the unchanging limitations of women in a male environment. From that tiny springboard, Livia created for herself a position of greater promin-ence, over a longer period of time, than had previously been enjoyed by any woman of the Republic.

Politically astute, she recognized that appearances were more import-ant than reality. In private she discussed a range of topics with Augustus. The *princeps* prepared himself for their discussions by committing his thoughts to paper in advance. Although Dio might claim of her, 'She occupied a very exalted station, far above all women of former days,' for the most part both she and Augustus took considerable pains to conceal the nature and degree of that exaltation.[6] It is reasonable to assume that Augustus both invited and, on occasion, accepted Livia's guidance in matters of a political complexion. Unlike Propertius, the *princeps* resisted broadcasting what in Roman terms amounted to role reversal. Although hostile sources insist that Livia demanded equality with Tiberius once the latter attained the principate, she maintained a stance of public deference towards Augustus. It was Ovid, not Livia her-self, who claimed for her the title '*princeps femina*', 'first lady'. A daughter of the Republican aristocracy, Livia had absorbed enough in her father's house to understand the impossibility of such a label.

Livia's behaviour during her marriage to Octavian-Augustus and the years of her widowhood under Tiberius demonstrates her exploitation of the art of the possible. She was not, as Tacitus would claim of Tiberius, 'disdainful of compliment'. As a priestess of the deified Augustus, she encouraged the development of the imperial cult from which she too benefited; there are no records of her attempting to restrict her own cult, which flourished outside mainland Italy even within her own life-time. Later historians have successfully darkened Livia's reputation: the silent testimony of nameless provincial worshippers is a powerful riposte.

For the most part her approach was cautious. She understood the bounds of acceptability and the limitations imposed on feminine advancement by Romans' ongoing engagement with the Republican concept of *virtus*.

Romans adopted a black and white approach to transgression. Mark Antony's wife Fulvia sought to exercise masculine powers, notably in a time of war. Her recompense was to forfeit her femininity. As Velleius Paterculus consigned her to posterity, nothing was womanly about Fulvia save her anatomy.[7]

Livia was a young woman at the time of Fulvia's prominence but evidently digested the lessons of her downfall. Not even Tacitus would deny Livia's womanliness. Her success was to create for herself a sphere of influence that arose directly from her woman's status as wife and mother but, unlike Propertius's Cynthia or his fearsome Cleopatra, included no sexual element. Livia's beauty was proverbial, but commentators refrain from mentioning it in connection with her public role. The 'Consolation to Livia' described her as 'one woman who has given so many benefits through her two offspring';[8] the Senate sought to create her 'Mother of her Country', and worshippers in a western province took the final leap and acclaimed her 'Mother of the World'. Was it Claudian pride which encouraged Livia to accept their homage – or a recognition that in such titles she had transcended the achievements of the heroines of Rome's past and could climb no higher? Her record would prove stubborn. Even Agrippina the Younger, Augustus's great-granddaughter who, as wife of the Emperor Claudius, came closer than Livia to playing a man's part, legitimized her pretensions through her status as 'the sister, wife and mother of men who ruled the world'.[9] Perhaps Tacitus's obituary notice of Livia, delivered with such invective, contains an unintended compliment. 'A compliant wife, a good match for the intrigues of her husband and the hypocrisy of her son', she was defined in death as in life by her relationship to men who occupied the highest public office. Adapting her behaviour to suit theirs may have been cynical; it demonstrated an assured grasp of the realities of Roman politics.

And what of Livy's assessment of the excessive cruelty and pride of the Claudii or Suetonius's record of a family tarnished by violence and arrogance? Did inherited failings direct Livia's life, as ancient biographers would insist they must?

Tennyson did not spare his own cruel heroine. 'Lady Clara Vere de Vere, There stands a spectre in your hall: The guilt of blood is at your door . . . You held your course without remorse.'

Are there spectres in Livia's atrium, shadowy figures of Marcellus, Gaius and Lucius Caesar, Marcus Agrippa, Augustus, Agrippa Postumus, Germanicus and the two Julias? The list is not a short one. But the answer, insofar as trustworthy evidence survives, is no and again no. Despite the best efforts of authors from Tacitus to Robert Graves, we cannot with certainty place the guilt of blood at Livia's door. That she held her course without remorse comes closer, grounds for a different history – the life of that woman who, as wife of Rome's leading citizen for half a century, unguided by precedent, became Rome's first, best-known and greatest empress.

Notes

CHAPTER 1: 'SUPERBISSIMA'

1 Flower, Harriet I., *Ancestor Masks and Aristocratic Power in Roman Culture* (Clarendon Press, Oxford, 1996), pp. 37–40.

2 Ibid., p. 37.

3 Suetonius, quoted in Grant, Michael, *The Twelve Caesars* (Weidenfeld and Nicolson, 1996), p. 105.

4 Kleiner, Diana E. E. and Matheson, Susan B., *I, Claudia: Women in Ancient Rome* (University of Texas Press, Austin, 1996), p. 119.

5 Milnor, Kristina, *Gender, Domesticity and the Age of Augustus: Inventing Private Life* (Oxford University Press, Oxford, 2005), pp. 103–4.

6 See Flower, op. cit., p. 203.

7 Beard, Mary, *Pompeii: The Life of a Roman Town* (Profile, London, 2008), pp. 102–3.

8 Martial, *Epigrams*, 12.57, quoted in Dalby, Andrew, *Empire of Pleasures: Luxury and Indulgence in the Roman World* (Routledge, London, 2000), p. 222.

9 Cassius Dio, *Roman History*, 39.9.2.

10 Goldsworthy, Adrian, *Caesar* (Weidenfeld and Nicolson, London, 2006), p. 34.

11 Suetonius, *The Twelve Caesars*, *Augustus*, 94.5.

12 Ibid., *Nero*, 6.1.

13 Syme, Ronald, *The Augustan Aristocracy* (Clarendon Press, Oxford, 1986), p. 19.

14 Treggiari, Susan, *Roman Marriage: Iusti Coniuges from the Time of*

Cicero to the Time of Ulpian (Clarendon Press, Oxford, 1991), p. 398.

15 Rawson, Beryl and Weaver, Paul, eds, *The Roman Family in Italy: Status, Sentiment, Space* (Oxford University Press, Oxford, 1999), p. 199.

16 For example, the death of Gaius Octavius. See Everitt, Anthony, *The First Emperor: Caesar Augustus and the Triumph of Rome* (John Murray, London, 2006), p. 16.

17 Rawson and Weaver, eds, op. cit, p. 199; Rawson, Beryl, ed., *The Family in Ancient Rome: New Perspectives* (Routledge, London, 1992), p. 216.

18 Aulus Gellius, *The Attic Nights*, 12.1.1–5, quoted in Dixon, Suzanne, *The Roman Mother* (Croom Helm, London, 1988), p. 106.

19 Balsdon, J. P. V. D, *Roman Women: Their History and Habits* (The Bodley Head, London, 1962), p. 201.

20 Rawson, ed., *The Family in Ancient Rome*, p. 214.

CHAPTER 2: IN THE BEGINNING . . . WERE THE CLAUDII

1 Cramer, Rev. J. A., *A Geographical and Historical Description of Ancient Italy* (Clarendon Press, Oxford, 1826), p. 122.

2 Dalby, *Empire of Pleasures*, p. 46.

3 Barrett, Anthony A., *Livia, First Lady of Imperial Rome* (Yale University Press, London, 2002), p. 8.

4 Goldsworthy, op. cit., p. 42.

5 Ibid., p. 33.

6 See Ferrero, Guglielmo, *The Women of the Caesars* (1911, repr. in trans. Loring and Mussey, New York, 1925), p. 22.

7 Treggiari, op. cit., p. 92.

8 Balsdon, op. cit., p. 198.

9 Dalby, *Empire of Pleasures*, p. 4.

10 Suetonius, op. cit., *Tiberius* 1.

11 Barrett, op. cit., p. 5.

12 Bourgeaud, Philippe, *Mother of the Gods: From Cybele to the Virgin Mary* (Johns Hopkins University Press, Baltimore, 2004), p. 61.

13 Ovid, *Fasti*, IV, 291ff., quoted in Staples, Ariadne, *From Goddess to Vestal Virgins: Sex and Category in Roman Religion* (Routledge, London, 1997), p. 117.

14 See Goldsworthy, op. cit., p. 257.

15   Ferrero, op. cit., p. 42.

16   Barrett, op. cit., p. 7.

17   Syme, op. cit., p. 199.

CHAPTER 3: 'INNOCENT OF GUILT'

1   Milnor, op. cit., p. 65.

2   Platner, Samuel Ball, *A Topographical Dictionary of Ancient Rome* (Oxford University Press, Oxford, 1929), p. 175.

3   Cassius Dio, op. cit., 38.17.6.

4   Polybius, *The Histories*, 53.9–54.4, quoted in Severy, Beth, *Augustus and the Family at the Birth of the Roman Empire* (Routledge, London, 2003), p. 169.

5   See Pliny the Younger, *Letters*, 50.

6   D'Ambra, Eve, *Roman Women* (Cambridge University Press, Cambridge, 2007), p. 78.

7   Pliny, op. cit., 46.

8   Brennan, T. Corey, *The Praetorship in the Roman Republic* (Oxford University Press, Oxford, 2000), p. 459.

9   Ryan, F. X., 'The Lex Scantinia and the Prosecution of Censors and Aediles', *Classical Philology*, Vol. 89, No. 2 (April 1994), p. 159.

10   Richlin, Amy, *The Garden of Priapus: Sexuality and Aggression in Roman Humor* (Oxford University Press, NY, 1992), p. 86.

11   Balsdon, op. cit., p. 211.

12   Dixon, op. cit., p. 133.

13   Vipstanus Messalla, *Dialogues*, 28, quoted in Dixon, ibid., p. 109.

14   Ibid., p. 105.

15   The minimum age for the consulship at this point was forty-one. Since Libo attained the consulship in 15 BC, it is possible to suggest a birth-date for him around 56 BC.

16   Syme, op. cit., p. 18.

17   Dixon, op. cit., p. 61.

18   Tregiarri, op. cit., p. 9.

19   Rawson, ed., op. cit., p. 45.

20   Cassius Dio, op. cit., 56.4.2.

21   Ibid., 56.3, trans. Ian Scott-Kilvert, *The Roman History: The Reign of Augustus* (Penguin, 1987), pp. 224–5.

22 Dixon, op. cit., p. 27.

23 Ibid., p. 25.

24 Ibid., p. 120.

25 Shakespeare, William, *Coriolanus*, I.III.

26 Dixon, op. cit., p. 131.

27 Quoted in Goldsworthy, op. cit., p. 10.

28 Horace, *Odes*, 3.6, trans. James Michie (Penguin, London, 1967), p. 155.

CHAPTER 4: 'VIRILITY TO HER REASONING POWER'

1   See Middleton, Conyers and Melmoth, William, *The Life and Letters of Marcus Tullius Cicero* (Moxon, London, 1839), p. 772.

2   Ibid., p. 771.

3   Ibid., p. 773.

4   Ibid., p. 772.

5   Cicero, *Pro Murena*, 75.

6   Ibid., quoted in Yakobson, Alexander, *Elections and Electioneering in Rome: A Study in the Political System of the Late Republic* (Franz Steiner Verlag, Stuttgart, 1999), p. 223.

7   Catullus, 81.

8   Suetonius, op. cit., *Tiberius*, 5.

9   Asconius, *Commentaries on Speeches of Cicero, For Milo*, 13.

10 Hemelrijk, Emily, *Matrona Docta: Educated Women in the Roman Elite from Cornelia to Julia Domna* (Routledge Classical Monographs, London, 2004), p. 22.

11 Cicero, *Brutus*, 211, quoted in Hemelrijk, ibid., p. 76.

12 Ibid., p. 91.

13 See Hallett, J., 'Queens, Princeps and Women of the Augustan Elite: Propertius's Cornelia Elegy and the Res Gestae Divi Augusti', in *The Age of Augustus* (Publications d'Histoire de l'art et d'archéologie de l'université catholique de Louvain XLIV, 1985), ed. Rolf Winkes, p. 80.

14 McAuslan, Ian, and Walcot, Peter, eds, *Women in Antiquity* (*Greece and Rome Studies*, Volume III, Oxford University Press, Oxford, 1996), p. 42.

15 Pomeroy, Sarah B., *Goddesses, Whores, Wives and Slaves: Women in Classical Antiquity* (Robert Hale and Co, London, 1976), p. 172.

16   Ibid., p. 170.

17   See Hemelrijk, op. cit., p. 62.

18   Ibid., p. 62.

19   Ibid., pp. 60–1.

20   Ibid., p. 91.

21   Milnor, op. cit., p. 87.

22   Broudy, Eric, *The Book of Looms: A History of the Handloom from Ancient Times to the Present* (Farnsworth Art Museum, Maine, 1993), p. 47.

23   McAuslan and Walcot, eds, op. cit., p. 41.

24   Balsdon, op. cit., p. 270.

CHAPTER 5: A YOUNG MAN OF NOBLE FAMILY. . .?

1   Rawson, ed., op. cit., p. 10.

2   McAuslan and Walcot, eds, op. cit., p. 43.

3   Ibid., p. 43.

4   Horace, *Odes*, 1.12, op. cit., p. 39.

5   Dixon, op. cit., p. 31.

6   McAuslan and Walcot, op. cit., p. 44.

7   Balsdon, op. cit., p. 173.

8   Treggiari, op. cit., p. 127.

9   Kleiner and Matheson, op. cit., p. 118.

10   Severy, op. cit., p. 7.

11   Horace, *Odes* 4.4, op. cit., p. 219.

12   Goldsworthy, op. cit., p. 494.

13   Barrett, op. cit., p. 10.

14   Suetonius, op. cit., *Tiberius* 4.1.

15   Fraschetti, Augusto, *Roman Women* (Chicago University Press, Chicago, 2001), p. 101.

CHAPTER 6: 'NIGHT WOULD LAST FOR EVER'

1   Ramsey, John T., and Licht, A. Lewis, *The Comet of 44 BC and Caesar's Funeral Games* (Oxford University Press, Oxford, 1997), p. 99.

2   Virgil, *Georgics*, I.466–8, quoted in Everitt, op. cit., p. 67.

3   See Kleiner and Matheson, op. cit., p. 132.

4   Treggiari, op. cit., p. 148.

5   Ibid., p. 152.

6   Ibid., p. 163.

7   Balsdon, op. cit., p. 183.

8   Ibid., p. 182.

9   Catullus, 64.

10 Beard, op. cit., p. 280.

11 Treggiari, op. cit., p. 164.

12 Flower, op. cit., p. 201.

13 Treggiari, op. cit., p. 166.

14 Ibid., p. 224.

15 Everitt, op. cit., p. 87.

16 Huzar, Eleanor Goltz, *Mark Antony* (Croom Helm, London, 1986), p. 119.

17 Matz, David, *Famous Firsts in the Ancient Greek and Roman World* (McFarland and Co., 1999), p. 40.

18 Suetonius, op. cit., *Augustus*, 27.

19 Appian, *The Civil Wars*, 4.23–4, quoted in Treggiari, op. cit., p. 431.

20 Everitt, op. cit., p. 88.

21 Barrett, op. cit., p. 14.

CHAPTER 7: FUGITIVE

1   Velleius Paterculus, *The Roman History*, II.75.2, trans. Frederick W. Shipley (Loeb, 1924), pp. 210–11.

2   Ibid., II.71.2, p. 204.

3   Goldsworthy, op. cit., p. 515.

4   Kleiner and Matheson, op. cit., p. 116.

5   See Milnor, op. cit., p. 30.

6   Huzar, op. cit., p. 119.

7   Treggiari, op. cit., p. 227.

8   Wyke, Maria, *The Roman Mistress: Ancient and Modern Representations* (Oxford University Press, Oxford, 2002), p. 215.

9   Everitt, op. cit., p. 90.

10 Pliny the Elder, *Natural History*, 34.1.

11 Balsdon, op. cit., p. 271.

12 Velleius Paterculus, op. cit., II.74.2, p. 208.

13   Everitt, op. cit., p. 130.

14   Velleius Paterculus, op. cit., II.75.3, p. 211.

15   Ibid.

16   Tacitus, *Annals*, III.33, trans. by Michael Grant (Penguin, 1956), p. 136.

17   Suetonius, op. cit., *Tiberius*, 6

CHAPTER 8: 'THE WHIMSICALITY OF FATE'

1   See Fraschetti, op. cit., pp. 5–6.

2   Petronius, *Satyricon*, 93: see Dalby, op. cit., p. 266; Sallust, *The Conspiracy of Catiline*, 9: see Dalby, op. cit., p. 11.

3   Seneca, *Epistles*, 55.

4   For the influence and role of Scribonia, see Barrett, op. cit., pp. 19–21.

5   Seneca, *Epistles*, 70.

6   Cassius Dio, op. cit., 48.15.3.

7   Bartman, Elizabeth, *Portraits of Livia* (Cambridge University Press, 1999), p. 3.

8   Cassius Dio, op. cit., 48.44.

9   Everitt, op. cit., p. 37.

10   See Rawson, Beryl, *Marriage, Divorce and Children in Ancient Rome* (Oxford University Press, Oxford, 1991), p. 59.

11   Tacitus, op. cit., I.10, p. 39.

12   Suetonius, op. cit., *Augustus*, 62; trans. by Robert Graves (Penguin, 1957), p. 84.

13   Velleius Paterculus, op. cit., II.75. 1, p. 210.

14   Horace, *Odes*, 3.14.

15   Treggiari, op. cit., pp. 135–6.

CHAPTER 9: 'AN EAGLE FLEW BY'

1   Pliny, *Natural History*, 15.137.

2   Suetonius, op. cit., *Galba*, 1, p. 243.

3   Cassius Dio, op. cit., 48.52.3.

4   Barrett, op. cit., p. 29.

5   Cassius Dio, op. cit., 48.43.4.

6   Suetonius, op. cit., *Augustus*, 92, p. 99.

7   Ibid., *Tiberius*, 14.1, p. 117.

8   Dixon, op. cit., p. 174.

9   Suetonius, op. cit., *Tiberius*, 14.1, p. 118.

10   Clark, Gillian, *Women in the Ancient World* (*Greece and Rome New Surveys in the Classics* No. 21, Oxford University Press, Oxford), p. 13.

11   Pomeroy, op. cit., p. 181.

12   Cassius Dio, op. cit., 48.34.3.

13   Winkes, ed., op. cit., p. 112.

14   Williams, Craig Arthur, *Roman Homosexuality* (Oxford University Press, Oxford, 1999), p. 74.

15   Cassius Dio, op. cit., 48.34.3.

16   See Harlow, Mary and Laurence, Ray, *Growing Up and Growing Old in Ancient Rome* (Routledge, London, 2001), p. 73.

17   Suetonius, op. cit., *Augustus*, 70, p. 89.

18   Bauman, Richard A., *Women and Politics in Ancient Rome* (Routledge, London, 1992), p. 95.

19   Ibid., p. 96.

20   Cassius Dio, op. cit., 48.44.3.

21   Martial, *Epigrams*, 6.29. See Gardner, Jane F. and Wiedemann, Thomas, *The Roman Household: A Sourcebook* (Routledge, London, 1991), p. 106.

22   Martial, *Epigrams*, 6.28; ibid., p. 105.

23   Suetonius, op. cit., *Augustus*, 62, p. 84.

CHAPTER 10: THE PRICE OF COMFORT

1   See Treggiari, op. cit., p. 85.

2   Everitt, op. cit., p. 14.

3   Suetonius, op. cit., *Augustus*, 6, p. 53.

4   *On Eutropius* 1, quoted in Cameron, Averil and Garnsey, Peter, *The Cambridge Ancient History*, Vol. 13 (Cambridge University Press, Cambridge, 1998), p. 153.

5   Suetonius, op. cit., *Augustus*, 2, p. 52.

6   Cassius Dio, op. cit., 56.3.

7   Plutarch, *The Life of Julius Caesar*, 68.1.

8   Everitt, op. cit., p. 63.

9   Cassius Dio, op. cit., 56.32; Suetonius, op. cit., *Augustus*, 101.

10   Severy, op. cit., p. 141.

11   Grant, op. cit., p. 69.

12   Suetonius, op. cit., *Augustus*, 79.2, p. 94.

13   Cassius Dio, op. cit., 56.46.1, p. 257.

CHAPTER 11: 'NO MAGIC CHANT WILL MAKE YOU A MOTHER'

1   Vitruvius, *On Architecture*, VIII 6.10–11.

2   Tacitus, *Annals*, 1.10.

3   Cassius Dio, op. cit., 48.52.4–53.1.

4   McAuslan and Walcot, eds, op. cit., p. 77.

5   Appian, *The Civil Wars*, 1.20, quoted in Fraschetti, op. cit., p. 59.

6   The 'Laudatio Turiae' is a funerary inscription for a much-loved wife, who has traditionally been associated with the Turia described by Valerius Maximus. It is now widely accepted that the two women are not in fact the same.

7   McAuslan and Walcot, eds, op. cit., p. 77.

8   Plutarch, *Life of Sulla*, 6.11. See Rawson, ed., op. cit., p. 9.

9   Ibid., p. 230.

10   Ibid., p. 231.

11   Lucretius, *On the Nature of the Universe*, 4.1227ff., trans. R. E. Latham (Penguin, London, 1951), p. 127.

12   Barrett, op. cit., p. 120.

13   Suetonius, op. cit., *Augustus*, 31.2, p. 68.

14   Brown, Norman O., 'XV. Kal. Mart. (February 15), Lupercalia', *New Literary History*, Vol. 4, No. 3, *Ideology and Literature* (Spring, 1973), p. 1 (541).

15   Gardner, Jane F., *Roman Myths* (British Museum Press, London, 1993), p. 77.

16   Ovid, *Fasti*, II.425ff., trans. A. J. Boyle and R. D. Woodard (Penguin, London, 2000), p. 39.

17   Parkin, Tim G., *Old Age in the Roman World* (Johns Hopkins University Press, Baltimore, 2003), p. 253; Dalby, Andrew, *Food in the Ancient World from A–Z* (Routledge, London, 2003), p. 118.

18   Parkin, op. cit., p. 253.

19   Barrett, op. cit., p. 109.

20   Dalby, *Food in the Ancient World*, p. 171.

21   Pliny, *Natural History*, 14.8.

CHAPTER 12: BY THE SIDE OF THE GODDESS

1   Appian, op. cit., II.102.

2   Kleiner, Diana E. E., *Cleopatra and Rome* (Harvard University Press, Harvard, 2005), p. 99.

3   Goldsworthy, op. cit., p. 496.

4   Cassius Dio, op. cit., 43.27.3.

5   Bartman, op. cit., p. 36.

6   Balsdon, op. cit., p. 52.

7   Hadas, Moses, *A History of Rome* (G. Bell and Sons, London, 1958), p. 68.

8   Plutarch, *Life of Antony*, 55.

9   Quintilian, *Institutio Oratoria*, XII.2.30.

10   Milnor, op. cit., p. 39.

11   Plutarch, *Life of Antony*, 60.

12   Everitt, op. cit., p. 184.

13   Plutarch, *Life of Antony*, 60.

14   Suetonius, *Augustus*, 69.2, quoted in Grant, op. cit., p. 69.

15   Kleiner and Matheson, eds, op. cit., p. 37.

16   Bartman, op. cit., p. 37.

17   Ibid., p. 36.

18   Kleiner, Diana E. E., and Matheson, Susan B., *I, Claudia II: Women in Roman Art and Society* (University of Texas Press, Austin, 2000), p. 32.

19   See Jones, Prudence J., *Cleopatra* (Haus Publishing, London, 2006), p. 40.

20   Kleiner and Matheson, eds, *I, Claudia*, p. 38.

21   Horace, *Odes*, I.38, op. cit., p. 87.

22   Kleiner, op. cit, p. 84.

23   See Milnor, op. cit., p. 82.

24   Clark, op. cit., p. 30.

25   See Jones, op. cit., p. 18.

26   Wyke, op. cit., p. 218.

27 Jones, op. cit., p. 96.

28 Pomeroy, op. cit., p. 219.

CHAPTER 13: SACROSANCT

1 See Severy, op. cit., p. 40.

2 Ibid.

3 Pliny, *Natural History*, 34.14.

4 Bartman, op. cit., p. 62.

5 Kleiner and Matheson, eds, op. cit., p. 36.

6 Pomeroy, op. cit., p. 149.

7 Kleiner and Matheson, eds, op. cit., p. 36.

8 *The Achievements of the Divine Augustus*, 8.5, trans. Brunt, P. A. and Moore, J. M. (Oxford University Press, Oxford, 1969).

9 Pliny, *Natural History*, 34.14.

10 Wood, Susan E., *Imperial Women, A Study in Public Images 40 BC–AD 68* (Brill, Leiden/Boston/Cologne, 1999), p. 32.

11 Kleiner, op. cit., p. 242.

12 Cassius Dio, op. cit., 49.38.1.

13 Wood, op. cit., p. 28.

14 Balsdon, op. cit., p. 258.

15 Wood, op. cit., p. 97.

CHAPTER 14: 'A CHARMING VIEW WITH MINIMAL EXPENSE'

1 Virgil, *Georgics*, IV.127–9, trans. Cecil Day Lewis (Jonathan Cape, London, 1940), p. 81.

2 Ibid., line 134.

3 Barrett, op. cit., p. 29.

4 Seneca, *Letters*, 55.

5 Pliny, *Natural History*, 35.37.116–17, quoted in Galinsky, Karl, ed., *The Cambridge Companion to the Age of Augustus* (Cambridge University Press, Cambridge, 2005), p. 274.

6 Vitruvius, *On Architecture*, VII.9.3.

7 Treggiari, op. cit., p. 54.

8 Laras, Ann, *Gardens of Italy* (Frances Lincoln, London, 2005), p. 12.

9   Ling, Roger, *Roman Painting* (Cambridge University Press, Cambridge, 1991), p. 150.

10   Laras, op. cit., p. 11.

11   Ibid., p. 12.

12   Pliny, *Natural History*, 15.39.

13   Barrett, op. cit., p. 113.

14   Ibid., p. 181.

CHAPTER 15: 'A MAN AND HIS FAMILY...'

1   Cassius Dio, op. cit., 56.35.5.

2   Levick, Barbara, *Tiberius the Politician* (Thames and Hudson, London, 1976), p. 15.

3   Bartman, op. cit., p. 108.

4   Milnor, op. cit., pp. 103–4.

5   Barrett, op. cit., pp. 326–8.

6   Suetonius, op. cit., *Augustus*, 72–3, pp. 91–2.

7   Iacopi, Irene, trans. Jeremy Scott, *The House of Augustus Wall Paintings* (Electa, Rome, 2008), p. 11.

8   Osgood, Josiah, *Caesar's Legacy: Civil War and the Emergence of the Roman Empire* (Cambridge University Press, Cambridge, 1996), p. 86.

9   Ibid.

10   Velleius Paterculus, op. cit., II.81.3, p. 223.

11   See Dalby, *Empire of Pleasures*, pp. 248–9.

12   Suetonius, op. cit., *Augustus*, 74, p. 92.

13   Grant, op. cit., p. 67.

14   Balsdon, op. cit., p. 71.

15   Syme, op. cit., p. 144.

16   Tacitus, *Annals*, 1.10.5.

17   Cassius Dio, op. cit., 56.9, p. 229.

18   Suetonius, op. cit., *Tiberius*, 7.1, p. 113.

19   Barrett, op. cit., p. 32.

20   Wood, op. cit., p. 35.

21   Syme, op. cit., p. 347.

22   Levick, op. cit., p. 15; Velleius Paterculus, II.94.2.

23   Suetonius, op. cit., *Augustus*, 63.

24   See Milnor, op. cit., p. 83.

25 See Grant, op. cit., p. 68.

26 Hemelrijk, op. cit., p. 28.

CHAPTER 16: 'THEY COMPELLED HIM . . .'

1   Everitt, op. cit., p. 231.

2   Cassius Dio, op. cit., 53.31, p. 153.

3   Propertius, *Elegies*, III.18, trans. A. S. Kline.

4   Cassius Dio, op. cit., 53.33.3, p. 154.

5   Ibid.

6   Suetonius, op. cit, *Augustus*, 69.1; Barrett, op. cit., p. 21.

7   Cassius Dio, op. cit., 53.4, pp. 128–9.

8   Ibid., 53.11.2, p. 134

9   *The Achievements of the Divine Augustus*, 34.

10 Velleius Paterculus, op. cit., II.93.1, p. 247.

11 Severy, op. cit., p. 68.

12 Dalby, *Empire of Pleasures*, p. 227.

13 Cassius Dio, op. cit., 51.21.8.

14 Seneca, *Consolation to Marcia*, 2, trans. John Davie (Oxford University Press, Oxford, 2007), p. 55.

15 Ibid.

16 Ibid., pp. 55–6.

17 Dalby, *Empire of Pleasures*, p. 53.

18 Propertius, *Elegies*, III.18.

19 Dalby, *Empire of Pleasures*, p. 52.

20 Syme, op. cit., pp. 314–15.

CHAPTER 17: 'BORN OF HIS SACRED BLOOD'

1   Cassius Dio, op. cit., 53.22.2; 53.25.1, pp. 145–7.

2   Holland, Richard, *Augustus* (Sutton, Stroud, 2004), p. 242.

3   Barrett, op. cit., pp. 34–5.

4   Flower, op. cit., p. 241.

5   Everitt, op. cit., p. 227.

6   Milnor, op. cit., p. 89.

7   Suetonius, op. cit., *Tiberius*, 8, p. 114.

8   Cassius Dio, op. cit., 53.26.1, p. 149.

9   Virgil, *Aeneid*, 6.791–2.

10 Tacitus, *Annals*, 4.52.4, trans. Michael Grant (Penguin, London, 1956, repr. 1996), p. 183; see Bauman, op. cit, p. 112.

11 Velleius Paterculus, op. cit., II.93.1–2, p. 247.

12 Catullus, 72.3–4.

13 Bauman, op. cit, p. 243 (footnote); Nepos, op. cit., NA 119.2–120.3.

14 Balsdon, op. cit., p. 72.

15 Cassius Dio, op. cit., 53.28, p. 150.

16 Velleius Paterculus, op. cit., II.89.4, pp. 238–9.

17 Ibid., II.89.1, p. 238.

18 Severy, op. cit., p. 114.

CHAPTER 18: 'HER SACRED OFFICE'

1   D'Ambra, op. cit., p. 155.

2   Cassius Dio, op. cit., 56.46.1, p. 257.

3   Velleius Paterculus, op. cit., II.130.5, p. 328.

4   Schultz, Celia E., *Women's Religious Activity in the Roman Republic* (University of North Carolina Press, 2006), p. 27.

5   Balsdon, op. cit., p. 249.

6   Kleiner and Matheson, eds, op. cit., p. 32.

7   Syme, Ronald, *History in Ovid* (Clarendon Press, Oxford, 1978), p. 23.

8   Kleiner and Matheson, eds, op. cit., p. 60.

9   D'Ambra, op. cit., p. 170.

10 See Dalby, *Empire of Pleasures*, p. 11.

11 See Everitt, op. cit., p. 252.

12 Iacopi, op. cit., p. 8.

13 Johnson, Patricia J., 'Ovid's Livia in Exile', *Classical World*, Vol. 90 No. 6 (1997), p. 407; Ovid, *Fasti*, 5.155–8, see Herbert-Brown, Geraldine, *Ovid and the Fasti: An Historical Study* (Clarendon Press, Oxford, 1994).

14 Dixon, Suzanne, *Reading Roman Women: Sources, Genres and Real Life* (Duckworth, London, 2001), p. 112.

15 Bartman, op. cit., p. 92.

16 Strabo, *The Geography*, 5.3.8: see Milnor, op. cit., p. 56.

17 Shakespeare, *Coriolanus*, V.III.

18 Wood, op. cit., p. 78.

CHAPTER 19: 'IF YOU COME TO ANY HARM...'

1   Suetonius, op. cit., *Augustus*, 81, p. 95.

2   Ibid.

3   Cassius Dio, op. cit., 55.16.3, p. 207.

4   See Everitt, op. cit., p. 230.

5   Cassius Dio, op. cit., 53.30, p. 152.

6   Velleius Paterculus, op. cit., II.93.1, p. 247.

7   Seager, Robin, *Tiberius* (Wiley Blackwell, repr. 2004), p. 16.

8   Cassius Dio, op. cit., 54.31, p. 183.

9   See Potter, David, *Emperors of Rome* (Quercus, London, 2007), p. 48.

10   Seager, op. cit., p. 16.

11   Cassius Dio, op. cit., 53.32, p. 153.

12   Flower, op. cit., p. 238.

13   Plutarch, *Life of Antony*, 87.2.

14   Cassius Dio, op. cit., 54.6, p. 161.

CHAPTER 20: THREE CITIES OF JUDAEA

1   Roller, Duane W., *The Building Program of Herod the Great* (University of California Press, Berkeley, 1998), p. 30.

2   Knoblet, Jerry, *Herod the Great* (University Press of America paperback, 2005), p. 152.

3   Barrett, op. cit., p. 37.

4   Strabo, *The Geography*, 16.2.2.

5   Cassius Dio, op. cit., 54.9, p. 163; Strabo, op. cit., 16.20.

6   Levick, op. cit., p. 26.

7   Cassius Dio, op. cit., 54.8–9.2, p. 163.

8   Levick, op. cit., p. 26.

9   Velleius Paterculus, op. cit., II.122.1, p. 309.

10   Barrett, op. cit., p. 37.

11   Ibid., p. 198.

12   Ibid.

13   Bartman, op. cit., p. 95.

14   Severy, op. cit., p. 112.

15   Ibid., p. 233.

16 Sicker, Martin, *Between Rome and Jerusalem: 300 Years of Roman-Judaean Relations* (Praeger, New York, 2001), p. 96.

17 Richardson, Lawrence, *A New Topographical Dictionary of Ancient Rome* (Johns Hopkins University Press, Baltimore 1992), p. 289.

CHAPTER 21: 'THE MAN SET APART...'

1   Wood, op. cit., p. 177.
2   Cassius Dio, op. cit., 54.10, p. 164.
3   Ibid., 51.11, p. 72.
4   Ibid.
5   Pliny, *Natural History*, 7.46.
6   Cassius Dio, op. cit., 54.3.2, p. 158.
7   Tacitus, *Annals*, 4.40, p. 177.
8   Bauman, op. cit., p. 102.
9   Pliny, *Natural History*, 36.59.2.
10 Kleiner and Matheson, eds, op. cit., p. 37.
11 Cassius Dio, op. cit., 54.18, p. 171.
12 Suetonius, op. cit., *Augustus*, 76, p. 93.
13 Dalby, *Empire of Pleasures*, p. 90.
14 Everitt, op. cit., p. 261.
15 Suetonius, op. cit., *Augustus*, 72, p. 91.
16 Treggiari, Susan, 'Jobs in the Household of Livia', Papers of the British School at Rome, 43 (1975), p. 63
17 Ibid., see pp. 48–64.
18 Ibid., p. 52.
19 Cassius Dio, op. cit., 54.23, p. 175.
20 Barrett, op. cit., p. 52.

CHAPTER 22: 'OUTSTANDINGLY VIRTUOUS'

1   Ovid, *Ex Ponto*, 3.1.114–18, quoted in Johnson, Patricia, J., 'Ovid's Livia in Exile', *Classical World*, Vol. 90, No. 6 (1997), p. 415.
2   Propertius, *Epistles*, II.1, trans. by Slavitt, David R. (University of California Press, Berkeley, 2002).
3   Ibid., I.2, see D'Ambra, op. cit., p. 4.
4   Edmondson, Jonathan and Keith, Alison, *Roman Dress and the Fabrics*

of Roman Culture (University of Toronto Press, Toronto, 2008), p. 194.

5   See Balsdon, op. cit., p. 254.

6   *The Achievements of the Divine Augustus*, 8.5.

7   Milnor, op. cit., p. 140.

8   Balsdon, op. cit., p. 75.

9   See ibid., p. 222.

10 Ibid., p. 215.

11 Cassius Dio, op. cit., 54.19, p. 172

12 Ibid., 54.16.2, pp. 169–70.

13 Ibid., p. 170.

14 Bartman, op. cit., p. 41.

15 Ibid.

16 Cicero, *Philippics*, 2.44, quoted in Sebesta, Judith Lynn and Bonfante, Larissa, *The World of Roman Costume* (University of Wisconsin Press, Wisconsin, 1994), p. 140.

17 Severy, op. cit., p. 55.

18 Tacitus, *Annals*, V.1, p. 195.

19 Pliny, *Natural History*, 9.58.1.

20 Velleius Paterculus, op. cit., II.97.1, p. 253.

21 Juvenal, *Satires*, 6.457–65: see D'Ambra, op. cit., p. 48.

22 Balsdon, op. cit., p. 263.

23 Clark, op. cit., p. 13.

24 Suetonius, op. cit., *Gaius Caligula*, 23, p. 160

25 Barrett, op. cit., p. 121.

CHAPTER 23: 'TIBERIUS CLOSER TO CAESAR'

1   Velleius Paterculus, op. cit., II.95.1–2, pp. 250–51.

2   Levick, op. cit., p. 30.

3   Velleius Paterculus, op. cit., II.97.2, p. 253.

4   Valerius Maximus, *Memorable Deeds and Sayings*, 3.3, trans. by Walker, Henry J. (Hackett Publishing, Indianapolis, 2004), p. 132.

5   Cassius Dio, op. cit., 54.29.2, p. 182.

6   Velleius Paterculus, op. cit., II.96.1, p. 252.

7   Cassius Dio, op. cit., 54.31, p. 183.

8   Tacitus, *Annals*, 4.38, p. 176.

9   Suetonius, op. cit., *Tiberius*, 7.2, p. 113.

10   Ibid., pp. 113–14.

11   Levick, op. cit., p. 153.

12   Tacitus, *Annals*, 5.1, p. 195.

13   Valerius Maximus, op. cit., 5.3, p. 181.

14   Anonymous, 'Consolation to Livia', 349–56: see Purcell, Nicholas, 'Livia and the Womanhood of Rome', *Proceedings of the Cambridge Philological Society* (1986), p. 78.

15   Barrett, op. cit., p. 108.

16   Suetonius, op. cit., *Claudius*, 1.5, p. 182.

17   Ibid., *Claudius*, 1.4; Tacitus, *Annals*, 2.82.3, p. 116.

CHAPTER 24: 'WHAT MORE CAN I ASK OF THE IMMORTAL GODS?'

1   Everitt, op. cit., p. 299.

2   Cassius Dio, op. cit., 55.10.4, p. 198.

3   Suetonius, op. cit., *Augustus*, 58.3, p. 83.

4   Velleius Paterculus, op. cit., II.100.2–3, pp. 258–9.

5   Pliny, *Natural History*, 7.46.

6   Propertius, *Elegies* IV.11, trans. A. S. Kline.

7   Severy, op. cit., p. 183.

8   Macrobius, *Saturnalia*, 2.5.8.

9   Seneca, *On Benefits*, 6.1–2: see Bauman, op. cit., p. 113.

10   Cassius Dio, op. cit., 55.10.7, p. 199.

11   Suetonius, op. cit., *Augustus*, 84, p. 96.

12   Ibid., *Augustus*, 101.2, p. 108.

13   Macrobius, *Saturnalia*, 2.5.4: see Milnor, op. cit., p. 88.

14   Suetonius, op. cit., *Augustus*, 65.2, p. 86.

15   Barrett, op. cit., p. 141.

16   See Bauman, op. cit., p. 116.

17   Severy, op. cit., p. 58.

18   Tacitus, *Annals*, 1.53, p. 63.

19   Bauman, op. cit., p. 112.

20   Suetonius, op. cit., *Tiberius*, 11.4, p. 116.

CHAPTER 25: 'TRY NOT TO GUESS WHAT LIES IN THE FUTURE'

1 Everitt, op. cit., p. 235.
2 Ibid., p. 274.
3 Horace, *Odes* I.9, p. 35.
4 Cassius Dio, op. cit., 54.25, p. 177.
5 Holland, op. cit., p. 255.
6 Dixon, *The Roman Mother*, p. 74.
7 Rossini, Orietta, *Ara Pacis* (Electa, Rome, 2006), p. 36.
8 Ibid.
9 Severy, op. cit., p. 124.
10 Suetonius, op. cit., *Tiberius*, 12, p. 116.
11 Ibid., *Tiberius*, 13, p. 117.
12 Velleius Paterculus, op. cit., II.91.1, p. 243.
13 Cassius Dio, op. cit., 55.9.4, p. 197.
14 Ibid., 55.11, p. 202.
15 Levick, op. cit., p. 39.
16 Valerius Maximus, op. cit., 5.5.3: see Milnor, op. cit, p. 199.
17 Treggiari, *Roman Marriage*, p. 344.
18 Cassius Dio, op. cit., 58.2.3.
19 Ibid., 55.16.4, p. 207.
20 Lomas, Kathryn, *Roman Italy 338 BC–AD 200: A Sourcebook* (Routledge, London, 1996), p. 247.

CHAPTER 26: 'PERPETUAL SECURITY'

1 Velleius Paterculus, op. cit., II.103.1–4, pp. 264–5.
2 Tacitus, *Annals*, 1.4.
3 Balsdon, op, cit., p. 67.
4 See Everitt, op. cit., p. 309.
5 Suetonius, op. cit., *Gaius Caligula*, 7, p. 152.
6 Levick, op. cit., p. 46.
7 Suetonius, op. cit., *Tiberius*, 15, p. 118.
8 Valerius Maximus, op. cit., p. 132.
9 Cassius Dio, op. cit., 60.2.1.
10 Barrett, op. cit., p. 127.

11   Cassius Dio, op. cit., 55.10A.5, p. 202.

12   Tacitus, *Annals*, 1.3.

13   Suetonius, op. cit., *Tiberius*, 70.

14   Velleius Paterculus, op. cit., II.102.2, p. 263.

15   Severy, op. cit., p. 188.

16   Cassius Dio, op. cit., 55.10A.5, p. 200.

17   Velleius Paterculus, op. cit., II.102.3, p. 263.

18   Suetonius, op. cit., *Tiberius*, 11.4, p. 116.

19   Ibid., *Claudius*, 3.2, p. 183.

20   Ibid., *Augustus*, 65.2, p. 86.

21   Tacitus, *Annals*, 1.3, p. 33.

22   Ibid.

23   Suetonius, op. cit., *Tiberius*, 21, p. 121.

24   Cassius Dio, op. cit., 55.13.2, p. 203.

CHAPTER 27: PURER THAN PARIAN MARBLE?

1   Pollini, John, 'The Augustus from Prima Porta and the Transformation of the Polykleiton Heroic Ideal: The Rhetoric Art', in Moon, Warren G., *Polykleitos, the Doryphorus and Tradition* (University of Wisconsin Press, Wisconsin, 1995), p. 268.

2   Horace, *Odes*, 1.19.5: see ibid.

3   Suetonius, op. cit., *Augustus*, 71, p. 90.

4   Cassius Dio, op. cit., 58.2.5.

5   Quintilian, *Institutio Oratoria*, 5.12.21: see Pollini, op. cit., p. 268.

6   Velleius Paterculus, op. cit., II.102.3, p. 263.

7   Cassius Dio, op. cit., 57.2.7.

8   Valerius Maximus, op. cit, 4.3.3, p. 132.

9   Wood, op. cit., p. 181.

10   Suetonius, op. cit., *Tiberius*, 15, p. 119.

11   Everitt, op. cit., p. 314.

12   Cassius Dio, op. cit., 55.32.1, p. 220.

13   Tacitus, *Annals*, 1.6, p. 35.

CHAPTER 28: 'BLOOD-RED COMETS'

1   Cassius Dio, op. cit., 56.29.1, p. 244.

2   Ibid., 56.29.3, p. 244.

3   Suetonius, op. cit., *Tiberius*, 21.5, p. 122.

4   Cassius Dio, op. cit., 56.26.2, p. 242.

5   Bartman, op. cit., p. 88.

6   Ovid, *Letters from the Black Sea*, 2.8, trans. A. S. Kline.

7   Horace, *Odes*, 4.5, p. 227.

8   Suetonius, op. cit., *Tiberius*, 20, p. 120.

9   Ibid., *Tiberius*, 17, p. 119.

10 Dalby, *Empire of Pleasures*, p. 193.

11 Levick, op. cit., p. 63.

12 Suetonius, op. cit., *Augustus*, 97, p. 104.

13 Cassius Dio, op. cit., 56.30, p. 245.

14 Velleius Paterculus, op. cit., II.123.2, p. 312.

CHAPTER 29: AUGUSTA

1   Suetonius, op. cit., *Tiberius*, 26, p. 124.

2   Barrett, op. cit., p. 149.

3   Cassius Dio, op. cit., 56.42, p. 255.

4   Suetonius, op. cit., *Claudius*, 4.2, p. 184.

5   Ibid.

6   Tacitus, *Annals*, 1.14.3, p. 41.

7   Suetonius, op. cit., *Tiberius*, 26, p. 124.

8   Tacitus, *Annals*, 4.38.2, p. 176.

9   Cassius Dio, op. cit., 56.46.2, p. 258.

10 Ibid., 56.47.1, p. 258.

11 Suetonius, op. cit., *Augustus*, 99.2, p. 106.

12 Ibid., *Augustus*, 101.3, p. 108.

13 Tacitus, *Annals*, 1.14.3, p. 41.

CHAPTER 30: 'HIS MOTHER LIVIA VEXED HIM'

1   Royal Collection, RCIN65160.

2   Seager, op. cit., p. 121.

3   Barrett, op. cit., p. 162.

4   Ibid., p. 211.

5   See Platt, David, *Imperial Cult in Roman Gytheum* (http://traumwerk.stansford.edu:3455/93/Home)

6   Severy, op. cit., p. 222.

7   Ibid., p. 220.

8   Cassius Dio, op. cit., 57.9.1.

9   Seager, op. cit., p. 122.

10   Tacitus, *Annals*, 4.37, p. 175.

11   Suetonius, op. cit., *Tiberius*, 50, p. 134.

12   Cassius Dio, op. cit., 57.12.3.

13   Hawley, Richard and Levick, Barbara, eds, *Women in Antiquity: New Assessments* (Routledge, London, 1995), p. 186.

14   Ibid.

15   Museum of Fine Arts, Boston (99. 109).

16   Kleiner and Matheson, eds, op. cit., p. 184.

17   Ibid.

18   Cassius Dio, op. cit., 56.46, p. 257.

19   Velleius Paterculus, op. cit., II.75.3, p. 211.

20   Tacitus, *Annals*, 1.72.5, p. 73.

21   Bauman, op. cit., p. 133.

22   Suetonius, op. cit., *Tiberius*, 59.1, p. 138.

23   Ibid., *Nero*, 7, p. 212.

CHAPTER 31: ABOVE THE LAW?

1   Tacitus, *Annals*, 12.69.

2   Barrett, op. cit., p. 183.

3   Ibid., p. 165.

4   Balsdon, op. cit., p. 94.

5   Tacitus, *Annals*, 2.34, p. 93.

6   Ibid., 4.21, p. 168.

7   Ibid., *Annals*, 2.34, p. 93.

8   Rawson, ed., op. cit., p. 221.

9   Tacitus, *Annals*, 2.41, p. 97.

10   Barrett, p. 168.

11   Tacitus, *Annals*, 2.69, p. 112.

12   Bauman, op. cit., p. 140.

13   Ibid., p. 142.

14   See Barrett, op. cit., p. 169.

15   Griffin, M. T., *Journal of Roman Studies* (1997), 252; lines 115–20: see

Lane Fox, Robin, *The Classical World: An Epic History of Greece and Rome* (Penguin, London, 2006), p. 486, footnote 5.

16   Tacitus, *Annals*, 4.3, p. 121.

17   Ibid., 3.64, p. 150.

18   Suetonius, op. cit., *Tiberius*, 51, p. 134.

19   Tacitus, *Annals*, 4.56, p. 186.

EPILOGUE

1   Propertius, *Elegies*, 3.11.1–2; see Wyke, op. cit., p. 195.

2   See McDonnell, Myles, *Roman Manliness: 'Virtus' and the Roman Republic* (Cambridge University Press, Cambridge, 2006).

3   Cicero, *Philippics*, 4.13.

4   Gurval, Robert Alan, *Actium and Augustus: The Politics and Emotions of Civil War* (University of Michigan Press, Michigan, 1998), p. 11.

5   Cassius Dio, op. cit., 58.2.3.

6   Ibid., 57.12.2.

7   Velleius Paterculus, op. cit., II.74.2, p. 209.

8   See Barrett, op. cit., p. 170.

9   Tacitus, *Annals*, 12.41.2.

Bibliography

PRIMARY SOURCES

Works by the following Classical authors were consulted during the research and writing of this book. Where appropriate, details of editions and translations used are provided in the endnotes. It is important to remember that, although termed 'primary' sources, a number of these works postdate Livia's life.

Appian
Aulus Gellius
Cicero
Diodorus Siculus
Dionysius of Halicarnassus
Horace
Juvenal
Livy
Lucan
Macrobius
Martial
Nepos
Ovid
Plautus
Pliny
Plutarch
Propertius
Ptolemy

Quintilian

Sallust

Seneca

Statius

Suetonius

Tacitus

Valerius Maximus

Velleius Paterculus

Virgil

Vitruvius

SECONDARY SOURCES

Balsdon, J. P. V. D., *Roman Women: Their History and Habits* (The Bodley Head, London, 1962)

Barrett, Anthony A., *Livia, First Lady of Imperial Rome* (Yale University Press, London, 2002)

Bartman, Elizabeth, *Portraits of Livia* (Cambridge University Press, Cambridge, 1999)

Bauman, Richard A., *Women and Politics in Ancient Rome* (Routledge, London, 1992)

Beard, Mary, *Pompeii, The Life of a Roman Town* (Profile, London, 2008)

Bourgeaud, Philippe, *Mother of the Gods: From Cybele to the Virgin Mary* (Johns Hopkins University Press, Baltimore, 2004)

Bradford, Ernle, *Cleopatra* (Hodder and Stoughton, London, 1971)

Broudy, Eric, *The Book of Looms: A History of the Handloom from Ancient Times to the Present* (Farnsworth Art Museum, Maine, 1993)

Clark, Gillian, *Women in the Ancient World* (Greece and Rome, New Surveys in the Classics No. 21, Oxford University Press, Oxford, 1989)

Cramer, Rev. J. A., *A Geographical and Historical Description of Ancient Italy* (Clarendon Press, Oxford, 1826)

Dalby, Andrew, *Empire of Pleasures: Luxury and Indulgence in the Roman World* (Routledge, London, 2002)

—, *Food in the Ancient World from A–Z* (Routledge, London, 2003)

D'Ambra, Eve, *Roman Women* (Cambridge University Press, Cambridge, 2007)

Dixon, Suzanne, *The Roman Mother* (Croom Helm, London, 1988)

—, *Reading Roman Women: Sources, Genres and Real Life* (Duckworth, London, 2001)

Edmondson, Jonathan and Keith, Alison, *Roman Dress and the Fabrics of Roman Culture* (University of Toronto Press, Toronto, 2008)

Everitt, Anthony, *The First Emperor: Caesar Augustus and the Triumph of Rome* (John Murray, London, 2006)

Falkner, Thomas M. and De Luce, Judith, *Old Age in Greek and Latin Literature* (State University of New York Press, NY, 1989)

Flower, Harriet I., *Ancestor Masks and Aristocratic Power in Roman Culture* (Clarendon Press, Oxford, 1996)

Forsythe, Gary, *A Critical Study of Early Rome: From Prehistory to the First Punic War* (University of California Press, Berkeley, 2005)

Frantantuono, Lee, *Madness Unchained: A Reading of Virgil's Aeneid* (Lexington Books, NY, 2007)

Fraschetti, Augusto, *Roman Women* (Chicago University Press, Chicago, 2001)

Galinsky, Karl, ed., *The Cambridge Companion to the Age of Augustus* (Cambridge University Press, Cambridge, 2005)

Gardner, Jane F. *Roman Myths* (British Museum Press, London, 1993)

Gardner, Jane F. and Wiedemann, Thomas, *The Roman Household: A Sourcebook* (Routledge, London, 1991)

Goldsworthy, Adrian, *Caesar* (Weidenfeld and Nicolson, London, 2006)

Grant, Michael, *The Twelve Caesars* (Weidenfeld and Nicolson, London, repr. 1996)

Gruen, Erich S., *Studies in Greek Culture and Roman Policy* (University of California Press, Berkeley, 1996)

Gurval, Robert Alan, *Actium and Augustus: The Politics and Emotions of Civil War* (University of Michigan Press, Michigan, 1998)

Hadas, Moses, *A History of Rome* (G. Bell and Sons, London, 1958)

Harlow, Mary, and Laurence, Ray, *Growing Up and Growing Old in Ancient Rome* (Routledge, London, 2001)

Hawley, Richard and Levick, Barbara, eds., *Women in Antiquity: New Assessments* (Routledge, London, 1995)

Hemelrijk, Emily, *Matrona Docta: Educated Women in the Roman Elite from Cornelia to Julia Domna* (Routledge Classical Monographs, London, 2004)

Herbert-Brown, *Geraldine, Ovid and the Fasti: An Historical Study* (Clarendon Press, Oxford, 1994)

Holland, Richard, *Augustus* (Sutton, Stroud, 2004)

Hughes-Hallett, Lucy, *Cleopatra: Histories, Dreams and Distortions* (Bloomsbury, London, 1990)

Huzar, Eleanor Goltz, *Mark Antony* (Croom Helm, London, repr. 1986)

Iacopi, Irene, *The House of Augustus Wall Paintings* (Electa, Rome, 2008)

Jones, Prudence J. *Cleopatra* (Haus Publishing, London, 2006)

Keaveney, Arthur, *Sulla: The Last Republican* (Croom Helm, London, 1983)

Kleiner, Diana E. E. and Matheson, Susan B., *I, Claudia: Women in Ancient Rome Exhibition 1996–7*, Yale University Art Gallery, New Haven (University of Texas Press, Austin, 1996)

Kleiner, Diana E. E., *I, Claudia II: Women in Roman Art and Society* (University of Texas Press, Austin, 2000)

—, *Cleopatra and Rome* (Harvard University Press, Cambridge, Mass., 2005)

Knoblet, Jerry, *Herod the Great* (University Press of America paperback, 2005)

Levick, Barbara, *Tiberius the Politician* (Thames and Hudson, London, 1976)

Ling, Roger, *Roman Painting* (Cambridge University Press, Cambridge, 1991)

Lloyd-Jones, Hugh, *Greek in a Cold Climate* (Barnes and Noble, NY, 1991)

Lomas, Kathryn, *Roman Italy 338 BC–AD 200: A Sourcebook* (Routledge, London, 1996)

Matz, David, *Famous Firsts in the Ancient Greek and Roman World* (McFarland and Co., Jefferson, 1999)

McAuslan, Ian and Walcot, Peter, ed., *Women in Antiquity* (Greece and Roman Studies, Volume III, Oxford University Press, Oxford, 1996)

McDonnell, Myles, *Roman Manliness: 'Virtus' and the Roman Republic* (Cambridge University Press, Cambridge, 2006)

Michie, James, trans. and intro., *The Odes of Horace* (Penguin, London, 1967)

Middleton, Conyers, Melmoth, William et al., *The Life and Letters of Marcus Tullius Cicero in One Volume* (Moxon, London, 1839)

Miles, Christopher with Norwich, John Julius, *Love in the Ancient World* (Weidenfeld and Nicolson, London, 1997)

Milnor, Kristina, *Gender, Domesticity, and the Age of Augustus: Inventing Private Life* (Oxford University Press, Oxford, 2005)

Moon, Warren G. 'Polykleitos, the Doryphoros and Tradition', in Pollini, John, *The Augustus from Prima Porta and the Transformation of the Polykleiton Heroic Ideal: The Rhetoric of Art* (University of Wisconsin Press, Wisconsin, 1995)

M. Tulii Ciceronis, *Orationes*, Vol. III, with a commentary by George Long (London, Whittaker and Co., 1856)

Osgood, Josiah, *Caesar's Legacy: Civil War and the Emergence of the Roman Empire* (Cambridge University Press, Cambridge, 1996)

Parkin, Tim G., *Old Age in the Roman World* (Johns Hopkins University Press, Baltimore, 2003)

Platner, Samuel Ball (as completed and revised by Thomas Ashby), *A Topographical Dictionary of Ancient Rome* (Oxford University Press, Oxford, 1929)

Pomeroy, Sarah B., *Goddesses, Whores, Wives and Slaves: Women in Classical Antiquity* (Robert Hale and Co., London, 1976)

—, ed., *Plutarch's Advice to the Bride and Groom and A Consolation to His Wife* (Oxford University Press, Oxford, 1999)

Potter, David, *Emperors of Rome* (Quercus, London, 2007)

Ramsey, John T. and Licht, A. Lewis, *The Comet of 44 BC and Caesar's Funeral Games* (Oxford University Press, NY, 1997)

Rawson, Beryl, *Marriage, Divorce and Children in Ancient Rome* (Oxford University Press, Oxford, 1991)

Richlin, Amy, *The Garden of Priapus: Sexuality and Aggression in Roman Humor* (Oxford University Press, NY, 1992)

Richardson, Lawrence, *A New Topographical Dictionary of Ancient Rome* (John Hopkins University Press, Baltimore, 1992)

Roller, Duane W., *The Building Program of Herod the Great* (University of California Press, Berkeley, 1998)

Rossini, Orietta, *Ara Pacis* (Electa, Rome, 2006)

Schultz, Celia E., *Women's Religious Activity in the Roman Republic* (University of North Carolina Press, Chapel Hill, 2006)

Seager, Robin, *Tiberius* (Wiley Blackwell, Oxford, repr. 2004)

Sebesta, Judith Lynn and Bonfante, Larissa, *The World of Roman Costume* (University of Wisconsin Press, Wisconsin, 1994)

Settis, Salvatore, *La Villa di Livia: le pareti ingannevoli* (Electa, Rome, 2008)

Shotter, David, *Tiberius* (Routledge, London, 2004)

Sicker, Martin, *Between Rome and Jerusalem: 300 Years of Roman-Judaean Relations* (Praeger, NY, 2001)

Southern, Pat, *Augustus* (Routledge, London, 1998)

—, *The Roman Army: A Social and Institutional History* (Oxford University Press, Oxford, 2007)

Staccioli, Romolo (trans. Francesco Caruso), *Villas of Ancient Rome* (Azienda di Promozione Turistica di Roma, Rome)

Staples, Ariadne, *From Goddess to Vestal Virgins: Sex and Category in Roman Religion* (Routledge, London, 1997)

Syme, Ronald, *The Roman Revolution* (Oxford University Press, Oxford, repr, 1968)

—, *The Augustan Aristocracy* (Clarendon Press, Oxford, 1986)

—, *History in Ovid* (Clarendon Press, Oxford, 1978)

Tatum, W. Jeffrey, *The Patrician Tribune: Publius Clodius Pulcher* (University of North Carolina Press, Chapel Hill, 1999)

Treggiari, Susan, *Roman Marriage*: Iusti Coniuges *from the Time of Cicero to the Time of Ulpian* (Clarendon Press, Oxford, 1991)

Williams, Craig Arthur, *Roman Homosexuality* (Oxford University Press, Oxford, 1999)

Winter, Bruce W., *Roman Wives, Roman Widows: The Appearance of New Women and the Pauline Communities* (Wm B. Eerdmands Publishing, 2003)

Wood, Susan E., *Imperial Women: A Study in Public Images 40 BC–AD 68* (Brill, Leiden/Boston/Cologne, 1999)

Wyke, Maria, *The Roman Mistress: Ancient and Modern Representations* (Oxford University Press, Oxford, 2002)

Yakobson, Alexander, *Elections and Electioneering in Rome: a Study in the Political System of the Late Republic* (Franz Steiner Verlag, Stuttgart, 1999)

PERIODICALS AND JOURNALS

Brown, Norman O., 'XV. Kal. Mart. (February 15). Lupercalia', *New Literary History*, Vol. 4, No. 3, *Ideology and Literature* (Spring, 1973), pp. 541–56

Cerutti, Steven M., 'The Location of the Houses of Cicero and Clodius and The Porticus Catuli on the Palatine Hill in Rome', *American Journal of Philology*, Vol. 118, No. 3 (Fall, 1997), pp. 417–26

Huzar, Eleanor G., 'Mark Antony: Marriages vs. Careers', *The Classical Journal*, Vol. 81, No. 2 (Dec. 1985–Jan. 1986), pp. 97–111

Jacobson, D. M. and Weitzman, M. P., 'What Was Corinthian Bronze?', *American Journal of Archaeology*, Vol. 96, No. 2 (April 1992), pp. 237–47

Johnson, Patricia J., 'Ovid's Livia in Exile', *Classical World*, Vol. 90, No. 6 (1997), pp. 403–20

Kuttner, Ann, 'Delight and Danger in the Roman Water Garden: Sperlonga and Tivoli', in *Landscape Design and the Experience of Motion*, ed. Michel Conan, 2003

Linderski, Jerzy, 'The Mother of Livia Augusta and the Aufiddii Lurcones of the Republic', *Historia* 23 (1974), pp. 463–80

Ling, Roger, 'Studius and the Beginnings of Roman Landscape Painting', *The Journal of Roman Studies*, Vol. 67 (1977), pp. 1–16

Pappano, Albert Earl, 'Agrippa Postumus', *Classical Philology*, Vol. 36, No. 1 (Jan. 1941), pp. 30–45

Perkell, Christine Godfrey, 'On the Corycian Gardener of Vergil's Fourth Georgic', *Transactions of the American Philological Association* (1974), Vol. 111 (1981), pp. 167–77

Platt, David, *Imperial Cult in Roman Gytheum* (http://traumwerk.stanford.edu:3455/93/Home)

Potter, Franklin H., 'Political Alliance by Marriage', *The Classical Journal*, Vol. 29, No. 9 (June 1934), pp. 663–74

Purcell, Nicholas, 'Livia and the Womanhood of Rome', *Proceedings of the Cambridge Philological Society* (1986), pp. 78–105

Ryan, F. X., 'The Lex Scantinia and the Prosecution of Censors and Aediles', *Classical Philology*, Vol. 89, No. 2 (April 1994), pp. 159–62

Semple, Ellen Churchill, 'Ancient Mediterranean Pleasure Gardens', *Geographical Review*, Vol. 19, No. 3 (July 1929), pp. 420–43

Shackleton Bailey, D. R., 'Tu Marcellus eris', *Harvard Studies in Classical Philology*, Vol. 90 (1986), pp. 199–205

Tenney, Frank, 'On Augustus and the Aerarium', *The Journal of Roman Studies*, Vol. 23 (1933), pp. 143–8

Tracy, Stephen V., 'The Marcellus Passage (*Aeneid* 6.860–886) and *Aeneid* 9–12', *The Classical Journal*, Vol. 70, No. 4 (April–May 1975), pp. 37–42

Treggiari, Susan, 'Jobs in the Household of Livia', *Papers of the British School at Rome* 43 (1975), pp. 48–77

Wiseman, T. P., 'The Mother of Livia Augusta', *Historia* 14 (1965), pp. 333–4

Glossary

aedile   One of the senatorial magistracies which together made up the 'cursus honorum' or sequence of offices followed by Roman politicians. Responsible for public and private buildings, roads, aqueducts and sewers, public lands, public spectacles and police, as well as the distribution of corn and markets, weights and measures.

arca   A coffer or large chest, often for keeping money in.

armarium   A cupboard, here made of wood, used to house wax portrait masks of ancestors.

atrium   The hall, close to the entrance of the Roman house; among the most important rooms of the house.

consul   The most senior magistracy of the 'cursus honorum'. Two consuls were appointed annually, with powers roughly akin to a shared prime ministership.

cubiculum   Usually a small room, often a bedroom; cubicula sited close to the atrium may have been used as smaller private meeting rooms with something of the function of the modern-day study.

denarius (pl. denarii)   The basic denomination of the Roman currency system, a small silver-coloured coin.

imagines maiorum   Romans' portraits of their ancestors. Sources suggest that these took the form of wax masks, and were worn or carried by actors in funeral processions.

imperium   A concept of power which implied sovereignty or command and the official right, among others, of inflicting punishment. It exceeded simple authority.

interrex   A provisional office of principal magistrate, rare in the late

302

Republic. Among traditional duties of the 'interrex' was overseeing the election of new consuls.

lar or **lares**   A form of Roman household god(s) with special responsibility for protecting the house and household, also associated with deceased ancestors or family members.

novus homo ('new man') A man not born into Rome's ruling class, who became the first member of his family to serve in the Senate.

paterfamilias   The male head of family who, possessing **patria potestas** ('the power of the father'), held far-reaching legal powers over descendants through the male line or adoption. In practice, by the late Republic, these powers had been significantly eroded.

patron/client   The patron/client relationship was one respectively of protection and dependency and existed between individuals – a wealthy Roman and his freedman, for example – and between influential individuals and communities, for example, a Roman senator and a community outside Rome who, as the senator's clients, could expect him to advance the community's needs in Rome. The patron offered support (including financial support and legal assistance) to his client; the client responded with attendance at the morning *salutatio* and support in public elections.

pontifex maximus   The chief priest of the Roman state cult, a lifelong appointment.

praetor   A magistracy of the 'cursus honorum', senior to the position of aedile, with responsibility for administering justice.

proscripti   Those whose names were publicly 'proscribed': their lives were forfeit and their property confiscated or sold. Proscription was developed in 82 BC by Sulla as a means of disposing of his enemies, and reintroduced by the second Triumvirate in 43 BC

salutatio   A morning meeting, partly akin to the levée; the formal morning greeting of a patron by his clients in the patron's atrium. The *salutatio* was also an informal business forum, in which favours were requested and bestowed; clients received from their patrons their *sportula* (monetary handout).

tablinum   A room, close to the atrium, used as an office.

tribune of the plebs   An elected office open to plebeians, the only form of plebeian representation in the Senate.

triumvirate   Historically a form of transitional government by three powerful men. The so-called First Triumvirate consisted of Julius Caesar, Pompey the Great and Marcus Licinius Crassus; the Second Triumvirate of Octavian, Mark Antony and Marcus Aemilius Lepidus.

virtus   A Roman virtue which overlapped with concepts of Roman-ness itself, encompassing courage, uprightness, excellence and idealized masculinity.

Index

Illustrations

1. Portrait bust of Livia Drusilla from a portrait group of the amphi-theatre of Arsinoe Crocodilopolis. (Copenhagen, Ny Carlsberg Glyptothek / Photo © akg-images)
2. *The Vestal Virgin Claudia and the Statue of Cybele* by Garofalo, originally Benvenuto Tisi (Rome, Galleria Nazionale, Pal. Barberini / Photo © akg-images / Andre Held)
3. *The Introduction of the Cult of Cybele at Rome, 1505-6* by Andrea Mantegna (The National Gallery, London / Scala, Florence)
4. Portrait head of Livia Drusilla with a veil over her hair. (Bochum, Kunstslg. der Ruhr-Universitaet / Photo © akg-images)
5. Portrait head of Livia Drusilla with a veil over her hair. (Bochum, Kunstslg. der Ruhr-Universitaet / Photo © akg-images)
6. Bust of Livia Drusilla (© Araldo de Luca / CORBIS)
7. Marble portrait bust of Livia Drusilla (Vatican Museums / Photo © akg-images)
8. Statue of Augustus from the Livia Villa at Prima Porta (Photo © akg-images / Erich Lessing)
9. Marble Augustus statue from the Villa Livia at Prima Porta. Marble, 1st century AD, copy after an original from c.20/17 BC. (Vatican Museums / Photo © akg-images)
10. Sardonyx Cameo bearing the profile of Livia wife of Emperor Augustus and Tiberius, 1st century AD (Kunsthistorisches Museum, Vienna, Austria / Photo © The Bridgeman Art Library)
11. Marble bust of Emperor Augustus (Photo © akg-images / Erich Lessing)

12. Basalt Head of Livia, 1st century BC (Louvre, Paris, France / Giraudon/ Photo © The Bridgeman Art Library)

13. *Antony & Cleopatra, Egyptian Theater 1866* by Alexis van Hamme (© Fine Art Photographic Library / CORBIS)

14. Marble Bust of Tiberius found in the amphitheatre of Arsinoe-Krokodilopolis, Lower Egypt (Copenhagen, Ny Carlsberg Glyptothek / Photo © akg-images)

15. Portrait head of Drusus maior (Tripolis, Archaeologisches Museum / Photo © akg-images / Gilles Mermet)

16. Portrait bust of Agrippa, (Photo © akg-images)

17. Augustinian Garden with fruit trees, flowers and birds. Detail from a fresco in the garden of the Villa Livia near Prima Porta. (Rome, Museo Nazionale Romano delle Terme / Photo © akg-images / Erich Lessing)

18. The Great Cameo of France, 1st century AD (Bibliotheque Nationale, Paris, France / © The Bridgeman Art Library)

19. Gold ring with an onyx cameo of Tiberius, Livia and female head (The Royal Collection © 2010 Her Majesty Queen Elizabeth II)

20. *Virgil reading the 'Aeneid' to Livia, Octavia and Augustus, 1819* by, Jean Auguste Dominique Ingres 1780–1867 (Musees Royaux des Beaux-Arts de Belgique, Brussels, Belgium / © The Bridgeman Art Library)

21. *Vergil reads from his 6th book of Aeneis* 1820, by Jean-Baptiste Joseph Wicar (Tremezzo, Villa Carlotta / Photo © akg-images / Electa)